Pentecostal Manifestos

James K. A. Smith and Amos Yong, *Editors*

PENTECOSTAL MANIFESTOS will provide a forum for exhibiting the next generation of Pentecostal scholarship. Having exploded across the globe in the twentieth century, Pentecostalism now enters its second century. For the past fifty years, Pentecostal and charismatic theologians (and scholars in other disciplines) have been working "internally," as it were, to articulate a distinctly Pentecostal theology and vision. The next generation of Pentecostal scholarship is poised to move beyond a merely internal conversation to an outward-looking agenda, in a twofold sense: first, Pentecostal scholars are increasingly gaining the attention of those outside Pentecostal/charismatic circles *as* Pentecostal voices in mainstream discussions; second, Pentecostal scholars are moving beyond simply reflecting on their own tradition and instead are engaging in theological and cultural analysis of a variety of issues from a Pentecostal perspective. In short, Pentecostal scholars are poised with a new boldness:

- Whereas the first generation of Pentecostal scholars was careful to learn the methods of the academy and then "apply" those to the Pentecostal tradition, the next generation is beginning to interrogate the reigning methodologies and paradigms of inquiry from the perspective of a unique Pentecostal worldview.
- Whereas the first generation of Pentecostal scholars was faithful in applying the tools of their respective trades to the work of illuminating the phenomena of modern Pentecostalism, the charismatic movements, and (now) the global renewal movements, the second generation is expanding its focus to bring a Pentecostal perspective to bear on important questions and issues that are concerns not only for Pentecostals and charismatics but also for the whole church.
- Whereas the first generation of Pentecostal/charismatic scholars was engaged in transforming the anti-intellectualism of the tradition, the second generation is engaged in contributing to and even impacting the conversations of the wider theological academy.

PENTECOSTAL MANIFESTOS will bring together both high-profile scholars and newly emerging scholars to address issues at the intersection of Pentecostalism, the global church, the theological academy, and even broader cultural concerns. Authors in PENTECOSTAL MANIFESTOS will be writing to and addressing not only their own movements but also those outside of Pentecostal/ charismatic circles, offering a manifesto for a uniquely Pentecostal perspective on various themes. These will be "manifestos" in the sense that they will be bold statements of a distinctly Pentecostal interjection into contemporary discussions and debates, undergirded by rigorous scholarship.

Under this general rubric of bold, programmatic "manifestos," the series will include both shorter, crisply argued volumes that articulate a bold vision within a field as well as longer scholarly monographs, more fully developed and meticulously documented, with the same goal of engaging wider conversations. Such PENTECOSTAL MANIFESTOS are offered as intrepid contributions with the hope of serving the global church and advancing wider conversations.

PUBLISHED

James K. A. Smith, *Thinking in Tongues: Pentecostal Contributions to Christian Philosophy* (2010)

Frank D. Macchia, *Justified in the Spirit: Creation, Redemption, and the Triune God* (2010)

Wolfgang Vondey, *Beyond Pentecostalism: The Crisis of Global Christianity and the Renewal of the Theological Agenda* (2010)

Amos Yong, *The Spirit of Creation: Modern Science and Divine Action in the Pentecostal-Charismatic Imagination* (2011)

The Spirit of Creation

Modern Science and Divine Action in the
Pentecostal-Charismatic Imagination

Amos Yong

WILLIAM B. EERDMANS PUBLISHING COMPANY

GRAND RAPIDS, MICHIGAN / CAMBRIDGE, U.K.

© 2011 Amos Yong

Published 2011 by
Wm. B. Eerdmans Publishing Co.
2140 Oak Industrial Drive N.E., Grand Rapids, Michigan 49505 /
P.O. Box 163, Cambridge CB3 9PU U.K.

Printed in the United States of America

17 16 15 14 13 12 11   7 6 5 4 3 2 1

Library of Congress Cataloging-in-Publication Data

Yong, Amos.
    The spirit of creation: modern science and divine action in the
    Pentecostal-charismatic imagination / Amos Yong.
        p.   cm.
    Includes indexes.
    ISBN 978-0-8028-6612-7 (pbk.: alk. paper)
    1. Religion and science.   2. Pentecostalism — Doctrines.
    I. Title.

    BL240.3.Y66   2011
    261.5′5 — dc22

                                    2011004119

www.eerdmans.com

For Aizaiah ~ 1 Cor. 2:9 & Eph. 3:20

Contents

Preface

I have been thinking about the issues discussed in this book for a long time, going all the way back through my seminary and even undergraduate education. The initial question, in brief, is this: Is the pentecostal-charismatic worldview within which I have been raised defensible in our contemporary scientific context? The following pages sketch only a very preliminary and programmatic response to this question. As pentecostal and charismatic readers will see, my answer is yes, albeit in a carefully qualified manner.

More importantly, however, I have also more recently come to believe two things: first, that my pentecostal concerns are not just my own, but that they pertain to a much wider swath of Christian believers in particular and perhaps even to monotheists and theists in general, and second, that some of the pentecostal-charismatic perspectives to be registered along the way are important for the wider theological discussion as well as the ongoing dialogue between theology and science. Might it indeed be the case that pentecostal-charismatic views regarding the dynamic presence and activity of the Spirit of God in the world have something to add to the theology and science discussion? Even more audaciously, might the pluralistic cosmology of many spirits in the pentecostal-charismatic worldview challenge the reigning paradigm at the intersection of theology and science? These questions not only animate this book; they are also intuitions that, if explicable, have the potential to open up discussions at the interface of theology and science in unprecedented directions. Thus I urge especially readers who are involved in the theology and science conversation or are at least interested in these matters to keep an open mind about this question: How might pentecostal-charismatic insights make a difference in the encounter between theology and science? This book is motivated by the bold intuition that a pentecostal-charismatic voice is important in this wider discussion. The specific proposals I make in response to concrete issues may not ultimately be plausible or appealing, but the issues they address will not be going away any time soon.

Books of this sort can be written only if the author incurs a great many debts. I want to express my deep appreciation to the following friends and colleagues who have given me feedback on this manuscript, and done so on short notice: Thomas Jay Oord, Nimi Wariboko, Dennis W. Cheek, Gregory R. Peterson (chapters 2, 5, and 6), Michael Palmer (especially on chapter 5), and Jamie Smith (my fellow series coeditor). The manuscript is vastly improved because of their comments, although they need to be absolved from any responsibility for what follows.

I also need to express my gratitude to my dean, Michael Palmer. He has provided me with institutional support that goes a long way toward enabling the completion of this book. Patty Hughson and her interlibrary loan team have once again been so incredibly efficient in helping me get my hands on the many items cited in this volume, while Kathy Schultz has cheerfully borne the added administrative burden of helping me to acquire various items dictated by my research. Thanks finally to my graduate assistant, Timothy Lim Teck Ngern, for his help with proofreading and indexing the volume.

This is my second book with Eerdmans. Jon Pott and his staff have been helpful at each step of the way. Thanks especially to Tom Raabe for his copyediting work on the manuscript.

As always, my wife Alma goes beyond the call of duty in encouraging my research and writing. Since many of the chapters of this volume saw their first iteration in other places, some going back six or seven years, the debts I owe to her for what has now been collected and revised within these pages stretch back longer than any other book I have written. Throughout, her patience has been admirable, her smile encouraging, and her love irreplaceable. Thank you again, Alma, for all you have done and continue to do. I cannot do any of this without you.

This book is dedicated to my firstborn son, Aizaiah — pronounced like the biblical Isaiah — who will be a college senior by the time he gets his copy. Aizaiah, no dad could be prouder of his son than I. This book probes many frontiers considered off-limits to the first few generations of

Pentecostals. But it represents at least in spirit a rudimentary vision of how I have attempted to make sense of my Christian faith in the twenty-first century, a vision that has been flowering in my heart as long as your mother and I have been blessed to have you in our life. I pass it on to you, with fond recollections of the many theological conversations we have had since your grade school days, but especially in eager anticipation of all the amazing things God is doing and will continue to do through your life for your generation that are far above and beyond what I couldn't even dream of doing for mine. I love you!

Chesapeake, Virginia

Permissions

I am grateful to the following for permission to use previously published material, in some cases greatly revised and expanded, for this book:

- Wipf and Stock Publishers (www.wipfandstock.com): "Poured Out on All Creation!? Searching for the Spirit in the Pentecostal Encounter with Science," in Amos Yong, ed., *Spirit, Grace, and Creation: Pentecostal Forays into Theology and Science* (Eugene, Oreg.: Pickwick Press, 2009), pp. xi-xxiii (for parts of chapter 1)
- William Kay, editor of the *Journal of the European Pentecostal Theological Association*: "The Spirit and Creation: Possibilities and Challenges for a Dialogue between Pentecostal Theology and the Sciences," *Journal of the European Pentecostal Theological Association* 25 (2005): 82-110 (for parts of chapter 2)
- Taylor & Francis Ltd (http://www.tandf.co.uk/journals): "The Spirit at Work in the World: A Pentecostal-Charismatic Perspective on the Divine Action Project," *Theology & Science* 7:2 (2009): 123-40 (for parts of chapter 3)
- Wiley-Blackwell: "Natural Laws and Divine Intervention in Theology and Science: What Difference Does Being Pentecostal or Charismatic Make?" *Zygon: Journal of Science and Religion* 43:4 (2008): 961-89 (chapter 4)
- Wm. B. Eerdmans Publishing Company, Grand Rapids, Michigan: "*Ruach*, the Primordial Waters, and the Breath of Life: Emergence Theory and the Creation Narratives in Pneumatological Perspective,"

in Michael Welker, ed., *The Work of the Spirit: Pneumatology and Pentecostalism* (Grand Rapids: Wm. B. Eerdmans, 2006), pp. 183-204 (for parts of chapter 5) — reprinted by permission of the publisher, all rights reserved

- Brill: "Academic Glossolalia? Pentecostal Scholarship, Multidisciplinarity, and the Science-Religion Conversation," *Journal of Pentecostal Theology* 14:1 (2005): 63-82 (for parts of chapter 6)

1 The Pentecostal Encounter with Science

Whence and Whither?

The "problem" addressed in this book can be simply put: What does a "premodern" supernaturalistic religion like pentecostalism have to do with the naturalistic and rationalistic world of modern science? What does Azusa Street, the iconic site of the pentecostal movement, have to do with MIT (Massachusetts Institute of Technology), one of the central educational institutions of the scientific establishment in our time? More importantly, does pentecostal theology have anything to say in, much less contribute to, the ongoing dialogue between theology and science?[1]

This book presents a preliminary response to these questions. In this introductory chapter, we will seek to locate the broader context of these issues first by sketching a bit of the history of the relationship between pentecostalism and science, and then by explicating the state of the contempo-

1. The word "pentecostalism" and its cognates are not capitalized throughout this book because they are broadly inclusive of the classical Pentecostal (capitalized) movements and churches coming out of the Azusa Street revival; of the charismatic movements in the mainline Protestant, Catholic, and Orthodox churches since the middle of the twentieth century; and of the many other related renewal movements in the global South that do not go by either name (neither pentecostal nor charismatic) but embrace, manifest, or value pentecostal- and charismatic-type phenomena, practices, and spirituality. I could just as easily have chosen to consistently use "charismatic" or "renewal" to describe this form of global Christianity, but am staying with "pentecostal" because this volume is being published in the Pentecostal Manifestos book series. For further discussion of this choice of nomenclature, see Amos Yong, *The Spirit Poured Out on All Flesh: Pentecostalism and the Possibility of Global Theology* (Grand Rapids: Baker Academic, 2005), pp. 18-21; cp. Mark J. Cartledge, *Encountering the Spirit: The Charismatic Tradition* (Maryknoll, NY: Orbis, 2007).

rary discussion between theology and science. Both exercises will set the stage for presenting the basic thesis and outlining the argument of this book.

Pentecostalism and Modern Science: A Brief History of Their (Missed?) Engagement

Ironically, pentecostalism as a religious movement was birthed during the period when science contributed to the parting of ways between what we now call fundamentalism and modernism.[2] Put positively, the early pentecostals sided with the fundamentalists in this debate not because they were against science but because they were motivated primarily by evangelistic concerns.[3] Pentecostal Bible institutes were focused first and foremost on developing pastors, missionaries, and church workers, and not at all on making scientific education part of a liberal arts curriculum. Their goal was world evangelization before the imminent return of Christ, and for that reason they found fundamentalists more congenial to their commitments than modernists.

The result, however, was that these otherworldly aspirations combined with a biblicist mind-set and worldview amidst a fundamentalist milieu to foster an anti-intellectualism among the vast majority of first-generation pentecostals. Leading up to and then following the Scopes trial of 1925, pentecostals increasingly came to understand themselves on the same side as the fundamentalists in defending the veracity of the scriptural account of God and creation against the modernist and liberal attacks.[4] Such an alignment led, inevitably, to a suspicion about higher education in general, as well as about scientific research in particular. This explains, at least in part,

---

2. See George M. Marsden, *Fundamentalism and American Culture: The Shaping of Twentieth Century Evangelicalism, 1870-1925* (New York: Oxford University Press, 1980), especially pp. 93-96 and 194-95, and Robert Mapes Anderson, *Vision of the Disinherited: The Making of American Pentecostalism* (New York: Oxford University Press, 1979).

3. For the evangelistic commitments of early pentecostalism, see James R. Goff Jr., *Fields White unto Harvest: Charles F. Parham and the Missionary Origins of Pentecostalism* (Fayetteville: University of Arkansas Press, 1988), and Allan Anderson, *Spreading Fires: The Missionary Nature of Early Pentecostalism* (London: SCM; Maryknoll, NY: Orbis, 2007).

4. See Gerald W. King, "Evolving Paradigms: Creationism as Pentecostal Variation on a Fundamentalist Theme," in *The Spirit Renews the Face of the Earth: Pentecostal Forays into Science and Theology of Creation,* ed. Amos Yong (Eugene, OR: Pickwick, 2009), pp. 93-114.

the resistance toward the (very gradual) transformation of pentecostal "Bible institutes" to "Bible schools" to "Bible colleges" to "liberal arts colleges" and, finally, to "universities."[5] The legacy of this anti-intellectualism has been the reluctance, even in the pentecostal academy, to seriously engage modern science until now.[6]

Hence science, insofar as it was understood by these early pentecostals, was an enemy of the faith, primarily because of the popularized claims of evolutionary geologists and paleontologists and their apparent presupposition of the nonexistence of God. At this point in pentecostal development, these popular claims appeared indistinguishable from the methodology and interests of other branches of science that were totally unknown territory. Since no pentecostal expertise was available to sort out the details, the sciences did not seem to be a safe venture. As with many conservative Protestants of their time, pentecostals rejected the Darwinian theory of evolution as being antithetical to a literal reading of the biblical creation narratives. The widespread influence of the *Scofield Reference Bible* (1909) among early pentecostals led many to adopt the gap theory of temporally ambiguous intervals between the Genesis narrator's first and second "days."[7]

Beginning in the 1930s and 1940s, a handful of second- and third-generation pentecostals were drawn out of curiosity and thoughtfulness to the study of the sciences, primarily biology, at universities, study not encouraged by the first generation.[8] It began to dawn on these students that

5. For an overview of these categories of pentecostal institutions of higher education, see Jeff Hittenberger, "The Future of Pentecostal Higher Education: The Ring, the Shire, or the Redemption of Middle Earth?" in *The Future of Pentecostalism in the United States,* ed. Eric Patterson and Edmund J. Rybarczyk (Lanham, MD: Lexington Books, 2007), especially pp. 84-86.

6. The stereotype of pentecostalism as being anti-intellectual continues to persist — e.g., Roger E. Olson, "Pentecostalism's Dark Side," *Christian Century* 123, no. 5 (March 7, 2006): 27-30. Pentecostals have recently begun to address the issue, however — e.g., Rick M. Nañez, *Full Gospel, Fractured Minds? A Call to Use God's Gift of the Intellect* (Grand Rapids: Zondervan, 2005).

7. See David S. Norris, "Creation Revealed: An Early Pentecostal Hermeneutic," in *The Spirit Renews the Face of the Earth,* pp. 74-92.

8. E.g., Stanley Horton, one of the first generation of pentecostal theologians, actually studied chemistry at the University of California at Berkeley in the 1930s, although he did not stay to complete a degree in that field; see Lois E. Olena with Raymond L. Gannon, *Stanley M. Horton, Shaper of Pentecostal Theology* (Springfield, MO: Gospel Publishing House, 2009), pp. 83-92.

medical missions created the need for biological sciences. At the same time, by distancing themselves from fundamentalism and affiliating with and being accepted by the emergent evangelical movement in the 1940s, pentecostals purchased some social space for members of the movement interested in the sciences.

By the 1950s and 1960s, the initial avoid-and-reject mentality toward an ancient earth remained among pentecostal leaders, but existed in tension with the discriminating worldview prevalent among the emerging group of college-educated adherents. Increasingly, Bible college and Bible institute educators and administrators sensed the need to provide an alternative "pentecostal" program of study for pentecostals desiring a college education. This led to the development of departments in the humanities and the sciences, and the offering of degrees in most of the liberal arts. But programs in the natural sciences proved expensive to develop and did not command the enrollment and tuition dollars of other subjects. The quest for regional accreditation was a strong motivating force, but outside scrutiny and pressure did not overcome the traditional resistance to pursuing competence in the sciences. Faculty was sought with at least graduate, if not terminal, degrees first in the humanities and in the liberal arts of mathematics, but only secondarily, during that time, in the natural sciences. But by the end of the twentieth century, these scientific traditions had become fairly well established at some of the leading pentecostal institutions like Oral Roberts University, Evangel University, and Lee University. Simultaneously, the emergence of pentecostal universities offering a full range of science majors meant that pentecostal scholars could no longer put off thinking theologically about science.[9]

In the meanwhile, pentecostal attitudes toward creation and, especially, an old earth theory continued to develop. The appearance of *Dake's Annotated Reference Bible* (1963) provided further impetus for the gap and day-age interpretations already popular among many pentecostals. The emergence in the 1960s of young earth creationism in fundamentalist and conservative evangelical circles gradually caused alarm among some pen-

9. One of the first published calls for a more integrative (rather than apologetic) approach to science within a pentecostal educational context was Robert O'Bannon, Lois Beach, and J. Patrick Daugherty, eds., *Science and Christianity: Friends or Foes? Proceedings of the 1977 Bible-Science Symposium Sponsored by Lee College and the Liaisons* (Cleveland, TN: Pathway Press, 1977). Yet not only are the dominant categories oppositional — e.g., as in the "Friends or Foes" subtitle — but the Lee faculty published in this volume all wrote from a "conservative evangelical" rather than an explicitly pentecostal frame of reference.

tecostal science departments, and the Society for Pentecostal Studies (formed in 1972) was warned early on concerning this assault on science by the head of the science department at Lee University, Dr. Myrtle Fleming, to "distinguish between fact and theory, original works (experimental evidence) and philosopher's thinking."[10] Some pentecostal administrators considered young earth creationism an embarrassment, and some institutions refused to hire faculty in any discipline, scientific or otherwise, who adhered to this position. On the other hand, pentecostal theologians and leaders realize that their pentecostal constituencies by and large not only embrace the young earth position, even a six twenty-four-hour-day creation, but also reject theistic evolution (macroevolution with divine guidance), believing it to be incompatible with their interpretation of the Bible.[11] What many do not realize is that this default to a young earth position is gaining ground globally as part of the explosive growth of conservative evangelical and renewal forms of Christianity.[12]

Another window into the ambiguous relationship between pentecostalism and the sciences is provided by pentecostal attitudes toward the use of medicine and the medical establishment. The biblicism of early pentecostalism led many to embrace the belief of divine healing. Given their lack of medical knowledge and the inaccessibility and inaffordability of medicinal supplies, many early pentecostals looked to God for their healing. As such, early pentecostal attitudes toward medical practitioners and their arts resonated well with faith healer John Alexander Dowie's (1847-1907) widely circulated pamphlet that identified the most dreaded disease as the *"bacillis lunaticus medicus."*[13] The result was that many sectarian pentecostal groups, especially in the rural parts of America, rejected medicine and relied solely on the healing power of God, sometimes resulting in the loss of life.

10. As cited in Ronald Numbers, *The Creationists: The Evolution of Scientific Creationism* (Berkeley: University of California Press, 1993), p. 307. See also Numbers, "Creation, Evolution, and Holy Ghost Religion: Holiness and Pentecostal Responses to Darwinism," *Religion and American Culture* 2, no. 2 (1992): 127-58.

11. Steve Badger and Mike Tenneson, "Does the Spirit Create through Evolutionary Processes? Pentecostals and Biological Evolution," in *Science and the Spirit: A Pentecostal Engagement with the Sciences,* ed. Amos Yong and James K. A. Smith (Bloomington: Indiana University Press, 2010), pp. 92-116.

12. For an explanation of this global phenomenon, see Michael Roberts, *Evangelicals and Science* (Westport, CT, and London: Greenwood Press, 2008), pp. 167-77.

13. See Bernie Van De Walle, "Cautious Co-belligerence? The Late Nineteenth-Century American Divine Healing Movement and the Promise of Medical Science," in *The Spirit Renews the Face of the Earth,* pp. 53-73.

Yet such early pentecostal polemics were rampant against not only the class of medical doctors, who also often made mistakes and appeared unreliable to some, but also the spiritual healing technologies of the Christian Science movement. Ironically, whereas North American pentecostals were wary of combining faith and spiritual healing, throughout Asia, sub-Saharan Africa, and Latin America, pentecostals have combined the belief in divine healing with shamanistic types of practices in order to address physical, emotional, psychological, and material ailments and needs. In the non-Western pentecostal world, such seemingly syncretistic practices continue to the present.[14]

However, pentecostals have always negotiated the tension between a robust belief in faith healing that repudiated medical technology entirely and the belief that faith healing and the use of medicine were indeed compatible. As Grant Wacker points out, medical doctors attended early pentecostal revival services and even participated as members in pentecostal communities of faith.[15] Over the generations, both the upward social mobility of many pentecostals and their medical missionary emphases led to an increasing acceptance of the use of medicine. In the 1970s, the establishment of a medical school at Oral Roberts University (ORU), a vanguard institution for neo-pentecostal and charismatic higher education, followed soon after by their City of Faith Medical and Research Center, signaled the full engagement of the medical sciences among pentecostals. Yet the ORU motto of educating "the whole man in spirit, mind and body" reflected at the same time the pentecostal concern for holistic health care strategies. Unsurprisingly, then, a recent poll of pentecostal ministers in Britain revealed that 93.7 percent believe that "modern medicine is a God-given blessing."[16] It is fair to assume that this percentage is reflective of Western pentecostal attitudes toward at least the medical, technological, engineering, and applied sciences. Even so, at the present time and at least in some circles, there remains the concern that overreliance on medicine will undermine authentic faith in God.

In one area, however, pentecostals have from the beginning been open

14. See Harvey Cox, *Fire from Heaven: The Rise of Pentecostal Spirituality and the Reshaping of Religion in the Twenty-First Century* (Reading, MA: Addison-Wesley, 1995), especially part III.

15. Grant Wacker, *Heaven Below: Early Pentecostals and American Culture* (Cambridge, MA: Harvard University Press, 2001), p. 198.

16. William Kay, "Approaches to Healing in British Pentecostalism," *Journal of Pentecostal Theology* 14 (1999): 113-25, quote from 121.

to science, at least in its applied forms: the sciences of communications and media technology. As pragmatists urgently focused on carrying out the Great Commission in anticipation of the imminent return of Christ, pentecostals have always availed themselves of the mass media. The first generation of pentecostals made good use of the printing press to spread their testimonies far and wide, and a few even opted, from the start, to use radio as an evangelistic tool.[17] As scientific advances have been made in the various communication technologies, pentecostals have been quick to adopt television, the big screen of film, and the Internet.[18] Contemporary pentecostals are globally networked using a wide range of electronic media. Given the prevalence of the use of media technologies in pentecostal mission and evangelism, the emergence of scholarship on the subject is not surprising, especially regarding developments in the global South.[19] However, most of these studies have been and are being done by outsiders to the movement, even as the absence of substantive theological reflection on these matters by pentecostal scholars or insiders is itself remarkable. In addition, what remains lacking is any analysis of the pentecostal encounter with science through this lens of media and technology.

In sum, almost from the beginning we can detect a "love-hate" rela-

17. On the use of radio in pentecostalism, see W. E. Warner, "Radio," in *The New International Dictionary of Pentecostal and Charismatic Movements,* ed. Stanley M. Burgess and Eduard M. Van Der Maas, rev. and expanded ed. (Grand Rapids: Zondervan, 2002), pp. 1015-16; Matthew Sutton, *Aimee Semple McPherson and the Resurrection of Christian America* (Cambridge, MA, and London: Harvard University Press, 2007), chapter 3 (on McPherson's media savvy); and Benjamin A. Wagner, "'Full Gospel' Radio: Revivaltime and Pentecostal Uses of Mass Media, 1950-1979," *Fides et Historia* 35, no. 1 (2003): 107-22.

18. D. J. Hedges, "Television," in *The New International Dictionary of Pentecostal and Charismatic Movements,* pp. 1118-20, and David Edwin Harrell, "Pentecost at Prime Time: Early Religious TV Presented Huge Challenges, Which Pentecostals Met Better Than Most," *Christian History* 49 (1996): 52-54. Contemporary pentecostal use of electronic media is covered through a case study of the Swedish Pentecostal movement *Livets Ord* ("Word of Life") by Simon Coleman, *The Globalization of Charismatic Christianity: Spreading the Gospel of Prosperity,* Cambridge Studies in Ideology and Religion 12 (Cambridge: Cambridge University Press, 2000).

19. E.g., Birgit Meyer, "Pentecostalism, Prosperity, and Popular Cinema in Ghana," in *Representing Religion in World Cinema: Filmmaking, Mythmaking, Culture Making,* ed. S. Brent Plate (New York: Palgrave Macmillan, 2003), pp. 121-45; J. Kwabena Asamoah-Gyadu, "Anointing through the Screen: Neo-Pentecostalism and Televised Christianity in Ghana," *Studies in World Christianity* 11, no. 1 (2005): 9-28; and Pradip Thomas, *Strong Religion, Zealous Media: Christian Fundamentalism and Communication in India* (Thousand Oaks, CA: Sage, 2008), especially part III.

tionship between pentecostalism and science. On the one hand, pentecostals were suspicious of any scientific advances that threatened to undermine belief in the reality, power, and personality of God and the Holy Spirit. On the other hand, pentecostals have been quick to avail themselves of at least the applied sciences insofar as developments in media and technology have enabled the cause of world missionization and evangelization. Given this history of what might be called "occasional encounters" between pentecostalism and science, it is not surprising that there has not been much theological reflection by pentecostals about medicine, the mass media, and other related scientific and technological matters.

But there may also be other explanations for this relative paucity of pentecostal theological engagement with the sciences. One reason is that pentecostal scholarship is still a fairly new phenomenon. The Society for Pentecostal Studies (SPS) was not established until the eighth decade of the modern pentecostal movement. Since its charter in the early 1970s, the SPS has steadily expanded its scholarly horizons, beginning first with history (reflecting the doctoral training of the majority of the SPS "founding fathers," who were seeking to preserve the oral history of the movement before the last eyewitnesses of the first generation passed from the scene), moving on to the biblical studies in the 1980s (a natural progression given pentecostalism's biblicistic orientation), and then to theological studies broadly conceived in the 1990s.[20] As part of a scholarly enterprise that is arguably still in its gestational stage, pentecostals in the academy have worked primarily in the arena of humanities in general, and in theological studies more specifically.

That pentecostal scholarship has focused more on the humanities is also suggestive of another reason internal to the logic of pentecostal spirituality and piety that has so far hindered a pentecostal engagement with science. Telford Work, an ecumenical theologian in the Foursquare Church, a classical Pentecostal denomination, has suggested that pentecostal intuitions and sensibilities will lead its practitioners to take up issues more relevant to certain aspects of the human sciences.[21] More specifically, like those in the Wesleyan tradition, in which are found the roots of modern pentecostalism, pentecostal scholars seem less interested in pursuing vocations in the natural sciences (or at least this is what the anecdotal "evi-

20. I provide an overview of these developments in my "Pentecostalism and the Theological Academy," *Theology Today* 64, no. 2 (2007): 244-50.

21. See Telford Work, "The Science Division: Pneumatological Relations and Christian Disunity in Theology-Science Dialogue," *Zygon* 43, no. 4 (2008): 897-908.

dence" suggests) and more predisposed to engage the humanities (especially history) and the social and behavioral sciences (e.g., psychology, sociology, and cultural anthropology). Perhaps the centrality of the experience of the Spirit in the pentecostal mode of being-in-the-world nurtures certain interests and provokes some questions rather than others, with the result being that initial pentecostal interfaces with the sciences on pentecostal terms — that is, where pentecostals engage the issues as pentecostals rather than as evangelicals or as Christians in general — have been more noticeable in these "softer" scientific disciplines, rather than the "harder" ones. Against this backdrop, the scholarly work of engaging with the sciences or with issues in the religion or theology and science encounter has been either off the radar altogether or deemed less pressing.

Nevertheless, over the past one hundred years pentecostal institutions of higher education have evolved from pastoral- and missionary-training institutes, to Bible institutes and colleges, to full-fledged colleges and universities in the liberal arts tradition. Along the way, pentecostal attitudes toward the sciences have also slowly changed: from suspicion and distrust of the "godlessness" of science, to an instrumental attitude toward the sciences, to a gradual engagement with the sciences and the work of scientists who have remained within pentecostal churches. Today, looking ahead into the second decade of the twenty-first century, I want to suggest three reasons why pentecostals not only cannot avoid engaging with modern science, but should wish to do so.

The first and most elementary reason is that pentecostals are themselves children of the modern world.[22] The emergence of pentecostalism in the early decades of the twentieth century can be understood, at least in part, as a reaction to liberalism and modernism. Yet while birthed as a reactionary movement, even earliest pentecostalism engaged its world instrumentally. And as the forces of modernization have continued in and through the processes of globalization, pentecostals have come to find themselves "at home" in the modern world, even as pentecostal movements in the developing world have also come to enjoy the advances of science. As pentecostals have awakened to increasing realization that science has defined and will continue to define their lives, I suggest they can no longer put off critical engagement with it.

22. David Martin calls pentecostalism "a major narrative of modernity"; see chapter 10 of his *On Secularization: Towards a Revised General Theory* (Aldershot, UK, and Burlington, VT: Ashgate, 2005).

This leads to my second rationale: failure to engage with modern science could undermine the vitality and future of pentecostal scholarship in particular and the pentecostal movement as a whole. Let me elaborate on this claim at three levels. From the perspective of pentecostal scholarship, currently focused on disciplines in the humanities like biblical studies, theology, history, and pastoral ministry (here, engaging especially the psychosocial sciences), to fail to engage the sciences in general and the natural sciences in particular is to leave it to those working in these disciplines to establish the plausibility structures for thinking as a whole and for worldview construction specifically. From the perspective of pentecostals working in the natural sciences, intentional pentecostal engagement with the sciences is requisite for breaching the bifurcation between spiritual life and vocational praxis. From the perspective of the next generation of pentecostals, perpetuation of this bifurcation between pentecostal spirituality and vocational science will result in a loss of our brightest minds, who may abandon pentecostal piety in search of careers in the sciences as there will be no role models to demonstrate how commitments to faithful living and empirical research can coexist in pentecostal communities.

What I am saying is that we must go beyond merely decrying scientific materialism, metaphysical naturalism, and positivistic empiricism, and engage the conversation. Rather than just denouncing evolutionary biology (concerned with life), for example, we must encourage ourselves and our students to enter into the discussion within the broader scientific context that ranges from quantum mechanics (the very small) to cosmological astrophysics (the very large).[23] Failure to do so will effectively ensure that pentecostalism remains merely a "religion for the masses,"[24] leaving the next generation of pentecostals without the role models to engage what will only be an even more scientifically shaped world. To be sure, pentecostalism as a "spirituality of the oppressed" will continue,[25] but if the movement does not begin to reflect theologically about pentecostal spirituality in relationship to modern science, it will be irrelevant

23. Darrel Falk, professor of biology and member of the Church of the Nazarene, has argued persuasively for the interconnectedness of the various fields of the natural sciences; see Darrel R. Falk, *Coming to Peace with Science: Bridging the Worlds between Faith and Biology* (Downers Grove, IL: InterVarsity, 2004).

24. As described by Christian Lalive d'Epinay, *Haven of the Masses: A Study of the Pentecostal Movement in Chile,* trans. Marjorie Sandle (London: Lutterworth, 1969).

25. Cheryl Bridges Johns has written *Pentecostal Formation: A Pedagogy among the Oppressed* (Sheffield: Sheffield Academic Press, 1993).

to the academic conversation and impotent against the ongoing developments in technology.

My third reason for why pentecostals should engage with modern science is internal to pentecostalism itself. Although pentecostalism was born
in the midst of the fundamentalist-modernist controversy, its genius, I
would suggest, is its distinctive response to the modern world. Unlike the
fundamentalists, who reacted to modernism using modernity's own scientific rationalism, pentecostals responded in part by unleashing a cry from
deep within the human spirit. Glossolalia, for example, can be said to be
both a symbol of the resistance of the masses against the hegemonic discourse of Enlightenment rationalism, and a representation of the prayerful
desire to be filled with the Holy Spirit. In this sense glossolalia symbolizes
a countermodernist "discourse" that turned on its head the "iron cages" of
Enlightenment rationalism. The belief in divine healing could also be seen
by sociologists as a protest against the failures of medical technology to
heal the ills associated with modernization and urbanization and as an ap-
propriation of New Testament thought regarding supernatural spiritual
gifts. As such, pentecostal spirituality signifies an eruption in the modern
world of the nonrational (not *ir*rational) elements of human feeling, expression, and experience that oppose not the methodologies of science and
engineering disciplines but the overextended claims of science. I thus suggest that recent scholarship about pentecostalism's holistic spirituality, af-
fective and embodied epistemology, and nonreductionistic worldview represents the best of pentecostal thinking in search of a way beyond the
impasses of (in no particular order) materialism versus spiritualism, rationalism versus empiricism, intellectualism versus emotionalism, individualism versus communalism, this-worldliness versus otherworldliness, naturalism versus supernaturalism, modernism versus postmodernism,
absolutism versus relativism, positivism versus fideism, etc.[26] Hence, pentecostals are spiritually and, in some respects, supernaturalistically oriented, but they are engaged with these dimensions of reality through the
concreteness of their embodiment, the sensitivies of their affections and
emotions, and the rationality (not rational*ism*) of their experiential, empirical, and pragmatic orientation.[27]

26. See James K. A. Smith, "Is the Universe Open for Surprise? Pentecostal Ontology
and the Spirit of Naturalism," *Zygon* 43, no. 4 (2008): 879-96, and "Is There Room for Surprise in the Natural World? Naturalism, the Supernatural, and Pentecostal Spirituality," in
Science and the Spirit, pp. 34-49.

27. On pentecostal pragmatism, see Grant Wacker, "Searching for Eden with a Satellite

My questions are these: When are pentecostals going to take this experientialism, empiricism, and pragmatism seriously enough to engage the sciences that are also driven by similar methodological dispositions? When are pentecostals going to counter the reductionistic interpretations of certain members of the scientific community with their own nonreductionistic portraits? When are pentecostals going to interpret their tongues — their testimonies — to a wider audience, not only so that their narratives can be judged and challenged (or validated) but also (perhaps even) so that the wonders of God can be declared to the ends of the earth? The recent coming of age of pentecostal scholarship means that we may now be ready to engage these matters. At the same time that the limits of scientific rationality have now been recognized and acknowledged by the scientific community, it invites pentecostal scholarly and theological engagement.

The Dialogue between Theology and Science: The Possibility of a Pentecostal Interjection?

That we can talk at all about a dialogue between theology and science suggests that it should be pretty easy to define "science." Unfortunately, as debates within many of the existing sciences reveal — for example, on (what some call radical) environmentalism within the ecological sciences, about design in the biological sciences, regarding alternative medicine in the health and nursing professions, and about paranormal phenomena in the human, social, and psychological sciences (which we will discuss in chapter 6) — the issue is not quite closed.[28] I prefer a more historical understanding of science as a cultural undertaking, whose demarcation from other fields of knowledge is constantly adjudicated by its practitioners.[29] In this sense, then, I want to privilege how scientists define their craft, even while recognizing that unanimity of opinion has not so far been and may never be achieved. Yet I do not therefore think that scientific inquiry can be understood merely as a social construction (unless we understand so-

---

Dish: Primitivism, Pragmatism, and the Pentecostal Character," in *The Primitive Church in the Modern World*, ed. Richard T. Hughes (Urbana: University of Illinois Press, 1995), pp. 139-66, and *Heaven Below*, pp. 267-68 and passim.

   28. See Alan Sokal, *Beyond the Hoax: Science, Philosophy, and Culture* (Oxford: Oxford University Press, 2008), chapter 8.

   29. E.g., as articulated in Frederick Grinnell, *Everyday Practice of Science: Where Intuition and Passion Meet Objectivity and Logic* (Oxford: Oxford University Press, 2009).

cial constructionism in the merely descriptive sense that all human cultural undertakings are socially construed). Rather, I think science is animated by certain ideal tasks: that of being a recognizably limited yet powerful means of inquiring after the cause-and-effect relations of the natural world involving observation, hypothesis formulation, theory, peer review, testing or experimentation, replicable results, and the communication and application of such findings.

I would affirm that, understood in this way, scientific inquiry proceeds according to a methodological naturalism — not a metaphysical naturalism, which would be a philosophic presupposition imposed on science — that recognizes its focus is limited to the exploration of nature or the natural world, and that there may be other methods of knowing that are more pertinent to other domains related to human existence or to other dimensions of reality.[30] At the same time, I am not completely happy with the "naturalism" label because it implies a dichotomy between that and whatever "supernatural" may entail. But I will nevertheless proceed with this as a preliminary definition, and later (in chapters 3 and 4, especially) show how we can affirm the principle of methodological naturalism without buying into any metaphysical dualism between the natural and the supernatural worlds.

Given this basic understanding of science, whither therefore the pentecostal encounter with science? As latecomers to the theology and science arena, of course, pentecostals have the advantage of learning from the history of the conversation. Whereas the conflict model has been widely published as characterizing a large part of the history of interactions between religion and science — such that disagreements or contradictions between theology and science mean that either the former trumps the latter (for religionists) or vice versa (for antireligious scientists)[31] — the last genera-

---

30. The notion of "methodological naturalism" was first explicated by Christian philosopher Paul de Vries, "Naturalism in the Natural Sciences: A Christian Perspective," *Christian Scholar's Review* 15, no. 4 (1986): 388-96, specifically to demarcate the focus of the sciences on the natural world, which in turn allowed for, if not required, theology to illuminate other domains of human experience, if not the totality of the world as a whole. I am grateful to Keith B. Miller, "The Misguided Attack on Methodological Naturalism," in *For the Rock Record: Geologists on Intelligent Design,* ed. Jill S. Schneiderman and Warren D. Allmon (Berkeley: University of California Press, 2009), pp. 117-40, especially 123-24, for initially pointing me to de Vries's fine article.

31. For the dispute in the nineteenth century and earlier, see John William Draper, *History of the Conflict between Religion and Science* (New York: Appleton, 1892), and Andrew Dickson White, *A History of the Warfare of Science with Theology in Christendom,* 2 vols.

tion has seen the emergence of other approaches including dialogue, consonance, convergence, mutuality, complementarity, as well as the view that each concerns separate domains of reality and human endeavor.[32] Within pentecostal circles, one might be able to find advocates all along the broad spectrum of positions.

For example, many working scientists who are pentecostals (that is, they are active members of or attend pentecostal churches) have published little about the specifically pentecostal questions they may ask about their science vocation or about the specifically scientific questions related to their practices or beliefs. Some live and work in two separate worlds, at the science workbench or in the lab on weekdays and tarrying at the altar or lifting up holy hands on weekends. Their science training neither encourages nor helps them to integrate their faith and their occupation (usually implicitly communicating that faith is an impediment to rigorous scientific work), and their pentecostal churches and traditions are ill equipped to handle such tasks. This kind of two-worlds approach is not unique to pentecostals, of course, and in many cases enables successful scientific careers and spiritual commitments simultaneously (albeit separately).

Yet, given the long alliance between evangelicalism and pentecostalism, an emerging number of pentecostals have taken up the task left over from previous generations of apologetic scholarship. The difference now, however, is at least twofold — first, for the most part, the natural theology approaches of the past have given way to the "humble approaches" of the present,[33] and second, pentecostal apologists are to be found not only on the traditional side of defending more-or-less accepted theistic commitments but also on the other (more progressive?) side of advocating for a

---

(New York: Appleton, 1897), although it should be noted that White's account is ideologically driven to argue that religion should be superseded by science. More recently, we have antireligious naturalists like Richard Dawkins and Daniel Dennett on the one side and those who wish to subordinate at least the social sciences to theology like folk in the Radical Orthodoxy movement on the other.

32. E.g., Alister E. McGrath, *The Foundations of Dialogue in Science and Religion* (Malden, MA: Blackwell, 1998); Ted Peters, ed., *Science and Theology: The New Consonance* (Boulder, CO: Westview Press, 1998); Ted Peters and Martinez Hewlett, *Evolution from Creation to New Creation: Conflict, Conversation, and Convergence* (Nashville: Abingdon, 2003); Alan G. Padgett, *Science and the Study of God: A Mutuality Model for Theology and Science* (Grand Rapids and Cambridge: Eerdmans, 2003); and Richard F. Carlson, ed., *Science and Christianity: Four Views* (Downers Grove, IL: InterVarsity, 2000).

33. John Marks Templeton, *The Humble Approach: Scientists Discover God*, rev. ed. (New York: Continuum, 1995).

more scientifically informed theology. Representative of the former is Paul Elbert, a physicist and New Testament scholar in the Church of God (Cleveland), whose publications on theology and science reflect an evangelical orientation toward identifying new theistic evidences especially in light of recent experimental findings in the cosmological sciences.[34] Representative of the latter is the pentecostal-charismatic biologist Denis Lamoureux, whose recent work has been devoted to defending a version of what he calls evolutionary creationism — which is a variant of theistic evolution — over and against young-earth and intelligent-design creationism.[35] Both Elbert and Lamoureux are insistent that God continues to be present and active personally in the human domain via the power of the Holy Spirit. They differ, however, about how the Spirit worked in the prehuman history of the world, with Elbert open to seeing certain events — the big bang, the origins of life, the origins of modern *Homo sapiens,* etc. — as signs of the Spirit's interventionist activity, while Lamoureux is more inclined to talk about evolutionary continuities even at these "junctures" so that the Spirit is understood to have worked immanently through the natural processes of the world instead of intermittently as in the traditional model.

The issues at stake in these parallel but perhaps ultimately diverging trajectories may be understood in terms of the debate in contemporary theology and science between those advocating for a revival of the natural theology project (which has fallen on hard times recently) and those proposing a scientifically informed theology of nature instead. These actually lie more across a spectrum than constitute polar opposites. Elbert's project will resonate with those working in the arena of natural theology in the

34. See Paul Elbert, review of *God of the Astronomers,* by Robert Jastrow, *Evangelical Quarterly* 52 (1980): 242-44; "Biblical Creation and Science: A Review Article," *Journal of the Evangelical Theological Society* 39, no. 2 (1996): 285-89; review of *Being a Christian in Science,* by Walter Hearn, *Ashland Theological Journal* 34 (2002): 177-80; and, most explicitly bringing his pentecostal sensibilities to bear on theology and science issues, "Genesis 1 and the Spirit: A Narrative-Rhetorical Ancient Near Eastern Reading in Light of Modern Science," *Journal of Pentecostal Theology* 15, no. 1 (2006): 23-72.

35. See Denis O. Lamoureux, *Evolutionary Creation: A Christian Approach to Evolution* (Eugene, OR: Wipf and Stock, 2008); Lamoureux, *I Love Jesus and I Accept Evolution* (Eugene, OR: Wipf and Stock, 2009); and Phillip E. Johnson, Denis O. Lamoureux, et al., *Darwinism Defeated? The Johnson-Lamoureux Debate on Biological Origins* (Vancouver, British Columbia: Regent College Publishing, 1999); see also my discussion of the latter volume, in "God and the Evangelical Laboratory: Recent Conservative Protestant Thinking about Theology and Science," *Theology and Science* 5, no. 2 (2007): 203-21, especially 209-11.

sense that his is also a quest to detect the fingerprints of God using experimental science.[36] His version is thus, arguably, one contemporary manifestation of the natural theology project most concretely epitomized in the divine watchmaker thesis of William Paley (1743-1805) at the beginning of the nineteenth century.[37] For Paley, and for others in his train, nature itself provides evidence for the existence of God, just as stumbling upon a watch in a desert suggests the existence of a watchmaker. The difference is that Paley, situated amidst the Enlightenment project, was inclined to think that nature's cues were self-evident signs of the deity's existence, while Elbert is more sensitive to the role of faith in discerning the divine imprint.

The project of natural theology, however, has been severely hampered in the wake of the Barthian critique. Barth's "Nein!" in reply to Emil Brunner's reference to a connection point between God and humanity challenged the very foundations of any natural theology project that presumed that the Creator's fingerprints could be easily read off nature's signs.[38] In addition, the withering of modern rationalism in our late modern, if not postmodern, situation, plus the growing realization that theistic arguments are much less proofs in the mathematical and scientific sense than they are intuitive and speculative hypotheses, have combined to take the wind out of the sails of the natural theology enterprise, at least as envisioned by Paley and others working in that tradition.[39] In its place, however, have ascended various versions of what had been called the theology of nature.

36. While I am sympathetic to Elbert's quest for what might be called a pneumatological theology of creation, my main question is his claim (if I understand him correctly) that the Genesis creation narrative has a prophetic character, one anticipating the experimental findings of modern science that in effect confirm the truthfulness of the creation myths. But this is like saying that after I reconstruct a historical event based on very few original sources, I later find other sources that corroborate my reconstruction, and this then leads me to label my original reconstruction as prophetic. I don't think this is the best way of treating the Genesis narratives. Thus, as should become clear, I'm less inclined to the more classical versions of natural theology than is Elbert, at least as I read him.

37. Paley's 1802 book continues to be reprinted, most recently as *Natural Theology: Evidence for the Existence and Attributes of the Deity, Collected from the Appearances of Nature,* ed. Matthew D. Eddy and David Knight, Oxford World Classics (Oxford: Oxford University Press, 2008).

38. See Peter Fraenkel, trans., *Natural Theology: Comprising "Nature and Grace" by Professor Dr. Emil Brunner and the Reply "No!" by Dr. Karl Barth* (1946; reprint, Eugene, OR: Wipf and Stock, 2002).

39. For a discussion of the waning of natural theology since Barth, see Alister E. McGrath, *The Open Secret: A New Vision for Natural Theology* (Malden, MA, and Oxford: Blackwell, 2008), part II.

In brief, theology of nature begins from the standpoint of faith and then seeks to "read" the world or nature through that lens.[40] The assumption is that the theistic conclusion is not foregone, much less the claim that any impartial assessment of the world of nature would lead observers to God (much less to the Christian deity). At the same time, theologians of nature base their work on the following premises: that the posture of faith does lead one to view, understand, and interact with the world and to engage in the scientific enterprise distinctively, at least in terms of the types of problems or questions one may choose to pursue; that theological perspectives derived from religious sources illuminate certain aspects of the world that otherwise remain hidden when engaged from merely naturalistic or materialistic assumptions; and that Christian theology itself would be bereft if it did not include self-critical reflection on the nature of the world as informed by modern science. In short, endeavors in the theology of nature are less interested in theistic proofs and apologetics directed toward those outside the camp (as were the older natural theologies) and are more committed to exploring the various ways in which faith commitments can be integrated with scientific learning.[41]

The discussion in theology of nature has thus, unsurprisingly, more recently reengaged with the more traditional work in theology of creation. Whereas the concept of "nature" has a more or less philosophical pedigree that contrasts with grace, particularly as these categories were promulgated by the medieval theologians,[42] the idea of "creation" is inherently biblical

40. The earliest versions were George S. Hendry, *Theology of Nature* (Philadelphia: Westminster, 1980), and Claude Y. Stewart Jr., *Nature in Grace: A Study in the Theology of Nature,* National Association of Baptist Professors of Religion Dissertation series 3 (Macon, GA: Mercer University Press, 1983); more recent articulations include R. J. Berry, *God's Books of Nature: The Nature and Theology of Nature* (London and New York: T. & T. Clark, 2003); Anna Case-Winters, *Reconstructing a Christian Theology of Nature: Down to Earth* (Burlington, VT, and Aldershot, UK: Ashgate, 2007); and John F. Haught, *Christianity and Science: Toward a Theology of Nature* (Maryknoll, NY: Orbis, 2007).

41. For further discussion of the continuities and discontinuities between the older project of natural theology and the newer forms of theology of nature, see Gert Hummel, ed., *Natural Theology versus Theology of Nature? Tillich's Thinking as Impetus for a Discourse among Theology, Philosophy, and Natural Sciences,* Theologische Bibliothek Töpelmann 60 (Berlin and New York: Walter de Gruyter, 1994).

42. See M.-D. Chenu, O.P., *Nature, Man, and Society in the Twelfth Century: Essays on New Theological Perspectives in the Latin West,* trans. Jerome Taylor and Lester K. Little (Chicago and London: University of Chicago Press, 1968), chapter 1, especially the section "The Discovery of Nature" (pp. 4-17).

and therefore distinctively theological, one that assumes a creator of the world (which for Christians and pentecostals is the God of Jesus Christ and of his Holy Spirit). Therefore the church has long had a doctrine of creation,[43] with the result that the current efforts in theology of nature and theology of creation overlap in many respects. It may be fair to say that theologians of nature privilege scientific categories, methods, and descriptions in their theological work even while approaching their work from a standpoint of faith, while theologians of creation emphasize biblical, dogmatic, or theological categories and frameworks instead, while trying to register scientific perspectives as well.[44] But we should not press this distinction too far, as Denis Lamoureux, for example, deploys and respects the scientific enterprise while self-identifying as a theologian of evolutionary creationism.

Yet the possibility of a theology of nature or of creation begs a range of methodological questions given the diversity of the Christian tradition. What counts theologically is contested across the global Christian movement. If biblical categories are utilized, then hermeneutical disputes inevitably arise. If a dogmatic framework is adopted, then the question surfaces: Which dogmatic tradition and on what grounds? If theological commitments are allowed to inform the theology and science conversation, there is pressure to keep them abstract, at the most general level, so as not to render the conversation unwieldy with the insertion of too many confessional or parochial perspectives.

While heeding these various concerns, surely important for any attempt (such as this volume) to provide a pentecostal-charismatic perspective on the theology and science dialogue, I want to identify two sets of developments that combine to embolden our efforts. The first is the emergence of more tradition-specific modes of inquiry that have provided models for how such approaches to the theology and science discussion can

43. E.g., as laid out in Langdon B. Gilkey, *Maker of Heaven and Earth: A Study of the Christian Doctrine of Creation* (Garden City, NY: Doubleday, 1959); more dogmatically oriented discussions can be found in Colin E. Gunton, *Christ and Creation: The Didsbury Lectures, 1990* (Carlisle, UK: Paternoster; Grand Rapids: Eerdmans, 1992), and Colin E. Gunton, ed., *The Doctrine of Creation: Essays in Dogmatics, History, and Philosophy* (Edinburgh: T. & T. Clark, 1997).

44. Examples of the latter include David A. S. Fergusson, *The Cosmos and the Creator: An Introduction to the Theology of Creation* (London: SPCK, 1998), and Karl Löning and Erich Zenger, *To Begin with, God Created . . . : Biblical Theologies of Creation*, trans. Omar Kaste (Collegeville, MN: Liturgical Press, 2000). Dorothee Soelle, with Shirley A. Cloyes, *To Work and to Love: A Theology of Creation* (Philadelphia: Fortress, 1984), is misleadingly titled, as it is more a theology of work than a theology of creation.

proceed. I am referring to contributions that refuse to settle on a generic "Christian" approach but instead seek to speak into the theology and science dialogue from out of the depths of the resources found in established theological traditions. Thus the Russian Orthodox scientist and theologian Alexei Nesteruk, for example, has brought classical and even patristic perspectives that have long served as the fountainhead of the Orthodox spiritual tradition to bear on the encounter between theology and science.[45] The genius of Nesteruk's work is his correlation between Orthodox theology and modern cosmology, one that seeks to illuminate contemporary physics, including discussions in ontology (the nature of things) and cosmology (the nature of the cosmos), from the standpoint of the Logos Christology (from John 1, for example) developed by the early church fathers. As a practicing scientist himself, then, Nesteruk suggests: "Scientific activity can be treated as a *cosmic eucharistic work* (a 'cosmic liturgy')."[46]

More recently, Wesleyan theologians like Michael Lodahl have also articulated a theology of nature from the resources in that ecclesial tradition.[47] In brief, Lodahl suggests that God graciously creates, sustains, and redeems/sanctifies all creation and does so by enabling creation to freely respond to the divine influence. This emphasis on creaturely freedom is, as those familiar with the Wesleyan tradition well know, central to Wesleyan theological instincts. So while Wesleyans may be surprised to find an untapped reservoir of resources in the writings of the Wesleys for a theology of nature, others interested in the science and religion conversation will find a deeply theological reading of the creation that nevertheless takes the sciences seriously. In fact, Lodahl's theology of nature and grace is potentially suggestive for thinking about an evolutionary creation (in which the world responds "freely" to the gracious initiative of God) as well as for responding appropriately to the environment (so that human beings can act ecologically in a manner consistent with God's prevenient grace).[48]

45. Alexei V. Nesteruk, *Light from the East: Theology, Science, and the Eastern Orthodox Tradition* (Minneapolis: Fortress, 2003). For another Orthodox viewpoint, albeit one that draws less explicitly on Orthodox sources, see Christopher C. Knight, *The God of Nature: Incarnation and Contemporary Science* (Minneapolis: Fortress, 2007).

46. Nesteruk, *Light from the East*, p. 2, italics in original.

47. Michael Lodahl, *God of Nature and of Grace: Reading the World in a Wesleyan Way* (Nashville: Kingswood Books, 2003).

48. For other Wesleyan voices in the theology and science dialogue, see Thomas Jay Oord, ed., *Divine Grace and Emerging Creation: Wesleyan Forays in Science and Theology of Creation* (Eugene, OR: Pickwick, 2009).

Understandably, pentecostals and charismatics with scientific training or with interest in the theology and science discussion (like Elbert and Lamoureux) are reluctant to engage in dialogue with their pentecostal or charismatic identities squarely on the table. Some of the reasons have already been highlighted in this introductory chapter. The result, however, has been that most pentecostal and charismatic scholars or scholar-scientists have been content with a generally evangelical or Christian identity. However, as the preceding discussion shows, it is possible that distinctive Christian theological traditions would have something unique to offer to the theology and science interface if they were to own rather than put aside their commitments. Is it possible that pentecostals and charismatics also have something inimitable to say if they come as themselves rather than as mere Christians/theists?

Before beginning to answer this question, however, I want to briefly survey a second set of developments in the last half-generation of theology and science conversations: those dealing with the willingness to probe more deeply into the role that specifically Christian commitments may play in the dialogue. By this I mean the increasing number of Christian theologians who are insisting that the conversation go further than general talk about God and ask what difference, if any, the insertion of the specificity of Christ — who, after all, is the fount apart from which Christianity is not — makes to the conversation. The result has been an overwhelmingly creative set of responses that have invigorated the discussion. There are at least two intertwined trajectories along these lines.

1. Most obviously, there have been attempts to rethink the various christological doctrines in light of the plausibility conditions established by modern science.[49] Thus, given what we now know about contemporary physics, evolutionary biology, the socio-cognitive sciences, etc., what can we say about the central doctrine of Christian faith: the incarnation of God in Christ?

2. More unexpectedly, strenuous efforts have been made in the other direction, one that asks: Given what Christians believe and confess about Christ, what kind of world should we expect modern science to

---

49. E.g., John Honner, "A New Ontology: Incarnation, Eucharist, Resurrection, and Physics," *Pacifica* 4 (1991): 15-50; Christopher C. Knight, *The God of Nature: Incarnation and Contemporary Science* (Minneapolis: Fortress, 2007); and F. LeRon Shults, *Christology and Science* (Grand Rapids and Cambridge: Eerdmans; Aldershot, UK: Ashgate, 2008).

unveil that would allow for such counterintuitive realities like the incarnation or that would make possible and illuminate other unfore-
seen events like the resurrection?[50] What does the nature of the life,
the death, and then the coming again to life of Christ reveal about the
way the world is and how God acts in the world?[51] Last but not least,
how, if at all, might this christologically charged vision interface with
contemporary science? In other words, christological commitments,
taken essentially by faith, frame questions that then impinge on scientific research projects.

These christological lines of inquiry have led, inexorably, toward Trinitarian proposals.[52] This should not be too surprising since from the beginning, Christian thinking about Christ has opened up to Trinitarian reflection. In the theology and science dialogue, once the specificity of
Christian doctrines regarding the person and work of Christ has been factored into the discussion, the whole Trinitarian dimension of the conversation emerges. Similarly, as with the christological theme, there have been
attempts to correlate Trinitarian theology with recent scientific advances
even as there have been efforts to chart methodological issues in theology
and science in light of Trinitarian perspectives.[53] At the same time, the
"Trinitarian turn" has proven to be an even more fecund source of creative
reflection and research at the theology and science intersection than may
have been anticipated when compared with christological proposals. In

50. This approach was launched initially by the Barthian theologian Thomas F.
Torrance, in his *Space, Time, and Incarnation* (London: Oxford University Press, 1969); see
also Tapio Luoma, *Incarnation and Physics: Natural Science in the Theology of Thomas F.
Torrance* (Oxford: Oxford University Press, 2002).

51. E.g., Ann Milliken Pederson, "The Centrality of Incarnation," *Zygon* 43, no. 1 (2008):
57-65; Niels Henrik Gregersen, "The Cross of Christ in an Evolutionary World," *Dialog* 40,
no. 3 (2001): 192-207; and Denis Edwards, "The Relationship between the Risen Christ and
the Material Universe," *Pacifica* 4 (1991): 1-14. Book-length discussions include George L.
Murphy, *The Cosmos in the Light of the Cross* (Harrisburg, PA, London, and New York: Trinity, 2003).

52. E.g., Denis Edwards, *The God of Evolution: A Trinitarian Theology* (New York and
Mahwah, NJ: Paulist, 1999).

53. For the former (Trinitarian correlations), see David N. Livingstone, "The
Thermodynamical Triple Point: Implications for the Trinity," *Perspectives on Science and
Christian Faith* 39, no. 1 (1987): 39-45; for the latter (methodological implications of Trinitarian theology), see K. Helmut Reich, "The Doctrine of the Trinity as a Model for Structuring
the Relations between Science and Theology," *Zygon* 30, no. 3 (1995): 383-405.

particular, there have been very ingenious suggestions to rethink the nature of time and temporality in conjunction with Trinitarian theology, especially taking into consideration the incarnational and pentecostal (referring to the events described in Acts 2, not to the modern pentecostal movement) events in salvation history, much of which has taken us deep into the mysteries of astrophysical cosmology, quantum physics, and the physics of thermodynamic processes.[54] Opposite these very abstruse (for most people, including scientists who work outside of the discipline of physics) discussions are the much more praxis-oriented proposals related to ecology and creation care that have also featured the creative interweaving of Trinitarian theology and the environmental sciences.[55]

One crest of this wave of Trinitarian contributions to the dialogue is John Polkinghorne's 2004 book *Science and the Trinity*.[56] What is Trinitarian about this volume is Polkinghorne's "bottom-up" approach that takes seriously the salvation history events at the heart of the Christian faith. Going further, however, Polkinghorne also says his theological method is based on what he calls a eucharistic or liturgy-assisted logic, that is, a type of Trinitarian logic that human beings experience sacramentally when gathered around the common meal (or Mass or communion). There is thus a "theological thickness" in the Trinitarian theology of nature pro-

---

54. Duane H. Larson, *Times of the Trinity: A Proposal for Theistic Cosmology*, Worcester Polytechnic Institute Studies in Science, Technology and Culture 17 (New York: Peter Lang, 1995); Robert W. Jenson, "Does God Have Time? The Doctrine of the Trinity and the Concept of Time in the Physical Sciences," *CTNS Bulletin* 11, no. 1 (1991): 1-6; Robert John Russell, "Is the Triune God the Basis for Physical Time?" *CTNS Bulletin* 11, no. 1 (1991): 7-19; Ted Peters, "The Trinity in and beyond Time," in *Quantum Cosmology and the Laws of Nature: Scientific Perspectives on Divine Action*, ed. Robert John Russell, Nancey Murphy, and C. J. Isham (1993; reprint, Vatican City State: Vatican Observatory; Berkeley, CA: Center for Theology and the Natural Sciences, 1999), pp. 263-89; and Michael Welker, "God's Eternity, God's Temporality, and Trinitarian Theology," *Theology Today* 55, no. 3 (1998): 317-28.

55. E.g., Loren Wilkinson, "The New Story of Creation: A Trinitarian Perspective," *ARC: The Journal of the Faculty of Religious Studies, McGill* 23 (1995): 137-52; Stephen R. Holmes, "Triune Creativity: Trinity, Creation, Art and Science," in *Trinitarian Soundings in Systematic Theology*, ed. Paul Louis Metzger (London and New York: T. & T. Clark, 2005), pp. 73-85.

56. John Polkinghorne, *Science and the Trinity: The Christian Encounter with Reality* (New Haven and London: Yale University Press, 2004). Polkinghorne is an elementary particle physicist turned Anglican priest and theologian; see my critical exposition, "From Quantum Mechanics to the Eucharistic Meal: John Polkinghorne's Vision of Science and Theology," in *The Global Spiral: A Publication of Metanexus Institute* 5, no. 5 (2005) (http://www.metanexus.net/magazine/ArticleDetail/tabid/68/id/9285/Default.aspx).

pounded in this book,[57] one that is serious about accounting for the richness of the Christian life, both that of the central event of the incarnation and all that is involved with it, and that of ongoing experiences of Christians, especially in their encounters with the risen Christ in the meal.

My major criticism of the Trinitarian vision of reality submitted in *Science and the Trinity* is its pneumatological deficiency. Polkinghorne does not say much about the Holy Spirit in this book other than that the Spirit combines with the Word as one of the Father's "two hands" (Irenaeus's metaphor) at work in the creation, and that the Spirit acts in a "hidden" manner within the world through "the input of information within its open history."[58] Other efforts to articulate a Trinitarian scientific theology, such as that of Alister McGrath, suffer from a similar neglect, with McGrath including only passing references to the Holy Spirit.[59] And when pneumatological references have emerged, they have inevitably been limited only to the sanctifying work of God in bringing the creation (or the cosmos) to its fulfillment.[60] Hence, even if much is said about the work of Christ, can we really have a viable Trinitarian theology when the Holy Spirit is absent, hidden, or neglected? Does not such result effectively in a binitarian theology instead?[61]

I am happy to report, however, that the Trinitarian turn in theology and science has not proceeded completely absent of pneumatological developments. While little of this pneumatological reflection has been registered in the theology and science discussion, we can note at least the following. First, the last generation has seen a gradual increase in pneumatological theologies of creation.[62] These would belong to the genre of

---

57. Chapter 3 of *Science and the Trinity* is titled "Theological Thickness."

58. Polkinghorne, *Science and the Trinity,* p. 84. See also John Polkinghorne and Michael Welker, *Faith in the Living God: A Dialogue* (Minneapolis: Fortress, 2001), chapter 5.

59. For the details of his Trinitarian scientific theology, see Alister E. McGrath, *A Fine-Tuned Universe: The Quest for God in Science and Theology* (Louisville: Westminster John Knox, 2009), especially chapter 6; the passing references to the Spirit appear on p. 72.

60. E.g., Keith Ward, *Religion and Creation* (Oxford: Clarendon, 1996), pp. 335 and 341, and David Ray Griffin, *Two Great Truths: A New Synthesis of Scientific Naturalism and Christian Faith* (Louisville and London: Westminster John Knox, 2004), chapter 2; cf. William L. Power, "The Doctrine of the Trinity and Whitehead's Metaphysics," *Encounter* 45, no. 4 (1984): 287-302.

61. As I argue has happened in general in the Christian theological tradition in my *Spirit-Word-Community: Theological Hermeneutics in Trinitarian Perspective* (Aldershot, UK, and Burlington, VT: Ashgate; Eugene, OR: Wipf and Stock, 2002), passim.

62. E.g., Jürgen Moltmann, *God in Creation: A New Theology of Creation and the Spirit*

theologies of creation (noted above), except that they are framed by pneumatological categories, concepts, and ideas. At the heart of this discussion is the notion of the world as the theater of the Holy Spirit's activity, and of the emergence of life as reflecting the life-giving and life-sustaining work of the Spirit. At the same time, there has been emphasis on the particularities of the creation's diversity as representing the creative activity of the world and of the creatures of the world in response to the Spirit.[63]

From this, second, have come more specific proposals toward a pneumatological theology of the environment. These can be considered either pneumatological eco-theologies (focused on creation care) or pneumatological cosmologies (seeking to comprehend the world beyond the bifurcation or dichotomy between matter and spirit).[64] The discourse here is in some cases dominated by green spirituality, but informed by pneumatological tropes: the earth suffers along with the wounded and divine spirit, while the world is also made alive by the same spirit.[65] Some might see in these proposals panentheistic frameworks with tendencies toward pantheism. I should say, though, that many of the theological moves seek to link deep ecology to the cruciform spirit.

Third, however, there have also been some efforts to engage pneumatology with theologies of nature.[66] Here attempts are made to correlate scientific notions — whether that of field theory, quantum mechan-

---

of God, trans. Margaret Kohl (Minneapolis: Fortress, 1993); Denis Edwards, *Breath of Life: A Theology of the Creator Spirit* (Maryknoll, NY: Orbis, 2004); and Clark H. Pinnock, "The Other Hand of God: God's Spirit in an Age of Scientific Cosmology," *Stone-Campbell Journal* 9, no. 2 (2006): 205-30.

63. See Colin E. Gunton, *The One, the Three, and the Many: God, Creation, and the Culture of Modernity* (Cambridge: Cambridge University Press, 1993), chapter 7, and Gunton, *Father, Son, and Holy Spirit: Essays toward a Fully Trinitarian Theology* (London and New York: T. & T. Clark, 2003), chapter 7.

64. Dawn M. Nothwehr, "The Ecological Spirit and Cosmic Mutuality: Engaging the Work of Denis Edwards," in *The Spirit in the Church and the World,* ed. Bradford E. Hinze, Annual Publication of the College Theology Society 2003, vol. 49 (Maryknoll, NY: Orbis, 2004), pp. 167-88; cf. W. J. Hollenweger, "All Creatures Great and Small: Towards a Pneumatology of Life," in *Strange Gifts? A Guide to Charismatic Renewal,* ed. David Martin and Peter Mullen (Oxford and New York: Basil Blackwell, 1984), pp. 41-53.

65. E.g., Mark I. Wallace, *Fragments of the Spirit: Nature, Violence, and the Renewal of Creation* (Harrisburg, PA: Trinity, 2002), and *Finding God in the Singing River: Christianity, Spirit, Nature* (Minneapolis: Fortress, 2005).

66. George L. Murphy, "The Third Article in the Science-Theology Dialogue," *Perspectives on Science and Christian Faith* 45, no. 3 (1993): 162-68.

ics, or information theory — with the Spirit.[67] Of course, the challenges here are at least twofold: that of subordinating biblical and theological themes to scientific concepts, and that of presuming, perhaps, that there is more than just an analogy that links the theological themes and scientific models under consideration. We will engage with some of these ideas later (see chapters 3–4).

Last but by no means least, then, we turn to the methodological bases for linking pneumatology and science. Here, philosophers like Philip Clayton have helpfully identified what might be called a pneumatological methodology that can contribute to the theology and science discussion, one that "involves a two-fold transformation of our own experience of spirit: (1) we extrapolate from the qualities of spirit known through the natural world and through encounters with other human persons, augmenting them to the level appropriate to divine Spirit, and (2) we seek to conceive the nature of Infinite Spirit based on our experience as embodied agents."[68] The result invites various pneumatological categories of research: spirit as a basic ontological category; spirit as neither monistic nor dualistic but relational; spirit as involving community; spirit as pointing to the dynamic character of reality; and God (who is spirit) and the world as neither separable nor indistinct. Might these kinds of pneumatological inquiries provide an open door for the insertion of pentecostal perspectives in the discussion?

Science and Theology of Creation in Pentecostal Perspective: Thesis and Overview of the Book

In my own work over the last few years, I have sought to contribute to the emerging discussion of theology of nature from a pentecostal and espe-

---

67. E.g., Wolfhart Pannenberg, *Systematic Theology,* trans. Geoffrey W. Bromiley, 3 vols. (Grand Rapids: Eerdmans, 1991-1994), 1:383 and 2:83-84; Wolfhart Pannenberg, *The Historicity of Nature: Essays on Science and Theology,* ed. Niels Henrik Gregersen (West Conshohocken, PA: Templeton Foundation Press, 2008), chapter 6; and Ernest L. Simmons, "Toward a Kenotic Pneumatology: Quantum Field Theory and the Theology of the Cross," *CTNS Bulletin* 19, no. 2 (1999): 11-16.

68. Philip Clayton, "In Whom We Have Our Being: Philosophical Resources for the Doctrine of the Spirit," in *Advents of the Spirit: An Introduction to the Current Study of Pneumatology,* ed. Bradford E. Hinze and D. Lyle Dabney, Marquette Studies in Theology 30 (Milwaukee: Marquette University Press, 2001), pp. 173-207, quotation from p. 194.

cially pneumatological perspective. Throughout, I have argued that while pentecostals have a very christocentric piety, their overall spirituality is also pneumatically oriented.[69] What I mean is that at the heart of pentecostal sensibilities is a specific kind of pneumatological imagination, one that infuses their being-in-the-world in a distinctive manner.[70]

I have already begun to apply this pneumatological imagination toward the construction of a specifically pentecostal approach to the theology and science conversation. What I have called a pneumatological theology of nature — or pneumatological theology of creation — starts with the Spirit (experientially and theologically), and from that vantage point seeks to engage, interact with, and perhaps even include scientific perspectives in attempting to comprehend the creation of God (the natural world). In this book, I wish to further develop such ideas by arguing two major and two minor theses. The major theses, with which we will begin, are methodological and theological.

Methodologically, I believe that a pentecostal perspective on the theology and science discussion can complement other approaches that emphasize a diversity of modes of engagement. My formulation of this principle of complementarity between theology and science has two aspects.[71] First, while I am intrigued by the argument for complementarity inspired by the quantum physicist Niels Bohr (1885-1962),[72] my own version is much more

69. Here I have built on the work of Harvey Cox, whose *Fire from Heaven* suggests that pentecostal piety partakes of a primal religiosity and spirituality characteristic of many indigenous traditions; see my interaction with Cox's thesis in Yong, *Discerning the Spirit(s): A Pentecostal-Charismatic Contribution to Christian Theology of Religions* (Sheffield: Sheffield Academic Press, 2000), pp. 17-20.

70. I develop my thinking about the pneumatological imagination in my *Spirit-Word-Community,* part II; see also Yong, "On Divine Presence and Divine Agency: Toward a Foundational Pneumatology," *Asian Journal of Pentecostal Studies* 3, no. 2 (July 2000): 167-88.

71. I have drawn from various sources — e.g., James E. Loder and W. Jim Neidhardt, *The Knight's Move: The Relational Logic of the Spirit in Theology and Science* (Colorado Springs: Helmers and Howard, 1992), especially section 1; Edward Mackinnnon, "Complementarity," in *Religion and Science: History, Method, Dialogue,* ed. W. Mark Richardson and Wesley J. Wildman (New York and London: Routledge, 1996), pp. 255-70; and briefly, Alister E. McGrath, *Science and Religion: An Introduction* (Oxford and Malden, MA: Blackwell, 2010), pp. 165-74. See also John Losee, *Religious Language and Complementarity* (Lanham, MD: University Press of America, 1992), especially chapters 9 and 11.

72. Bohr's complementarianism had to do with how quantum phenomena could be measured either as wavelike or as particle-like, but never in the same measurement. This notion has initiated a range of proposals suggesting that theology (and religion) and science are complementary in ways similar to quantum phenomena. See the full yet succinct discus-

pragmatic and theological. What I mean is that science, which studies the natural world — theologically: the creation of God — reveals the character of the Creator in ways that complement what can be learned from the revelatory sources of religious traditions.[73] Truth is, in a theological sense, unitary, and so the data from which truth is derived cannot ultimately be contradictory. If there appears to be any contradiction between theology and science, it may be because both are in error, or the revelatory sources of religious traditions have been misunderstood, or the experimental findings of scientists have been misinterpreted. My complementarianism might involve situations when theology and science speak to altogether distinct realities, but it may also be that on other occasions they converge on the same thing, or that the lines between what they are addressing are blurred. In other words, while in some respects some might want to affirm the autonomy and distinctiveness of theology and science,[74] in other respects no consensus has yet been reached (for example, when it comes to the parapsychological sciences, as we shall see later).[75]

The second aspect of the complementarity between theology and science is that neither theology nor science is homogeneous, which means there will be numerous ways in which the discourses of theology and the findings of various scientific disciplines can and do complement each other. This explains in part why there are various ways through which the theology and science dialogue itself is being conducted.[76] I will present in

sion by Henry J. Folse, *The Philosophy of Niels Bohr: The Framework of Complementarity* (Amsterdam: North-Holland Physics Publishing, 1985).

73. As a Christian, I affirm the Old and New Testaments as being revelatory, although as a catholic Christian, I am sympathetic with how the Jewish and Christian traditions play essential roles in our understanding of what these revelatory documents say; see my argument in *Spirit-Word-Community,* part III.

74. E.g., as affirmed by the late Pope John Paul II; see "Message of His Holiness Pope John Paul II," in *Physics, Philosophy, and Theology: A Common Quest for Understanding,* ed. Robert J. Russell, William R. Stoeger, and George V. Coyne (Vatican City State: Vatican Observatory; Notre Dame, IN: University of Notre Dame Press, 1988), pp. M1-M14, especially M8.

75. So, while I appreciate Steven Gould's attempt to distinguish the authority of science and religion as nonoverlapping magisteria, I don't think it's really possible to demarcate or compartmentalize them as he does. See Stephen Jay Gould, "Nonoverlapping Magisteria: Science and Religion Are Not in Conflict, for Their Teachings Occupy Distinctly Different Domains," *Natural History* 106, no. 2 (1997): 16-22 and 60-62; and *Leonardo's Mountain of Clams and the Diet of Worms: Essays on Natural History* (New York: Three Rivers Press, 1998), chapter 14.

76. See, e.g., Niels Henrik Gregersen and J. Wentzel van Huyssteen, eds., *Rethinking Theology and Science: Six Models for the Current Dialogue* (Grand Rapids: Eerdmans, 1998).

this volume a theological justification for such a pluralistic methodology that derives from the heart of the pentecostal experience. In brief, pentecostal piety features the spiritual practice of glossolalia, which pentecostals believe to be speaking in tongues according to the model provided by the Day of Pentecost phenomenon as described in Acts 2. Pentecostal scholars have argued that the many tongues of the Day of Pentecost can be understood not only historically and linguistically but also theologically, so that the plurality of glossolalic utterances has ecumenical significance with regard to the diversity of Christian communions and their gifts, or postcolonial relevance with regard to the many cultures, ethnicities, and people groups that characterize the contemporary landscape of global renewal and world Christianity.[77] Building on this methodological platform, I have already presented extended book-length arguments that the many tongues of Pentecost not only suggest a theological anthropology that recognizes the diversity of human ways of being in and knowing the world but also illuminate a pluralistic theology of interfaith practices as well as a public theology of various political, social, civil, and economic postures.[78]

How might such a pentecostal and pluralistic theology be applied to the theology and science conversation? First, I suggest that a pentecostal theology of many tongues invites consideration of how the various models for theology and science engagement are valid, albeit in different respects. Thus we will privilege theological categories and commitments even as we are constrained by the empirical data produced by the sciences, albeit in various respects. There would also be situations in which we treat theological and scientific discourses as nonoverlapping domains, while there may be other contexts in which we seek convergence, and still others where we persist in mutual truth-seeking dialogue even when the way forward is not very clear. Various phases of the argument in this volume will highlight how these very diverse models for theology and science engagement can be

77. The ecumenical argument for tongues has been made by Frank D. Macchia, "The Tongues of Pentecost: A Pentecostal Perspective on the Promise and Challenge of the Pentecostal/Roman Catholic Dialogue," *Journal of Ecumenical Studies* 35, no. 1 (1998): 1-18, while the cultural argument has been presented by Samuel Solivan, *The Spirit, Pathos, and Liberation: Toward an Hispanic Pentecostal Theology* (Sheffield: Sheffield Academic Press, 1998), pp. 112-18. See also my further synthesis in *Spirit Poured Out*, chapter 4.

78. See Yong, *Theology and Down Syndrome: Reimagining Disability in Late Modernity* (Waco, TX: Baylor University Press, 2007); *Hospitality and the Other: Pentecost, Christian Practices, and the Neighbor* (Maryknoll, NY: Orbis, 2008); *In the Days of Caesar: Pentecostalism and Political Theology* (Grand Rapids: Eerdmans, 2010).

operative. As a theologian, however, I will continually reflect on how the many tongues of Pentecost metaphor can serve as a theological guide for such a variegated methodological approach.

Second, I propose also that the many pentecostal tongues can be understood analogically as providing a theological rationale for the many scientific disciplines. In this framework, the various sciences — natural, social, and human — function like distinct languages, each with its own presuppositions, traditions of practices (inquiries), and explanations. The many tongues analogy thus underwrites, theologically, both the multidisciplinary and interdisciplinary character of the theology and science encounter. Multiple disciplines are involved, and we have to heed the relative autonomy of each discipline. At the same time, there is an increasing interdisciplinarity as well in terms of the ways in which various disciplines influence and inform others.[79] This book on theology and science is already at least bidisciplinary in subject matter. A pentecostal perspective would suggest that this involves a translation of languages that interprets the values, presuppositions, and practices of each side to the other. This volume as a whole will seek to perform such an interpretation of tongues so that by the end, readers will be able to discern if in fact the methodologically pluralistic theology upon which it proceeds is successful. An affirmative response would indicate that the many tongues metaphor illuminates the disparate character of theology and science engagement as well as its multi- and interdisciplinary character. A negative reply would suggest that the tongues analogy is more forced than helpful, more a theological imposition than one with heuristic power.

Besides this dual methodological proposal, I will also present and attempt to defend a theological hypothesis, one motivated by my conviction that a pentecostal perspective on the theology and science discussion can help further the discussion in pneumatological theologies of nature and of creation that we introduced above. In the main, I believe that pneumatological theologies of nature and creation assist in countering the scientistic and positivistic reductionisms of the world that leave the realm of spirit eviscerated and that promote materialistic and naturalistic exaggerations instead. Yet, while we need a science and even a metaphysics of spirit, the

---

79. See J. Wentzel van Huyssteen, *The Shaping of Rationality: Toward Interdisciplinarity in Theology and Science* (Grand Rapids; Eerdmans, 1999), and Christine Ledger and Stephen Pickard, eds., *Creation and Complexity: Interdisciplinary Issues in Science and Religion* (Adelaide, Australia: ATF Press, 2004).

route toward such ends is fraught with all sorts of pitfalls. If modernity first severed the spiritual from the material and then took leave of the former altogether, postmodernity's reenchanted world threatens to overwhelm the material with the spiritual and leave us levitating in the world of the New Age instead.[80] Is it possible that pentecostal perspectives, despite the fantastic nature of some aspects of pentecostal spirituality, might help us recover an enspirited world, but one that empowers rather than eviscerates the scientific enterprise?[81] The result would be not only a theological ethic that helps us to navigate our way in a pneumatologically charged world,[82] but also an orientation that perhaps also returns to inform both the theology and science conversation and the ongoing scientific enterprise.

While in a real sense this whole book will be an exploration of this theological hypothesis — that is, that a pentecostal perspective has something unique to contribute to the ongoing discussions in pneumatological theologies of nature and of creation — the following pages will also explicitly take up two specific tasks within this overarching framework: developing a theology of divine action in light of the long-term discussions of this topic in the theology and science dialogue, and sketching a pneumatological cosmology that is sensitive to both the pentecostal worldview and the contemporary cosmological and astrophysical sciences. Efforts in these two directions represent my two minor theological theses. Let me briefly locate these tasks within the broader framework of this volume.

---

80. An example of "New Age science" writ large would be Ted Andrews, *Enchantment of the Faerie Realm: Communicate with Nature Spirits and Elementals* (St. Paul: Llewellyn Publications, 1993). Much more in touch with the scientific establishment but still considered by many to be on the fringes where "real science" meets the "New Age" is Ervin Laszlo, *Science and the Reenchantment of the Cosmos: The Rise of the Integral Vision of Reality* (Rochester, VT: Inner Traditions, 2006).

81. More mainstream theological proposals for "reenchantment" include David Ray Griffin, *The Reenchantment of Science: Postmodern Proposals* (Albany: State University of New York Press, 1988), and Alister E. McGrath, *The Re-enchantment of Nature: Science, Religion, and the Human Sense of Wonder* (London: Hodder and Stoughton, 2002), reprinted in North America as *The Reenchantment of Nature: The Denial of Religion and the Ecological Crisis* (New York: Doubleday, 2003). A secularist attempt to rehabilitate Darwinism for an enchanted late modernity is George Levine, *Darwin Loves You: Natural Selection and the Reenchantment of the World* (Princeton: Princeton University Press, 2006).

82. As intuited by fellow pentecostal theologian Andrew Gabriel, "Pneumatological Perspectives for a Theology of Nature: The Holy Spirit in Relation to Ecology and Technology," *Journal of Pentecostal Theology* 15, no. 2 (2007): 195-212.

The theory of divine action is motivated precisely by routine claims regarding the presence and activity of the Holy Spirit in pentecostal spirituality and piety. Given the pervasiveness of the Spirit's work in pentecostal testimonies, and given the living expectation that the Spirit of God is active in the world to heal, deliver, meet needs, and bring about otherwise impossible events in the world, any pentecostal engagement with the sciences must squarely confront this issue. In this book, I take up this question of the Holy Spirit's action in the world by engaging with the existing debates regarding divine action within the theology and science dialogue. My proposal, a teleological model of divine action, attempts to reimagine pentecostal self-understandings of the Spirit's activity while simultaneously acknowledging the world's causal processes as illuminated by modern science.

The pneumatological cosmology that I will sketch — and I can do no more than briefly outline my ideas on this matter in this volume — attempts to account for the "enchanted universe" that pentecostals in particular but also many Christians believe they inhabit. What scientific sense can we make of the world of spirits, angels, and demons that populate the pentecostal and charismatic imagination? If modern scientific reductionism has evacuated the cosmos of spiritual beings, creatures, and powers,[83] pentecostal and popular Christian piety strains under the burden of having to make do in a world of competing spiritual forces. In this book, I take seriously such pentecostal and charismatic Christian self-understandings regarding the nature of the cosmos, but simultaneously attempt to locate such perspectives in relationship to the dominant scientific narratives — even myths[84] — that shape and structure our late modern state of knowledge. My thesis is to suggest, very tentatively, an emergentist cosmology that provides nonreductionistic accounts for pneumatic or spiritual realities while, at the same time, challenging dualistic construals about the relationship between the spiritual and material world.

83. As was pointed out long ago by anthropologist Paul Hiebert, in his now classic essay "The Flaw of the Excluded Middle," *Missiology* 10, no. 1 (1982): 35-47. See also Hiebert's *Anthropological Reflections on Missiological Issues* (Grand Rapids: Baker, 1994), chapter 12.

84. By "myth" I don't mean that the deliverances of science are mythological in the popular sense of being made up and untrue to reality; rather, I mean that the narrative of science has now emerged as modernity's own myth about human and cosmic origins, with its own explanatory power as well. Here, I am in agreement with and follow Adam Frank, *The Constant Fire: Beyond the Science vs. Religion Debate* (Berkeley: University of California Press, 2009), especially part II, who helps us see how modern science functions mythically in our time.

In both of these minor theses — that regarding a pneumatological theology of divine action and that involving the quest for a pneumatological cosmology — our motivation comes primarily from the depths of the pentecostal experience. Thus both queries contribute to the major theological hypothesis — a pneumatological theology of nature and of creation — that drives the inquiry of this volume. And the theological thesis and methodological proposal also cohere in that both follow out the intuitions embedded in pentecostal piety and practice, and both are attuned to pentecostal sensibilities and commitments.

If successful, then, this volume will not merely contribute to the theology and science discussion, but will perhaps also do its part in overturning the regnant modernist paradigm that still holds sway even in such circles. By this I mean that any privileging of positivistic methodologies and materialistic ontologies will need to be tempered to acknowledge that there may be other viable methods of inquiry as well as pneumatic, if not pneumatological, modes of reality that need to be factored into the discussion. The result will be that pentecostal perspectives will undoubtedly be chastened, even corrected; but simultaneously, pentecostal insights will also potentially inform, maybe even transform, the reigning discursive practices operating at the intersection of theology and science. At the very least, the dialogue between theology and science will not be able to proceed as if pentecostal Christianity had never arrived at the dialogue table; even more disruptive might be that the paths of scientific inquiry will hereafter more intentionally be informed not just by generically theistic or even vaguely Christian (or evangelical) perspectives, but also by pentecostal and pneumatological ones.

Here is what the reader can expect in the following pages. Chapter 2 presents scientific explorations of pentecostalism and asks both methodological and theo-anthropological questions; the goal here is to realize both the potential and the limits of science in illuminating pentecostal phenomena, and then to query what this means for a contemporary theological anthropology informed by the pentecostal encounter with science. The next two chapters successively interact with the Divine Action Project that has been ongoing in theology and science circles for over twenty years in order to develop a more Trinitarian theology of divine action that is informed by robustly pneumatological, eschatological, and teleological perspectives,[85] and then test the plausibility of this model of pneumatological

---

85. I should note up front that my teleological proposal is thoroughly theological in

divine action in conversation with theories about the laws of nature. The result intends to contribute to the articulation of an authentic pentecostal witness at the theology and science table while it also enables a more plausible and coherent account of divine action for pentecostal piety and Christian practice in the twenty-first century. I then step back from the debates of divine action theory to sketch a rudimentary pneumatological theology of creation in two steps: a pneumatological and eschatological theology of evolutionary emergence (chapter 5) that builds on the methodological pluralism and the teleological theory of divine action of the preceding chapters, and a fairly novel pneumatological ontology and cosmology (chapter 6) that explore what it means to talk about not only a Spirit-infused and Spirit-suffused but also a spirit-filled world. An epilogue concludes the volume.

---

conceptualization, being driven by an eschatological orientation informed by the life and teachings of Christ. Part of the burden of this book is to make the argument that teleological thinking can be incorporated into the theology and science discussion without jeopardizing work in the latter domain.

2 The Science of Pentecostalism

Spirit and Interdisciplinarity in Theology and Science

In this chapter we take our initial steps toward a constructive dialogue between pentecostalism and science. Our goal here is to display the illuminative power of science regarding pentecostalism while yet also securing a noneliminative or nonreductionistic interpretation of the latter.[1] If we are successful, we will see how pentecostalism in particular and, by extension, religion in general have nothing to fear from science. Rather, there is a dual relationship: on the one hand, religious phenomena are open to and even invite scientific investigation; but on the other hand, the peculiarities of human religiosity resist facile reductionism to any single scientific perspective. In pentecostalism, the neuropsychological and social sciences can help us understand a great deal; at the same time, pentecostalism and pentecostal phenomena throw up distinctive questions that chart scientific research agendas even as these questions persist against the grain of totalizing explanations within any disciplinary or explanatory horizon.

We begin with scientific investigations of pentecostalism and then, in a methodological reversal, ask whether there are specifically pentecostal approaches to the various sciences. Our chapter commences with psychological investigations of pentecostal glossolalia (tongues speaking), which will include more recent cognitive scientific explorations. We then turn to so-

1. As Edward Slingerhand, "Who's Afraid of Reductionism? The Study of Religion in the Age of Cognitive Science," *Journal of the American Academy of Religion* 76, no. 2 (2008): 375-411, notes, all explanations are reductive in some respect, so the goal of any disciplinary inquiry should be *noneliminative* reductionism, a reductionism that recognizes but does not do violence to other, especially insider, accounts of the phenomenon.

ciological studies of pentecostalism, observing the evolution of social scientific analyses of the movement in relationship to the secularization thesis and the Weberian theory of charisma and routinization. These (cognitive) psychological and sociological overviews will set the stage for our sketch of what I call a pluralistic and interdisciplinary methodology for theology and science, one informed distinctively by pentecostal spirituality.

Within the broader scheme of this volume, this chapter seeks to contribute in general to its two major theses. On the one hand, I will endeavor to demonstrate the plausibility of the methodological approach that is derived analogically from the many tongues of the Pentecost narrative and from the pentecostal experience; hence I suggest that the various disciplinary perspectives brought to bear on the study of pentecostalism each speak truly in some way from those points of view and with regard to those levels of analysis. On the other hand, I suggest that when pentecostal self-understandings are factored in as well, that in turn invites a recognition of the multidimensional character of human life, one that acknowledges the ontological complexity that constitutes the interface of the spiritual and the material domains of this world. Both theses, of course, support and sustain each other.

The (Cognitive) Psychology of Pentecostalism:
Many Tongues, Many Interpretations

Not surprisingly, there have been psychological assessments of pentecostalism almost from the very beginning of the movement in the early twentieth century because of the prevalence of glossolalia in pentecostal spirituality.[2] In most pentecostal self-understandings, of course, glossolalia is a sign of the presence and activity of the Holy Spirit, although we will bracket out this theological claim for the moment and return to it in our concluding section of this chapter. Nor surprisingly, the manifestation of glossolalia has perennially captured the interests of outside observers, and psychologists have been no less fascinated by it. In the following discus-

---

2. My survey is rather selective, according to my own agenda. An earlier overview is James T. Richardson, "Psychological Interpretations of Glossolalia: A Reexamination of Research," in *Speaking in Tongues: A Guide to Research on Glossolalia*, ed. Watson E. Mills (Grand Rapids: Eerdmans, 1986), pp. 369-79; more recently, a fairly exhaustive discussion of behavioral-science studies is provided by Mark J. Cartledge, *Charismatic Glossolalia: An Empirico-Theological Study* (Aldershot, UK, and Burlington, VT: Ashgate, 2002), pp. 85-102.

sion, I want to briefly focus on two strands of research: behavioral-psychological studies and newer cognitive scientific investigations. Each strand, I suggest, is illuminative of pentecostal piety even if found to be sorely wanting when taken as a total explanation.

The first psychological assessments appeared not long after the Azusa Street revival and were mostly critical of the phenomenon. Alexander Mackie, a Presbyterian minister, was motivated in his inquiry by the claim by "unthinking Christians" that the present revival involved a restoration of the apostolic charismata.[3] He focused on the Shakers, the Irvingites, and the primitive Mormons, convinced that, phenomenologically, they exhibited the same mental and physiological traits as the modern pentecostals, and concluded that all were behaviorally and psychologically pathological. Tongues speech was inevitably, in his view, accompanied by falling, jerking, barking, and uncontrollable laughing, if not also by ethically objectionable features like perverse sexual tendencies, egomania, and habitual lying. The mental state of someone speaking in tongues was thus comparable with "a pathological condition as in alcoholic intoxication or in epilepsy."[4]

A few years later George Cutten, the sitting president of Colgate University who had earned a Ph.D. in psychology, published another historical survey that included a chapter on the psychology of tongues speaking.[5] While likening glossolalia to ecstatic experiences, catalepsy, and hysteria, Cutten was careful to acknowledge that these were phenomenological descriptions rather than etiological or even theological explanations. Yet after deploying various personal disintegration models then prevalent in the psychological sciences of his day to discuss the personal instability and subconscious elements that precipitated or seemed to be consistently associated with tongues speech, he concluded: "As far as I know there is no case of speaking in strange tongues which has been strictly and scientifically investigated that cannot be explained by recognized psychological laws."[6] While not wishing to be reductionistic, Cutten ends up relying on questionable empirical data, resulting in an interpretation of glossolalia in particular and pentecostal experience in general that discounted the inward subjective experience or conscious understanding of tongues speakers.

3. Alexander Mackie, *The Gift of Tongues: A Study in Pathological Aspects of Christianity* (New York: George H. Doran Co., 1921), p. vii.
4. Mackie, *The Gift of Tongues*, p. 263.
5. George Barton Cutten, *Speaking with Tongues: Historically and Psychologically Considered* (New Haven: Yale University Press, 1927), chapter 9.
6. Cutten, *Speaking with Tongues*, p. 181.

These "scientifically established results" held sway for the next few generations.[7] Even after the dawn of the charismatic renewal movement in the mainline churches, Baptist scholars like Wayne Oates suggested that glossolalic mentalities could be illuminated through the study of the thought patterns of children or of the mentally ill.[8] Oates concluded that tongues speakers

> had weak egos, confused identities, high levels of anxiety, and unstable personality. They had chaotic religious backgrounds and a remarkable degree of emotional deprivation. Emotion deprivation does not follow socio-economic lines. It appears in the homes of the most affluent where communication is non-existent and where clear expressions of open trust are absent. The terrible isolation and loneliness of successful people in the middle-class churches has broken out in other forms and manners in this generation. The hyperdependence upon alcohol, the high incidence of psychosomatic disorders, the absence of a clear-cut family structure, and the conventionalization of the church life all provide a fertile soil for the sudden chaotic breakthrough represented in glossolalia.[9]

Clearly, for Oates, tongues speakers were regressive and repressed, if not psychologically disturbed, personalities. That Oates and his colleagues would see glossolalia in such light should not have been surprising given their cessationist convictions about charismatic manifestations after the apostolic period.

Yet the explosive growth of the charismatic renewal through the 1960s could not help but leave an impact on the psychological study of pentecostalism. The Lutheran minister and psychologist John Kildahl produced the important study *The Psychology of Speaking in Tongues*.[10] Kildahl concluded that glossolalists may be more suggestible or submissive personali-

7. Even more recently, there have been assessments of glossolalia in terms of hysteria; see Emma Gonsalvez, "A Psychological Interpretation of Religious Behaviour of Pentecostals and Charismatics," *Journal of Dharma* 7 (1982): 408-29.

8. Wayne E. Oates, "A Socio-Psychological Study of Glossolalia," in Frank Stagg, E. Glenn Hinson, and Wayne E. Oates, *Glossolalia: Tongues Speaking in Biblical, Historical, and Psychological Perspective* (New York and Nashville: Abingdon, 1967), pp. 76-99.

9. Oates, "Socio-Psychological Study of Glossolalia," p. 97.

10. John P. Kildahl, *The Psychology of Speaking in Tongues* (New York: Harper and Row, 1972).

ties, more easily influenced by authoritative, charismatic leaders or peer pressure (especially individuals seeking social acceptance), and that there is a correlation between the openness to tongues speaking and hypnotizability (even if the two are distinct). And rather than being seen as a psychological (or psychotic) aberration, glossolalia was indeed "a learned phenomenon,"[11] one that involved a more or less predictable sequence of events including the personal realization of an existential crisis, the establishment of relationship within a larger community, the emergence of a satisfactory rationale, and an inviting atmosphere.[12] The result was that tongues speech was a more "normal" rather than less "normal" psychological state of being.

The most important scientific study of tongues since Kildahl's is the longitudinal collaborative research of psychologists H. Newton Malony and A. Adams Lovekin.[13] After critically evaluating previous assessments of glossolalia as anomalous, aberrant (pathological), or extraordinary (i.e., trance-induced or deprivation-based) behavior, Malony and Lovekin attempted to track the effects of glossolalia. Tongues speaking, they found, did not effect measurable physical changes, but it did alleviate depression and enabled coping with anxiety. Addictive behaviors, among other behavioral changes, seemed to have been effected as well, although it is impossible to isolate glossolalia as the causal variable from the wider milieu within which tongues speech occurs. Perhaps most importantly, glossolalia produced attitudinal and axiological transformations in personal self-understanding. Not as many were motivated toward sociopolitical engagement, but many recounted how glossolalic prayer reoriented them especially in their relationship with God.

From this, Malony and Lovekin concluded that the glossolalic experience is best understood as a manifestation of what B. J. Mawn calls "transcendency deprivation," that which drives the quest for "more immediate religious experience."[14] Thus, they classified the glossolalic phenomenon

11. Kildahl, *The Psychology of Speaking*, p. 74.

12. See also John P. Kildahl, "Psychological Observations," in *Speaking in Tongues: A Guide to Research on Glossolalia*, ed. Watson E. Mills (Grand Rapids: Eerdmans, 1986), pp. 347-68, especially 352-55.

13. H. Newton Malony and A. Adams Lovekin, *Glossolalia: Behavioral Science Perspectives on Speaking in Tongues* (New York and Oxford: Oxford University Press, 1985).

14. Malony and Lovekin, *Glossolalia*, p. 259, referring to B. J. Mawn, "Testing the Spirits: An Empirical Search for the Socio-Cultural Situational Roots of the Catholic Pentecostal Religious Experience" (Ph.D. diss., Boston University, 1975).

under the category of *mysticism,* as defined by historian of religion Ernst Troeltsch (1865-1923). For Troeltsch, mysticism characterized a kind of religiously-individualistic and inwardly-spiritualistic orientation toward the transcendent that, at least in some instances, functioned experientially to legitimate participation and membership in religious groups.[15] Malony and Lovekin preferred this Troeltschean approach because it "avoids the errors of reductionism and functionalism" by taking seriously participants' own perspectives while allowing, even encouraging, the ongoing scientific study of the issues.[16]

Malony and Lovekin's research took into consideration the self-understanding of glossolalists as it changed over time. Several aspects of this present trend of research in the psychology of pentecostalism can be observed. First, involving pentecostal insiders in such studies gives them opportunity to register their own perspective to the researcher. This can happen at both the quantitative and the qualitative level. Quantitatively, for example, pentecostals or glossolalists can complete questionnaires of various sorts that in turn produce cumulative and comparable data. One study suggested that glossolalia on its own did not correlate significantly with integrated personalities, although a more positive correlation was found for those who participated in charismatic environments and activities over extended periods of time.[17]

In another case, however, William Kay and Leslie Francis queried 364 (British) pentecostal ministry candidates with the widely used Eysenck Personality Questionnaire, and concluded that these candidates, compared with Anglican ministry candidates and general public samples, were nei-

15. For discussion of Troeltsch's category of mysticism, see William R. Garrett, "Maligned Mysticism: The Maledicted Career of Troeltsch's Third Type," *Sociological Analysis* 36, no. 3 (1975): 205-23. Karl-Fritz Daiber, "Troeltsch's Third Type of Religious Collectivities," *Social Compass* 49, no. 3 (2002): 329-41, however, reminds us that Troeltsch's mysticism type also tended to renounce religious community and its commitments, and in that respect would fit pentecostalism less exactly than his sect-type. In the next section we discuss other scholars who categorize the pentecostal phenomenon in Troeltschean sect terms.

16. Malony and Lovekin, *Glossolalia,* p. 261. See also William R. Garrett, "Troublesome Transcendence: The Supernatural in the Scientific Study of Religion," *Sociological Analysis* 35, no. 3 (1974): 167-80, who argues that a phenomenological approach that explores the consequences or effects of beliefs in or experiences of the transcendent allows social scientists to avoid both reductionism and functionalism while also taking emic perspectives into consideration.

17. Adams Lovekin and H. Newton Malony, "Religious Glossolalia: A Longitudinal Study of Personality Changes," *Journal for the Scientific Study of Religion* 16, no. 4 (1977): 383-93.

ther more or less extroverted nor more or less psychotic or neurotic. More interestingly, and here in direct contrast to the Lovekin and Malony study, the data also suggested that glossolalic practice — which was *the* characteristic that distinguished pentecostal from nonpentecostal ministry candidates — not only "promotes positive aspects of psychological health" but also more than likely "functions to reduce tension or to integrate personality."[18] The difference may have been, at least in part, that Lovekin and Malony focused on American Roman Catholic charismatics in contrast to the subjects of Kay and Francis's study.

Qualitatively speaking, the research of empirical theologian Mark Cartledge has also shown how pentecostal insider or emic perspectives can further our understanding of glossolalia as a psycho-behavioral phenomenon.[19] Along with studies such as Kildahl's that emphasized the social aspects of glossolalia as learned behavior, William Samarin had explicitly identified a more important role for family and friends in the nurturing of glossolalics.[20] In his ethnographic study of pentecostalism, however, Cartledge determined that the role of friends and family, while present, is overestimated. Rather, building on but also developing Kildahl's observations, he asserts that the "most significant influences are personal Bible study and church leadership."[21] People come into the "tongues experience" as much because of their own personal religious searches as because they experience "peer pressure" from significant others. Yet there are also documented instances of glossolalics who had embraced tongues speaking without prior exposure, which cautions against overemphasizing the social character of the phenomenon.[22]

Cartledge's study also reveals that emic data inevitably opens up to and invites a more substantial religious and theological account. This is

18. Leslie J. Francis and William K. Kay, "The Personality Characteristic of Pentecostal Ministry Candidates," *Personality and Individual Differences* 18, no. 5 (1995): 581-94, quotes from 589-90; cp. William K. Kay and L. J. Francis, "Personality, Mental Health and Glossolalia," *Pneuma* 17, no. 2 (1995): 253-63.

19. Mark J. Cartledge, *Practical Theology: Charismatic and Empirical Perspectives* (Carlisle, UK, and Waynesboro, GA: Paternoster, 2003).

20. William J. Samarin, *Tongues of Men and Angels: The Religious Language of Pentecostalism* (New York and London: Macmillan, 1972).

21. Cartledge, *Practical Theology,* p. 226.

22. See William K. Kay, "The Mind, Behaviour and Glossolalia: A Psychological Perspective," in *Speaking in Tongues: Multi-Disciplinary Perspectives,* ed. Mark J. Cartledge (Milton Keynes, UK, and Waynesboro, GA: Paternoster, 2006), pp. 174-205, especially 204-5 n. 100.

because the self-understanding of religious practitioners includes explicitly religious and theological dimensions that a reductionistic social scientific approach either has to reject or else can only ignore. It is for this reason that previous research "fails to come to grips directly with the experience of tongues-speaking as a patently personal religious phenomenon."[23] In other words, the religious dimension of glossolalia needs to be factored in, and this is accessed, at least in part, from the practitioner's point of view. For the purposes of the theology and science conversation, Cartledge reminds us also that "theology cannot be entirely reduced to social science without serious loss of identity. Rather, the practical theological approach affirms the idea that within the *charismata* grace works in and through human nature, including socialization processes [which] can only explain or interpret glossolalia partially (the hypotheses were corroborated only partially)."[24]

Another relatively recent approach, studying glossolalia from the perspective of cognitive psychology, broadly considered, emerged initially in the early 1970s in the work of linguist and cultural anthropologist Felicitas Goodman (1914-2005). In her landmark volume, *Speaking in Tongues: A Cross-Cultural Study of Glossolalia,* Goodman correlated glossolalia with dissociative psychological states in which the mind is thought to detach itself from the body.[25] Through the study of Spirit-possession rites among

23. Richard A. Hutch, "The Personal Ritual of Glossolalia," in *Speaking in Tongues: A Guide to Research on Glossolalia,* ed. Watson E. Mills (Grand Rapids: Eerdmans, 1986), pp. 381-95, quote from 382.

24. Cartledge, *Practical Theology,* p. 227, italics in original. See also Cartledge's essay, "The Socialization of Glossolalia," in *Sociology, Theology, and the Curriculum,* ed. Leslie J. Francis (New York and London: Cassell, 1999), pp. 125-34.

25. Felicitas D. Goodman, *Speaking in Tongues: A Cross-Cultural Study of Glossolalia* (Chicago and London: University of Chicago Press, 1972). More expansively, Steven Jay Lynn and Judith W. Rhue, eds., *Dissociation: Clinical and Theoretical Perspectives* (London and New York: Guilford Press, 1994), understand dissociation as referring to the "experience" of multiple (two or more) mental processes/contents that are not integrated or associated; to activation of different mental modules/systems inaccessible to consciousness or that function independently of conscious experience; or to altered states of consciousness (as in clinical syndromes of depersonalization and derealization) that serve as defense mechanisms. In their book, studies of dissociation involve the following contexts: dreams and dreaming; abuse (physical, sexual, and psychological); severe experiences of trauma or even posttraumatic stress disorder (PTSD); captivity in cults; transference theory; hypnosis; neurological conditions (e.g., temporal lobe epilepsy, sleep loss, strokes, severing of cerebral commissure); accounts of out-of-body experiences; automatisms; multiple personality disorder; and altered states of consciousness or trance.

largely indigenous Mexican and Central American Yucatanian pentecostal groups, this thesis emerged: "in many societies the mental state of dissociation could serve as the environment of some other activities: dance, drama, singing. While in this state, people might fall into catatoniclike states, some saw visions, others talked."[26] This understanding of glossolalic utterance as a feature of trance or alternative states of consciousness, as it then was and still is known in the wider literature, is then ethnographically detailed through a phenomenology of tongues speaking, kinetic behavior, and the "reassociation" process wherein the glossolalist emerges from the trance experience and regains personal autonomy.[27] Along the way, Goodman draws also from the disciplines of linguistic psychiatry and cognitive physiology, and locates glossolalic trance amidst the wider field of comparative religious anthropology and ritual theory, particularly that focused on indigenous cultural practices of shamanistic flight.[28]

This linkage between glossolalia and dissociative or trance states has been further explored by ethnomusicologist Judith Becker.[29] In one section of her book she focuses briefly on Pentecostal Holiness worship services close to her residence in Michigan, and discusses the role of music in pentecostal liturgy, the processes of cultivating the Holy Spirit's palpable

26. Goodman, *Speaking in Tongues*, p. ix. See also Jeannette H. Henney, Esther Pressel, and Felicitas D. Goodman, *Trance, Healing, and Hallucination: Three Field Studies in Religious Experience* (New York: Wiley, 1974).

27. While trance is not necessarily linked to glossolalia — see, e.g., Nicholas P. Spanos and Erin C. Hewitt, "Glossolalia: A Test of the 'Trance' and Psychopathology Hypotheses," *Journal of Abnormal Psychology* 88, no. 4 (1979): 427-34, and Heather Kavan, "Glossolalia and Altered States of Consciousness in Two New Zealand Religious Movements," *Journal of Contemporary Religion* 19, no. 2 (2004): 171-84 — we should not underestimate Goodman's proposals, grounded concretely as they are in careful phenomenological and ethnographic study. I would only add that what happens among indigenous Mexican or indigenous Central American pentecostals may not happen consistently among the global renewal community. David M. Beckman's "Trance: From Africa to Pentecostalism," *Concordia Theological Monthly* 45 (1974): 11-26, is not very helpful because of his essentialist and stereotypical assessment of African religiosity.

28. These ideas are developed by Goodman in later studies, especially *Ecstasy, Ritual, and Alternate Reality: Religion in a Pluralistic World* (Bloomington: Indiana University Press, 1988), and *Where the Spirits Ride the Wind: Trance Journeys and Other Ecstatic Experiences* (Bloomington: Indiana University Press, 1990). See also Sidney M. Greenfield, *Spirits with Scalpels: The Cultural Biology of Religious Healing in Brazil* (Walnut Creek, CA: West Coast Press, 2008), part III.

29. Judith Becker, *Deep Listeners: Music, Emotion, and Trancing* (Bloomington and Indianapolis: Indiana University Press, 2004).

manifestation through singing, praying (often in tongues), "tarrying," and other means. Her guiding questions are: "How are the outward characteristics of religious trance (dance, prophecy, speaking in tongues, speaking in voices of spiritual beings) correlated with inner physiology and what is the role of music in facilitating these events?"[30] The ensuing explorations are set within a wider theoretical framework of "deep listening" that draws from the disciplines of biology, neurology, philosophical phenomenology, and philosophy of mind.

In brief, deep listening is a holistic activity that is embodied, emotional, cognitive, and even spiritual, in which people enter variously into dissociative states — in many cases remaining fully conscious although, paradoxically, quite apart from a recognized autobiographical self — amidst a musical background.[31] Against previous understandings that defined trancers as people with certain kinds of "disorders," deep listeners are persons who are highly skilled in negotiating the interface between their embodiment, various levels of consciousness, and their interpersonal and interspiritual relationships within the context of their community. Thus, trancers who participate in spirit-possession ceremonies do so within a religio-cultural contextual framework that allows for and even encourages openness to the expanding of the self with other aspects of the self or even replacing the self with other selves. In this perspective, pentecostal glossolalists who revel in the "baptism of the Holy Spirit" during the service do so "through the group processes of recurrent interactions between co-defined individuals in a rhythmic domain of music that is intrinsically social, visibly embodied, and profoundly cognitive."[32]

Goodman and especially Becker postulate a neurophysiological theory of pentecostal experience in general and glossolalia in particular that is being increasingly studied using the ever-expanding techniques of the cogni-

30. Becker, *Deep Listeners,* p. 4.

31. The plausibility of these theoretical and empirical interpretations of glossolalia should not be taken to mean that I think trance is intrinsic to pentecostal tongue-speaking. Rather, as Kilian McDonnell has said, trance is not necessarily constitutive of glossolalia, and even when present, means neither that pentecostal behavior is aberrant nor that its religious or theological significance is thereby undermined. See McDonnell, "The Function of Tongues in Pentecostalism," *One in Christ* 19, no. 4 (1983): 332-54, at 333; see also n. 27 above.

32. Becker, *Deep Listeners,* p. 129. Becker's hypothesis also illuminates especially the trance rituals of snake-handling pentecostal sects in the Appalachian Mountains — see Ralph W. Hood Jr. and W. Paul Williamson, *Them That Believe: The Power and Meaning of the Christian Serpent-Handling Tradition* (Berkeley: University of California Press, 2008), especially chapter 6.

tive sciences. One of the earliest brain studies described glossolalia in terms of seizure, like electrical activity in the temporal lobe.[33] A more tightly controlled study hypothesized that glossolalia activity involved greater activation of right cerebral hemisphere processes, associated historically with mystical states or experiences, in contrast with discursive reading activity, a presumed left-hemisphere task.[34] Using an infrared radiometer that measured blood flow in both hemispheres after ten minutes each of tongues speaking and, later, of reading a scholarly article, nothing was observed that refuted the hypothesis. But the sample was small, with only five participants, since many glossolalists at this evangelical Christian university were reluctant to submit to experimental analysis. With regard to this specific study, there persists the question about dividing mental activity too acutely between right and left cerebral spheres, an assumption that is increasingly problematic in light of the latest developments in the cognitive sciences.

One final nuclear-imaging study deserves mention. Andrew Newberg and his colleagues measured regional cerebral blood flow in five women glossolalists using a SPECT (single photon emission computed tomography) scan.[35] Among a number of hypotheses, two appeared to be supported: that there would be a decrease in parietal frontal lobe (PFL) activity when compared with singing, since the PFL is involved with willful behaviors, and that there would be no significant decreases in the superior parietal lobe (SPL) when compared with meditation, since the SPL had been shown to deactivate commensurate with the experience of a loss or altered state of consciousness. A third hypothesis, that activity would increase in limbic areas like the amygdala in accordance with the emotional arousal related to tongues speaking, was neither confirmed nor disconfirmed; thus this study did not show glossolalia to be a more or less emotional experience relative to nonglossolalic states. If this study is accurate, then at least the hypotheses regarding the PFL and the SPL are consistent with glossolalist claims that while they are active in the sense of vocal-

33. Michael A. Persinger, "Striking EEG Profiles from Single Episodes of Glossolalia and Transcendental Meditation," *Perceptual and Motor Skills* 58, no. 1 (1984): 127-33.

34. Ron Philipchalk and Dieter Mueller, "Glossolalia and Temperature Change in the Right and Left Cerebral Hemispheres," *International Journal for the Psychology of Religion* 10, no. 3 (2000): 181-85.

35. Andrew B. Newberg et al., "The Measurement of Regional Cerebral Blood Flow during Glossolalia: A Preliminary SPECT Study," *Psychiatry Research: Neuroimaging* 148, no. 1 (November 22, 2006): 67-71.

izing sounds, there is also an element of passivity in the experience; theologically, of course, such passivity is correlated with the activity of the Holy Spirit, who is believed to enable the glossolalic utterance. We will return to this issue below.

What are the theological implications of such cognitive scientific studies of pentecostal phenomena? Here the work of John Pilch and others connected with the Context Group: A Project on the Bible in Its Socio-Cultural Context (see http://www.contextgroup.org/) is relevant. In *Visions and Healing in the Acts of the Apostles,* Pilch's background in cultural and medical anthropology is brought to bear on understanding early Christian experiences.[36] In addition, however, Pilch suggests that recent advances in the cognitive neurosciences can also illuminate the Lukan narratives. Briefly, a central part of his argument is that ecstatic or trance experiences enabled by the neurological "hardware" of human brains are the means of receiving healing or divining answers to existential and concrete problems of life, and of experiencing a transformative encounter with the realm of the transcendent or with God. Early Christian experiences of visions and healing, then, may be illuminated through contemporary neuroscience.

Drawing on the work of both Goodman and Newberg, Pilch calls attention to the empirical data for the following neurological processes: (1) that sustained concentration on a thought or intense visual focus on an object often induces trance experiences; (2) that such trance experiences are triggered by meditation (from the "top down") or by overstimulation of the nervous system (from the "bottom up" — e.g., through strenuous physical or ritual activity, rhythmic hand-clapping, drumming, dancing, fasting, even sleeplessness); and (3) that prolonged meditative activity brings about different levels of consciousness in the brain that, when mapped through electroencephalograms, correlate with the kinds of colors that are seen, with the brighter colors signaling deeper trance experiences. He concludes that trance experiences enable access to alternate realms of reality not normally accessible in the more usual modes of perception, even as such experiences are explained according to the dominant social and intellectual ideas that are present.

From this, Pilch suggests that the visionary and healing experiences of the first-century Christians can be understood in part as altered states of consciousness or trance experiences that opened up another reality under-

36. John J. Pilch, *Visions and Healing in the Acts of the Apostles: How the Early Believers Experienced God* (Collegeville, MN: Liturgical Press, 2004).

stood in terms of God, angels, miracles, and the "supernatural." He applies this hypothesis to the Acts narrative and suggests, among other proposals, the following:

- that "looking intently" or "staring" was a means of precipitating alternative states of consciousness and accessing the realm of the "supernatural" (e.g., Acts 1:10; 3:4; 7:55; 13:9-10; 14:9);[37]
- that fasting also appears to have provided a point of entry into trance and visionary experiences (e.g., Paul in Acts 9:9-12; Peter in 10:10; members of the church in Antioch in 13:1-3);
- that intense concentration and meditative activity induced visionary experiences (e.g., Paul's intense focus on persecuting followers of Jesus precipitated his vision of Jesus); and
- that reports of seeing bright lights signified trance experiences (e.g., Stephen's face in Acts 6:15; Peter in jail in 12:7; and Paul in 9:3-6; cf. 22:4-11 and 26:9-18).[38]

In these cases, Pilch suggests, mental states explicable in terms of neurophysiological processes brought the early Christians into contact with the reality of God in ways that resulted in healing, exorcism, and transformed lives.[39]

The preceding discussion is extremely selective, as no attempt has been made to be exhaustive in our account. But it should be evident that it holds important implications for the theology and science dialogue. For the moment, however, it should be clear there is no one metascientific narrative about glossolalia in particular or about pentecostalism in general. This is not to say that helpful or illuminating studies have not been conducted. It is only to say that each study is limited in its scope and fallible in its conclusions. From a scientific point of view, none of this is surprising; but the

---

37. Pilch writes that "gazing or staring or looking intently . . . might not only be the sign of being in trance but also a technique for inducing trance. . . . From the perspective of cognitive neuroscience, such intense concentration can induce a trance 'from the top down.' This level of consciousness originates primarily in the brain either by clearing the mind of all thought or focusing intensely on a thought" (*Visions and Healing,* p. 41).

38. Parallel comments on these texts can be found in Bruce J. Malina and John J. Pilch, *Social-Science Commentary on the Book of Acts* (Minneapolis: Fortress, 2008).

39. I discuss the work of Pilch and Becker in more detail in my "Academic Glossolalia? Pentecostal Scholarship, Multi-disciplinarity, and the Science-Religion Conversation," *Journal of Pentecostal Theology* 14, no. 1 (2005): 63-82.

theological implications of this might be disconcerting at least for some people. I will take up the theological issues at stake later in this chapter.

The Sociology of Pentecostalism:
Social Deprivation, Secularization, and Routinization

If in the earliest pentecostal accounts the revival originated not with individual or even collective effort but was a result of the Holy Spirit's sovereign outpouring, "suddenly, from heaven,"[40] sociological analyses have focused on the environmental factors that may have precipitated the movement. Over the last forty years, such studies of pentecostalism have taken off. As there is no hope of being comprehensive in the following, we will focus our lenses on three trajectories of inquiry — an earlier one in which pentecostal emergence and growth were considered according to social deprivationist theories, and two more current discussions in terms of secularization theory and the Weberian model of the evolution of charisma. As we have already seen, different sociological accounts take into consideration diverse "facts," and these all contribute to sociological understandings (sociolog*ies,* to be exact) of pentecostalism.

An initial and persisting sociological thesis regarding the origins of pentecostalism was an extension of the aforementioned Troeltschean sociology of Protestantism that distinguished between established churches and upstart sects.[41] Churches persist because they find ways to accommodate themselves to the wider culture and other secular or worldly institutions, while sects oftentimes emerge from a critical reaction to ecclesial complicity with existing cultural arrangements, demand a heightened degree of voluntary commitment from their members, and aspire to a more perfectionist expression of ecclesial life. As a corollary, members of sectarian organizations, groups, or movements are generally on the margins rather than closer to the center of the sociopolitical, economic, and cultural institutions with which their lives remain more or less entangled.

One of the first extended applications of this Troeltschean model to pentecostalism was the study of the Chilean version of the movement by

40. This was the title of one of the official denominational histories: Carl Brumback, *Suddenly . . . from Heaven: A History of the Assemblies of God* (Springfield, MO: Gospel Publishing House, 1961).

41. Most clearly and extensively articulated in Ernst Troeltsch, *The Social Teaching of the Christian Churches,* trans. Olive Wyon (New York: Harper Torchbooks, 1960), vol. 2.

the Swiss sociologist and theologian Christian Lalive d'Epinay.[42] Carried out under the auspices of the Committee for World Mission and Evangelization of the World Council of Churches (WCC), the study was motivated in part by the fact that two fledgling pentecostal denominations in Chile were the first to join the WCC in the early 1960s (a very ecumenical and un-pentecostal thing to do). Thus d'Epinay observed that while from a Troeltschean standpoint pentecostalism in Chile surely fit the sectarian profile, it was nevertheless a dynamic and heterogeneous movement. Within the church-sect framework, pentecostalism could be understood to have offered to the masses of lower-class members in the movement a "mythical religious mentality . . . , faith in a god of love, the certainty of salvation, security in a community, and a sharing in responsibility for a common task to be fulfilled. It thus offers them a humanity which society denies them."[43]

It should now be clear why d'Epinay linked the title of his book to the Marxist idea about religion being the "opiate of the masses."[44] But contrary to the Marxist thesis about the proletariat being the carriers of a revolutionary power against the bourgeoisie, Chilean pentecostals were basically apolitical, even though some of their leaders were sufficiently progressive to have led their congregations into the orbit of the WCC. From this sociology of development perspective, d'Epinay concluded: "Pentecostalism — like any kind of a-politicism — is an ideology of order and not movement, of conservatism and not change."[45] In short, Chilean pentecostalism fit the sect-type category in terms of its socially marginalized constituency's perfectionist ideals forged partly in reaction to the wider religious and political (predominantly Roman Catholic) environment.[46] But pentecostalism's religious ideology lacked

42. Christian Lalive d'Epinay, *Haven of the Masses: A Study of the Pentecostal Movement in Chile,* trans. Marjorie Sandle (London: Lutterworth, 1969).

43. D'Epinay, *Haven of the Masses,* p. 224.

44. See Marx's introduction of his 1843 work *A Contribution to the Critique of Hegel's Philosophy of Right,* in Marx, *Early Writings,* trans. Rodney Livingstone and Gregor Benton (New York: Vintage, 1975), p. 244.

45. D'Epinay, *Haven of the Masses,* p. 225.

46. This is because, as d'Epinay put it later, Marxism as an ideology is disseminated from the workplace while the locus of operation for pentecostalism is in the home; see d'Epinay, "Political Regimes and Millenarianism in a Dependent Society: Reflections on Pentecostalism in Chile," trans. Paul Burns, in *New Religious Movements,* ed. John Aloysius Coleman, Gregory Baum, and Marcus Lefébure (Edinburgh: T. & T. Clark; New York: Seabury Press, 1983), pp. 42-54, especially 44. Even in this later work, however, d'Epinay as a

the capacity to foster the kind of sociopolitical change hoped for in the Marxist dialectic.[47]

More famous than d'Epinay's study is Robert Mapes Anderson's *Vision of the Disinherited: The Making of American Pentecostalism*.[48] While Anderson as a historian rightly chastises any psychological reductionism of pentecostalism,[49] by the end of his otherwise very helpful and informative study he engages in his own reductionistic explanation, one that locates the origins and emergence of at least North American pentecostalism amidst the various social and economic forces of the early twentieth century. These statements in Anderson's concluding chapter capture the gist of his thesis:

- "I would hazard the hypothesis that status deprivation and an anti-rationalist, anti-bureaucratic — i.e., anti-modern — temper has combined to predispose most of the recruits to the neo-pentecostal movement. Pentecostals, old and new, have typically testified that before their conversion to pentecostalism they felt empty and hungry for God or for something they could not articulate. In short, they felt deprived."[50]
- "Pentecostalism provided a catharsis for the troubled; by creating close-knit, primary religious fellowships, it restored a sense of community to the displaced and ostracized; by holding forth the promise of an imminent Kingdom, it offered hope and solace for the despairing."[51]

---

sociologist is quite confident that although the evolution of any social group, pentecostalism included, varies according to both external (social) and internal (agency) factors, deep knowledge of pentecostalism and of its environment does enable fairly stable generalizations about group dynamics. I discuss this point in the final section of this chapter.

47. Another sociological study of Latin American pentecostalism about a decade later was Cornelia Butler Flora, *Pentecostalism in Colombia: Baptism by Fire and Spirit* (Cranbury, NJ, and London: Associated University Presses; Rutherford, NJ: Fairleigh Dickinson University Press, 1976). The strength of this analysis, a structural-functional analysis of pentecostalism, is also its weakness — a lack of historical perspective regarding the dynamics of social movements vis-à-vis cultural change.

48. Robert Mapes Anderson, *Vision of the Disinherited: The Making of American Pentecostalism* (1979; reprint, Peabody, Mass.: Hendrickson, 1992).

49. Early in his book, he writes: "Speaking in tongues is a cultural phenomenon that cannot be reduced to a psychological or linguistic phenomenon merely. It need not and probably will not lend itself, without exception, to any uniform psychological or linguistic definition" (*Vision of the Disinherited*, p. 18).

50. Anderson, *Vision of the Disinherited*, pp. 228-29.

51. Anderson, *Vision of the Disinherited*, p. 235.

- "Rejected by the world, the Pentecostals in turn rejected the world. Lacking the skills and opportunities to improve their fortunes in this world, they renounced worldly success and developed their talents within the limits of the community of the Spirit. Denied the satisfaction of social relationships devoid of prejudice and condescension, they found salvation in a sublime experience of union with the Divine that carried them above their grueling, insipid lives, and in the fantastic contemplation of an imminent reversal of social roles and rewards. . . . The root of the Pentecostal movement was social discontent. . . . The radical social impulse inherent in the vision of the disinherited was transformed into social passivity, ecstatic escape, and, finally, a most conservative conformity."[52]

In short, for Anderson, pentecostalism, in both its original and neoclassical forms, was a movement of the "disinherited" that met the needs of the socially marginalized and deprived.

Part of the issue with Anderson's assessment was that it did not appear to take seriously sociological evidence that had emerged in the intervening years since d'Epinay's work that problematized the social deprivation thesis. Already by the mid to late 1960s, researchers were questioning the plausibility of understanding pentecostalism according to the social deprivation and social disorganization models then on offer.[53] To be sure, some measures revealed a relative deprivation of status or power, but these still cautioned that "deprivation and disorganization should be considered facilitating rather than causal conditions of the movement."[54] It was no longer viable to simply see the marginalized and deprived as swept up in the euphoria of pentecostal experience. Indeed, the opposite might have just as much evidence going for it: that conversion to pentecostalism produced ideological changes that motivated explicitly sociocultural and, in rarer instances, political opposition (i.e., an anti-Catholic or anti-indigenous religious set of discursive practices).[55]

---

52. Anderson, *Vision of the Disinherited*, p. 240.

53. Virginia H. Hine, "Pentecostal Glossolalia: Toward a Functional Interpretation," *Journal of the Society for the Scientific Study of Religion* 8, no. 2 (1969): 211-26, especially 451.

54. Virginia H. Hine, "The Deprivation and Disorganization Theories of Social Movements," in *Religious Movements in Contemporary America*, ed. Irving I. Zaretsky and Mark P. Leone (Princeton: Princeton University Press, 1974), pp. 646-61, especially 660.

55. Luther P. Gerlach, "Pentecostalism: Revolution or Counter-Revolution?" in *Religious Movements in Contemporary America*, pp. 669-99.

In a study of the charismatic renewal in the mainline churches published in the same year as Anderson's book, Cecil Bradfield, a Lutheran pastor and sociologist, observed that there was no strong correlation between economic or social deprivation and the emergence of neo-pentecostalism.[56] Perhaps "non-objective forms of deprivation such as psychic and ethical, can be instrumental in the emergence of sectarian movements like neo-Pentecostalism,"[57] but if so, then this highlighted the importance of attending to "insider" factors for conversions to neo-pentecostalism. In other words, we need to go "beyond deprivation" to identify some of the motivating personal, ethical, or countercultural reasons for the attraction of neo-pentecostalism. If this happened, as A. G. Miller later insisted, we would not so easily equate spiritual hunger with emotional lack or deprivation.[58] In short, we need a sociological approach that privileges, or at least considers, the agency and self-understanding of pentecostals rather than persisting in reducing the phenomenon to underlying social forces and dynamics.

The sociological analyses of David Martin and Margaret Poloma push forward the sociology of pentecostalism by attending to emic pentecostal perspectives, albeit in different ways. Martin is a sociologist in the classical mold, always after the formulation of a more adequate general sociological theory.[59] His work is unique, however, in that rather than attempting to squeeze pentecostalism into an existing sociological framework, it revises the contours of sociological theory in light of the phenomenon that is global pentecostalism. So when it was observed that the prediction about the inability of religion to resist the forces of secularization was unraveling,[60] Martin looked deeply at global pentecostalism in order to understand the issues.

56. Cecil David Bradfield, *Neo-Pentecostalism: A Sociological Assessment* (Washington, DC: University Press of America, 1979).

57. Bradfield, *Neo-Pentecostalism*, p. 56.

58. A. G. Miller, "Pentecostalism as a Social Movement: Beyond the Theory of Deprivation," *Journal of Pentecostal Theology* 9 (1996): 97-114.

59. Yet even general sociological theories are bound to the empirical data; thus Martin's *A General Theory of Secularization* (New York: Harper and Row, 1978) was clear that any general theory of secularization needed to take into consideration a host of socio-empirical factors such as the relationships of churches to the state, the extent of denominational pluralism in any given country or region, whether the dominant religion is Catholic or Protestant, etc.

60. I.e., Harvey G. Cox, *The Secular City: Secularization and Urbanization in Theological Perspective* (New York: Macmillan, 1965).

What Martin found has been encapsulated in two books, one on Latin American pentecostalism and the other on the global renewal movement.[61] In brief, his study of pentecostalism has helped him to see secularization itself as a multifaceted process, perhaps one that has many types of historical expressions. In the present time, Martin writes of "the viable core of secularization as the sub-theory of social differentiation. Serious doubts can be raised about the sub-theory of rationalization, and an important work by José Casanova criticizes the sub-theory of privatization."[62] To be more precise, the phenomenon of global pentecostalism has led Martin to see contemporary secularization more as a process of social differentiation than as a process of rationalization or privatization.

This means that pentecostalism, rather than being a carryover of premodernity in a modern world, is itself "a major narrative of modernity."[63] Being in effect a descendant of the genius of Methodism, pentecostalism is better seen as "a harbinger of modernity throughout the developing world,"[64] not because it acquiesces to Enlightenment rationalism but because it rejects social totalization and strives for, celebrates, and exerts pressures toward social and cultural pluralism. On a global scale, pentecostalism empowers discrete voluntary associations that operate in differentiated spheres, and generates free (nonhierarchical and more or less noninstitutionalized) spaces within which social groups can flourish amidst more complex religious and political environments.[65] This flows from the fact that pentecostalism as a metanarrative "is not based on rationalization and bureaucracy but rather on story and song, gesture and empowerment, image and embodiment, enthusiastic release and personal discipline. One has to view this potent combination of empowerment with release as just as viable in terms of advancing modernity as rationalization."[66] Thus when one pays closer attention to what is happening on the pentecostal ground, one sees that it "offers a narrative of transformations

61. David Martin, *Tongues of Fire: The Explosion of Protestantism in Latin America* (Oxford: Blackwell, 1990), and *Pentecostalism: The World Their Parish* (Oxford: Blackwell, 2002).

62. David Martin, *On Secularization: Towards a Revised General Theory* (Aldershot, UK, and Burlington, VT: Ashgate, 2005), p. 17. Martin refers here to José Casanova's *Public Religions in a Modern World* (Chicago: University of Chicago Press, 1994).

63. This is part of the title of chapter 10 of Martin, *On Secularization*.

64. Martin, *On Secularization*, p. 141.

65. For an overview, see my *In the Days of Caesar: Pentecostalism and Political Theology — the Cadbury Lectures, 2009* (Grand Rapids: Eerdmans, 2010), chapter 1.

66. Martin, *On Secularization*, p. 142.

and transfigurations rather than a logic of linear implication or a theoretical rendering of tested empirical linkages. You can dismiss these modes of superstitions, illusions which mysteriously linger into what ought to be austere and rigorous human adulthood . . . , or you can suppose that there are other forms of encounter through testimony, gesture, song, and healing, which do not lie under the guillotine of progress but are intrinsic to the human condition."[67]

Ironically, then, pentecostalism flourishes in part because of secularization and even supports it by providing its adherents with "an internal compass and a portable identity, a protected environment for revisions of consciousness and social organization, including the nuclear family."[68] So in a sense, pentecostalism's participation in modernity resists any hegemonic expression of the modern, and thus supports the emergence of postcolonial, post-Western, and post-Enlightenment sensibilities in all their variety on the transnational ground. This is not the traditional form of political modernity, that characterized by a rational nation-state; rather it is a culturally and socially diffused version of the late modern world, one featuring the effusion of the many tongues and practices of pentecostalism. Yet precisely because pentecostalism operates at the level of cultural differentiation rather than at the political level, where most scholarly energies are focused, it has flown under the radar of scholarly research. Thus Martin is both a general theorist and a detailed empiricist, one who lets pentecostal self-identity inform his sociological accounts of pentecostalism while simultaneously shifting the field of the sociology of pentecostalism into the twenty-first century in ways that recognize pentecostal agency.[69]

Margaret Poloma is not just a Christian sociologist, as is Martin, but also a longtime participant in the charismatic movement, first in Roman Catholic circles but then within the wider renewal world. In her work, there is a twofold registration of pentecostal perspectives and agency: that of her own views as a participant-observer and that of other agents or insiders to

67. Martin, *Pentecostalism*, p. 176.

68. Martin, *On Secularization*, p. 151.

69. See also Bernice Martin, "From Pre- to Postmodernity in Latin America: The Case of Pentecostalism," in *Religion, Modernity, and Postmodernity*, ed. Paul Heelas (Oxford and Malden, MA: Blackwell, 1998), pp. 102-46, and Graham Howes, "The Sociologist as Stylist: David Martin and Pentecostalism," in *Restoring the Image: Essays on Religion and Society in Honour of David Martin*, ed. Andrew Walker and Martyn Percy (Sheffield: Sheffield Academic Press, 2001), pp. 98-108.

the movement. This personal involvement in and engagement with various facets of the movement she has studied for over three decades explains, at least in part, her interest not just in describing pentecostalism sociologically but in its ongoing vitality. Poloma's social scientific expertise has thus been consistently brought to bear on the questions pertaining to the perpetuation and longer-term effects of pentecostal and charismatic renewal.

Each of Poloma's four books (to date) on pentecostalism and the renewal thus reflects both social scientific and personal interests.[70] Thus her first volume, *The Charismatic Movement: Is There a New Pentecost?* acknowledges both that it emerged at least in part out of her own "search for truth" and that the results of at least this initial leg of her research enabled her to "respond affirmatively to the question-title of this book."[71] She intertwined social scientific research and theological analysis, the latter informing her assessment that the charismatic renewal as the object of study was indeed the most recent rendition of the biblical Pentecost as described in the book of Acts.

In this first book Poloma raised concerns about the routinization of charisma. Within the Weberian framework, there are various understandings of the notion of charisma, although almost all of them refer in some respect or other to the special powers that undergird the authority of certain people, leaders, and set them apart from ordinary persons. Routinization refers to the processes of institutionalization and traditionalization that happen to groups when, upon the demise of their charismatic founders, successors are established through noncharismatic and increasingly professionalized techniques and processes (e.g., educational achievements, ritual events, hereditary appointments).[72] Even within the short space of fifteen to twenty years, the charismatic renewal movement in mainline Protestantism and in the Catholic Church was already succumbing to the

---

70. Margaret Poloma, *The Charismatic Movement: Is There a New Pentecost?* (Boston: Twayne, 1982); *The Assemblies of God at the Crossroads: Charisma and Institutional Dilemmas* (Knoxville: University of Tennessee Press, 1989); *Main Street Mystics: The Toronto Blessing and Reviving Pentecostalism* (Walnut Creek, CA: AltaMira Press, 2003); and with Ralph W. Hood Jr., *Blood and Fire: Godly Love in a Pentecostal Emerging Church* (New York: New York University Press, 2008).

71. See the preface to Poloma, *The Charismatic Movement*, which is unnumbered.

72. A short overview is Max Weber, *The Theory of Social and Economic Organization*, ed. Talcott Parsons (New York: Free Press, 1964), pp. 358-73. See also Weber, *On Charisma and Institution Building: Selected Papers*, ed. S. N. Eisenstadt (Chicago and London: University of Chicago Press, 1968), part VII.

forces of routinization. Bureaucratic models of leadership were displacing the egalitarian dynamics of the early days of the movement, and concerns with "the size, financial status, and prestige of the organization" were extinguishing the yearning for manifestations of the charismatic gifts.[73]

Poloma next explored charismatic routinization in a substantial study of a pentecostal denomination founded in 1914, the Assemblies of God (AOG). After about seventy years, the strains of routinization were quite evident, she observed. Yes, the AOG had been quite successful among classical pentecostal groups in its ongoing "protest against modernity,"[74] especially in its ability to perpetuate charismatic expressions like glossolalia (especially linked to the doctrine of the baptism of the Holy Spirit as its physical evidence), divine healing, and prophecies (not to mention visions and dreams). Yet the denomination also showed unmistakable signs of institutionalization and routinization: the gradual decline of women in ministry (revealing the influence of the movement's alignment with broader evangelical commitments toward a more patriarchal understanding of ordained ministry),[75] emergence of a denominational bureaucracy and constitutionalized administrative structures (in place of prophetic leadership), accommodation to social and especially political powers (reflecting the upward mobility of the AOG constituency), and assumptions of charismatic manifestations by the ecclesial and pastoral hierarchy (rather than their diffused expression among the rank and file). Poloma thus concludes: "In some ways the dilemmas and the spirit of charisma remain alive and well, allowing the breath of mysticism to animate the organization. In other ways, the freshness of mysticism is jeopardized by institutional successes and related accommodative forces. Paradoxically, the institution which has developed out of charisma and has been strengthened by fresh outbursts also seeks to tame and domesticate the charismatic spirit."[76]

Poloma's third book explored further how mysticism, in this case the Toronto Blessing revival that exploded in 1993, works within pentecostalism to rejuvenate its institutions. Revitalization here was brought about, again,

73. Poloma, *The Charismatic Movement,* pp. 230-33, quote from 231.

74. This is the subtitle of chapter 1 of Poloma's *Assemblies of God at the Crossroads.*

75. See also David G. Roebuck, "'Cause He's My Chief Employer': Hearing Women's Voices in a Classical Pentecostal Denomination," in *Philip's Daughters: Women in Pentecostal-Charismatic Leadership,* ed. Amos Yong and Estrelda Y. Alexander (Eugene, OR: Pickwick, 2009), pp. 38-60.

76. Poloma, *Assemblies of God,* p. 212.

by charismatic manifestations, especially healing and prophecy. In this volume, however, Poloma deployed the cultural anthropological and ritual theory of Victor Turner (1920-1983) to understand the Toronto Blessing.[77] But rather than focusing only on Turner's major theory of liminality — which understood religious rites to be "in-between" spaces and times that enabled participants to escape the status quo of their conscripted daily lives in order to creatively realize novel possibilities, understandings, and even identities — Poloma turns to one of the last essays Turner wrote before his death, which attempted to understand religious ritual and mysticism from within a cerebral neurological framework.[78] What emerges is a cognitive-anthropological and sociological assessment of pentecostal renewal.

For example, Poloma, with the help of Turner's analysis, identifies some of the revival's most noticeable phenomena — thrashing, rolling, falling down, etc. — as expressions of the instinctual elements of the brain that are responsible for alertness and the coordination or control of consciousness with bodily movement. Other manifestations, like laughing or crying, derive from the limbic system that includes the hypothalamus — which is involved in the expression of the major emotions, among other functions — and can be correlated with both positive affect (in the case of laughing, corresponding to joy, happiness, or peace) or negative emotional states (in the case of crying or weeping, connecting to feelings of sadness, pain, grief, depression, etc.). Ritual healing was facilitated at least in part through the music of the revival and mediated through physical and emotional experiences of the participants.[79] In short, the Blessing renewed individuals, and this renewal of individuals constituted the revival of pentecostalism itself.

Poloma's account takes firsthand testimonies of the renewal experience seriously. In fact, she describes her own personal experience of receiv-

77. See Turner's anthropological classic text, *The Ritual Process: Structure and Anti-Structure* (Chicago: Aldine, 1969).

78. Poloma cites Turner's essay, "Body, Brain, and Culture," in *Brain, Culture, and the Human Spirit: Essays from an Emergent Evolutionary Perspective,* ed. James B. Ashbrook (Lanham, MD: University Press of America, 1993), pp. 77-108, which was originally published in *Zygon* 18 (1983): 247-69. In this piece, Turner adapted the brain theory of physician and neuroscientist Paul D. MacLean (1913-2007), whose proposals in *The Triune Brain in Evolution: Role in Paleocerebral Functions* (New York: Plenum, 1990) remain contested. For discussion, see Gerald A. Cory Jr. and Russell Gardner Jr., eds., *The Evolutionary Neurotheology of Paul MacLean: Convergences and Frontiers* (Westport, CT, and London: Praeger, 2002).

79. Poloma's discussion and application of Turner's cerebral-neurological theory is found in *Main Street Mystics,* pp. 74-80, 105-10, and 137-42.

ing a prophetic word, also in terms of Turner's neurological theory.[80] Here, as elsewhere in her work, she honestly portrays her research as a very delicate "dancing between involvement and detachment."[81] Yet she does not claim her own experiences as normative in any naive manner; rather they are illuminated by those of others, even while all contribute to the sociological whole. Thus she has walked a fine line, almost from the beginning of her scholarly writing on the neo-pentecostal and charismatic renewal movement, between allowing her faith to inform her sociological work and bringing her scholarly vocation to bear on challenging, critiquing, and even at times correcting her faith.[82]

What is evident sociologically in Poloma's research, however, is that despite the institutional dilemmas that pentecostalism confronts, not even the processes of secularization can inexorably predetermine routinization. Instead, the charismatic renewal revives classical pentecostalism, even as another wave of revivals — that is, the Toronto Blessing — rejuvenates a stagnating charismatic movement. Individual churches in the renewal come (and go) unpredictably as well,[83] unexpectedly resisting the tides of institutionalization or else succumbing to the routinization of charisma faster than anticipated. But all are said by pentecostals to be workings of the Holy Spirit — which raises the question: Aren't these activities of the Spirit reducible to psychological or sociological processes after all?

The Spirits of Pentecostalism: The Emergence of Methodological Pluralism in Theology and Science

The preceding overview is selective, almost in the extreme; we have not attempted to survey the breadth of the sociological literature on pentecostal-

80. Poloma, *Main Street Mystics,* pp. 124-27.
81. Poloma, *Main Street Mystics,* p. 248.
82. See also Poloma's preface titled "A Research Chronicle: Being a Sociological Witness to Dialogue," in *The Charismatic Movement;* part of the appendix, "A Research Saga: Presenting a Methodological Account," in *The Assemblies of God at the Crossroads;* chapter 10, "Narrative and Reflexive Ethnography: A Concluding Account," in *Main Street Mystics;* appendix A, "Margaret Poloma's Reflections on a Research Journey," in Poloma and Hood, *Blood and Fire;* and "Is Integrating Spirit and Sociology Possible? A Postmodern Research Odyssey," in *Science and the Spirit: A Pentecostal Engagement with the Sciences,* ed. Amos Yong and James K. A. Smith (Bloomington: Indiana University Press, 2010), pp. 174-91.
83. This is the story told in Poloma and Hood, *Blood and Fire,* about which we have neither time nor space to comment any further.

ism, much less engaged in depth with the interlocutors we have mentioned. But our goals are much more modest: to get a sense of how scientific analyses of pentecostalism, especially in the psychological and sociological sciences, can illuminate the phenomenon. From such analyses, however, the following observations and questions arise. First, we have encountered various modes of inquiry, in particular, the sociological, psychological, and cognitive scientific. Is each of these valid in its own way, and if so, how? Second, we have had occasion to note the importance of pentecostal self-understandings even in these scientific accounts. Are the ways in which pentecostal perspectives have informed scientific inquiry legitimate, or do they contaminate the scientific quest for "objective" truth? Finally, we have mentioned in passing the pentecostal belief that glossolalia and other charismatic manifestations are signs of the human interface with the realm of the transcendent, with the person and work of the Holy Spirit in particular. Is science able to undertake an investigation of such a claim? Are those working at the intersection of theology and science prohibited from asking, much less pursuing, such questions?

In the following pages, I want to establish a framework for reflecting on these matters, and will do so in two steps. Initially, I will sketch the rudiments of what I have elsewhere called an emergentist anthropology,[84] focusing especially on the noneliminative character of mind at both the personal/individual and social levels. Next, such a multidimensional anthropology requires, correspondingly, an interdisciplinary method. Together, these considerations help us to think philosophically about the nature of human complexity in ways that invite, rather than disdain, the tools of inquiry available in both theology and science.

An Emergentist Anthropology

The concern here is to guard against an ontological reductionism of the social level to that of the psychological level, or of both to the level of our biological substrate. Instead, I am eager to avoid both neural/biological and social determinism, each of which eliminates the explanatory power available at other levels. Emergence theory helps us see how the higher and more complex levels of reality appear unpredictably from, and are consti-

---

84. See my *Theology and Down Syndrome: Reimagining Disability in Late Modernity* (Waco, TX: Baylor University Press, 2007), pp. 180-91.

tuted and self-organized by, lower-level parts yet activate novel properties and even behaviors that are not explicable in terms of the sum of those parts.[85] Chemical properties, for example, emerge from their underlying molecular structures, just as classical physical phenomena emerge from the quantum world. In chapters 5 and 6, I will present a wider framework for thinking about emergence, but in the meanwhile, I want to explore how the mind or consciousness emerges from the brain.

Noted Christian psychologists Malcolm Jeeves and Warren Brown have recently provided a lucid overview of the various principles of brain operations that show us how the mind is constituted by but irreducible to the brain.[86] They note, first, that the brain is part of an organic system connected with the nervous system and the body's sensory-motor organs, and that the brain is nested within this loop of action-feedback interactions. Yet the brain can also engage in "off-line" action emulation (i.e., undertake abstract thinking that does not necessarily have motor-sensory consequences). They note also that the complexity that is the brain is constituted by several support systems, all of which work distinctly and yet together; that many distinctive functions of the brain have been confirmed as localized to various support systems or neural areas, even while such localized areas also serve as important nodes or connection points of the brain understood as a "widely distributed processing network";[87] that the brain thus seems to have evolved out of a genetic blueprint most congenial to the adaptability and survival of the human species on the one hand, but exhibits a self-organizing impulse and plasticity in response to and in interaction with its environment (both within and outside the body) on the other hand; that such plasticity reflects the dynamic nature of the brain's learning capacities across the life span; and that these neuropsychological principles invite a dynamic core hypothesis of the mind as dependent upon but irreducible to the ever-changing neural states involving differentiated neural networks and their interactions with the brain's various support systems. In sum, given these latest developments in the field of neuropsychology, Jeeves and Brown recommend their theory of the emer-

85. See Harold Morowitz, *The Emergence of Everything: How the World Became Complex* (New York: Oxford University Press, 2002), for a synoptic account. We will explicate more of Morowitz's work in chapter 5.

86. Malcolm Jeeves and Warren S. Brown, *Neuroscience, Psychology, and Religion: Illusions, Delusions, and Realities about Human Nature* (West Conshohocken, PA: Templeton Foundation Press, 2009), chapter 4.

87. Jeeves and Brown, *Neuroscience, Psychology, and Religion*, p. 47.

gent mind as supporting the existing experimental data, as coherently demonstrating how the whole of the mind is both greater than the sum of the (biological) parts and simultaneously constituted by nothing more or less than those parts, and as allowing for genuine "top-down" causation (so that the mind is in turn capable of influencing the brain and the body).

I wish to further expand on this idea of mind or consciousness as emergent from correlative brain and body states in dialogue with two philosophers who have played a major role in the theology and science conversation, Nancey Murphy and Philip Clayton. Murphy, who teaches at Fuller Theological Seminary, has long advocated a nonreductive physicalist or supervenience theory of human nature and the mind-brain relationship.[88] Three central features in Murphy's account stand out for our purposes. First, and most obviously, nonreductive physicalism rejects dualism in favor of a monistic view of the human person as essentially and ontologically a corporeal or physical being; hence, there is no "vital force" or other metaphysical entity that is needed to explain higher-level or emergent phenomena such as consciousness. But second, nonreductive physicalists acknowledge that once having emerged, mind or consciousness also exerts top-down or downward causal influence on the physical world and in that sense is dependent upon but causally irreducible to the brain. Murphy defines downward causation as "a matter of the laws of the higher-level selective system determining in part the distribution of lower-level events and substances."[89] Thus downward causation, "in the sense of environmental selection of neural connections and tuning of synaptic weights, provides a plausible account of how the brain becomes structured to perform rational operations. The larger system — which is the brain in

---

88. Murphy has published widely on this topic — e.g., Nancey Murphy, *Anglo-American Postmodernity: Philosophical Perspectives on Science, Religion, and Ethics* (Boulder, CO: Westview Press, 1997), especially chapter 10, "Supervenience and the Nonreducibility of Ethics to Biology"; "Supervenience and the Nonreducibility of Ethics to Biology," in *Evolutionary and Molecular Biology: Scientific Perspectives on Divine Action*, ed. Robert John Russell, William R. Stoeger, S.J., and Francisco J. Ayala (Vatican City State: Vatican Observatory Publications; Berkeley: Center for Theology and the Natural Sciences, 1998), pp. 463-89; and "Nonreductive Physicalism: Philosophical Issues," in *Whatever Happened to the Soul? Scientific and Theological Portraits of Human Nature*, ed. Warren S. Brown, Nancey Murphy, and H. Newton Malony (Minneapolis: Fortress, 1998), pp. 127-48.

89. Murphy, "Neuroscience and Human Nature: A Christian Perspective," in *God, Life, and the Cosmos: Christian and Islamic Perspectives*, ed. Ted Peters, Muzaffar Iqbal, and Syed Nomanul Haq (Aldershot, UK, and Burlington, VT: Ashgate, 2002), pp. 357-89, quote from 372.

the body interacting with its environment — selects which causal *path-ways* will be activated."[90] Finally, downward causation also operates "from higher-order evaluative or supervisory systems within the agent's cognitive system that reshapes the agent's goals and strategies for achieving them."[91]

This leads, then, to an understanding of the mind and brain existing in a relationship of supervenience. For Murphy, "higher-level properties supervene on lower-level properties if they are partially constituted by the lower-level properties but are not directly reducible to them. Thus, for example, mental properties can be said to supervene on properties of the neurological system; moral properties supervene on psychological or sociological properties."[92] Thus M(ind) supervening on B(rain) entails that something about B in circumstances *c* entails M, but not vice versa: for example, while the signal "I'm home" (M) supervenes on the lighted lamp at the window (B) when agreed upon by neighbors *(c)*, the signal cannot be reduced to this set of physical circumstances as the lamp could be on for another reason, or the neighbors could have agreed to use another signal.[93] To be sure, this concept of supervenience has stirred up intense debate.[94] However, I see it linked closely to emergence theory, and at present do not know of better overall metaphysical hypotheses that can adjudicate between the methodological naturalism of scientific inquiry and the metaphysical pluralism of theological reflection. Hence we continue tentatively with Murphy's notion of supervenience in anticipation of our further discussion (especially in chapter 5).

What results, then, is a nondualistic theory of mental causation supervenient on indeterministic quantum states of the brain that is essential to the notions of both libertarian freedom and moral responsibility. This is Murphy's argument for ethics as a science between the social sciences and theology/metaphysics: on the one hand, ethics cannot be re-

90. Murphy, "Neuroscience and Human Nature," p. 374, italics in original.
91. Murphy, "Neuroscience and Human Nature," p. 384.
92. Nancey Murphy and George F. R. Ellis, *On the Moral Nature of the Universe: Theology, Cosmology, and Ethics* (Minneapolis: Fortress, 1996), p. 23.
93. Murphy, "Nonreductive Physicalism," p. 135.
94. The resistance to the concept has been led by the analytic philosopher Jaegwon Kim, especially his *Supervenience and Mind: Selected Philosophical Essays* (Cambridge and New York: Cambridge University Press, 1993), and *Supervenience* (Aldershot, UK, and Burlington, VT: Ashgate, 2002). For further discussion, see Elias E. Savellos and Umit D. Yalçin, eds., *Supervenience: New Essays* (Cambridge and New York: Cambridge University Press, 1995).

duced to neurological, psychological, social, or political dimensions, although it emerges from or supervenes on their combination; on the other hand, the nonreductive physicalist account of human nature "needs to be completed by a theological account in which descriptions of divine action supervene on descriptions of natural and historical events, but without being reducible to them."[95] While Murphy grants that such a nonreductive physicalist theory (like its dualist or reductionist competitors) can never be scientifically confirmed, it can serve fruitfully as the hard-core notion undergirding a (Lakatosian) scientific research program.[96]

Keep in mind that Murphy formulates her nonreductive physicalism as a hypothesis to be tested rather than as an obvious metaphysical axiom. This is important especially in light of the criticisms raised against the idea of supervenience. The major question — besides that concerning what it means to "supervene" — can be approached from two angles. On the one side, if Murphy is serious about her physicalism, then the "nonreductive" qualifier becomes vacuous; on the other side, if mind is truly irreducible to the brain, then Murphy becomes an advocate of dualism instead of monism. Murphy is not oblivious to the seriousness of these critical questions, but insists that nonreductive physicalism serves as a sufficiently coherent metaphysical hypothesis to sustain ongoing empirical research.

But there is another side to Murphy's nonreductive view of mind. Although her focus has been, so far, on the downward or mental causation aspects of mind's irreducibility, the emergence theory of mind also points to other dimensions, including what some scholars have called the "hard problem of consciousness."[97] For those working on this issue — many in the philosophy of mind — the problem, to put it in Murphy's supervenience terms, is that the lower-level brain states and patterns simply cannot account for the correlative mental feeling, sense, or experience. It is precisely this "hard problem" that has also led some researchers to insist that mental subjectivity cannot merely be studied "objectively" as in

95. Murphy, "Nonreductive Physicalism," p. 147.

96. See Imre Lakatos, *The Methodology of Scientific Research Programmes* (Cambridge and New York: Cambridge University Press, 1978).

97. See David Chalmers's essay and the responses and discussion in Jonathan Shear, ed., *Explaining Consciousness — the "Hard Problem"* (London and Cambridge, MA: MIT Press, 1997). Contrary to the claims of philosophers like Daniel Dennett, this "hard problem" of consciousness is nowhere near to being resolved, and some might even say that as mind is an ontologically emergent level of complexity, this problem will resist scientific resolution within the current paradigm.

the dominant trends of the psychological sciences, but must be accessed in the first person.[98] From this perspective, emic accounts are essential to providing a more complete picture of what is happening.

Philip Clayton, who teaches at Claremont University, has been motivated precisely by this "hard problem" issue to provide a more expansive account of the emergence of the human spirit from its material, biological, and neurological underpinnings.[99] His hypothesis proceeds as follows. (1) The neuroscientific evidence for a one-to-one correlation between brain states and mental states does not appear to be forthcoming anytime soon. Yet this is not just a matter of epistemic ignorance that will be gradually dismissed by the ongoing march of the cognitive sciences. Rather, it is a matter of the mind as an emergent property with a level of complexity and capacity to act that is constituted by but ontologically irreducible to the brain and the body. (2) Once emergent, human mentality produces, dialectically, self-consciousness, asymptotic freedom (for all intents and purposes even if people are only conditionally free), teleological directedness (goal orientation), moral responsibility, social relations, cultural artifacts, and symbolic languages. Each of these levels of emergent behavior is characterized by the freedom of self-transcendence, the capacity of human agents and social groups to aspire for and act toward ideals and attempt to achieve unrealized goals.[100] This signifies, for Clayton, the emergence of spirit, both of human persons as individuals and of social or communal groups as collectives.[101]

---

98. As argued for by Buddhist scholar B. Alan Wallace, *The Taboo of Subjectivity: Toward a New Science of Consciousness* (New York: Oxford University Press, 2000); *Contemplative Science: Where Buddhism and Neuroscience Converge* (New York: Columbia University Press, 2007); *Hidden Dimensions: The Unification of Physics and Consciousness* (New York: Columbia University Press, 2007); and *Mind in the Balance: Meditation in Science, Buddhism, and Christianity* (New York: Columbia University Press, 2009). See also my discussion of Wallace's work in Yong, "Tibetan Buddhism Going Global? A Case Study of a Contemporary Buddhist Encounter with Science," *Journal of Global Buddhism* 9 (2008) (http://www.globalbuddhism.org/).

99. Philip Clayton, *In Quest of Freedom: The Emergence of Spirit in the Natural World*, Religion Theologie und Naturwissenschaft/Religion Theology and Natural Science 13 (Göttingen: Vandenhoeck & Ruprecht, 2009).

100. This is argued by Frederick L. Ware, "Can Religious Experience Be Reduced to Brain Activity? The Place and Significance of Pentecostal Narrative," in *Science and the Spirit*, pp. 117-32.

101. See also Philip Clayton, *Adventures in the Spirit: God, World, Divine Action* (Minneapolis: Fortress, 2008).

I am less enthused about Murphy's physicalist language although I believe her notion of supervenience, while not unambiguous, can be usefully adapted within an emergentist anthropological framework much like the one sketched by Clayton. Understood in this way, human beings are minimally constituted by their bodies in an existing environmental web.[102] Apart from this embodiment and environmental rootedness, mind is nonexistent and incapable of appearing.[103] Yet once emergent, certain personal properties are activated that cannot be explained as merely the sum of the constitutive parts. This holds true both psychologically at the level of the individual and socially at the level of the group or community. Hence, the actions of any individual are constrained even if not completely predetermined by brain waves and patterns, even as the actions of any collective group of self-conscious agents are constricted even if not wholly preordained by any individual member. Similarly, the emergentist principle of "no brains or bodies, no minds," can be extended to say, "no minds, no social groups or social realities."[104] From the emergentist or top-down perspective, however, it is also just as accurate to say, "no social interactions, no minds," thus reflecting the social character of human consciousness. In evolutionary terms, this suggests that the emergence of self-consciousness depends on the emergence of sociality and relationality.[105]

This brief sketch suggests that any theological anthropology will need

102. Melvin Konner, *The Tangled Wing: Biological Constraints on the Human Spirit* (New York: Holt, Rinehart and Winston, 1982).

103. Many other Christians are being drawn toward a monistic anthropological account — viz., Kevin Corcoran, *Rethinking Human Nature: A Christian Materialist Alternative to the Soul* (Grand Rapids: Baker Academic, 2006), and Joel B. Green, *Body, Soul, and Human Life: The Nature of Humanity in the Bible* (Grand Rapids: Baker Academic, 2008).

104. This is not to say, of course, that there are still no (traditional or revisionist) dualists — e.g., John W. Cooper, *Body, Soul, and Life Everlasting: Biblical Anthropology and the Monism-Dualism Debate* (Grand Rapids: Eerdmans, 1989), and J. P. Moreland and Scott B. Rae, *Body and Soul: Human Nature and the Crisis in Ethics* (Downers Grove, IL: InterVarsity, 2000). Although the reader will have to wait until later in this book to see my rationale for avoiding dualism in these matters, some of my reasons are found in Yong, "Christian and Buddhist Perspectives on Neuropsychology and the Human Person: *Pneuma* and *Pratityasamutpada*," *Zygon* 40, no. 1 (2005): 143-65.

105. See, e.g., the arguments of Leslie Brothers, *Friday's Footprint: How Society Shapes the Human Mind* (New York and Oxford: Oxford University Press, 1997), and William Irwin Thompson, *Self and Society: Studies in the Evolution of Consciousness* (Charlottesville, VA: Imprint Academic, 2004); cp. George Herbert Mead, *Mind, Self, and Society: From the Standpoint of a Social Behaviorist*, ed. Charles W. Morris (Chicago: University of Chicago Press, 1934).

to be informed by at least three levels of ontological analysis: that of the material level of the human body, perhaps best accessed through the biological and cognitive sciences; that of the mental level of human life, perhaps most appropriately approached by the psychological sciences; and that of the relational level of human sociality, illuminated most effectively by the social sciences.[106] My claim, and my use of emergence theory here and later in this book (chapters 5–6), is based on the view that scientific analysis of the parts does not suffice to explain the whole, but that each ontological level of analysis adds new perspective not only for the emergent level but also, potentially, for all the lower levels. Of course, these ontological domains overlap, which means that the methodological tools utilized at one level may be helpful for the others as well, although how that is the case will need to be carefully discerned. What are the implications of such an emergentist anthropology for theology and science?

The Emergence of Interdisciplinarity

In this final part of this chapter, I will suggest that an emergentist anthropology opens up an interdisciplinary framework for the theology and science dialogue, but that it does so for both scientific and theological reasons. Scientifically, the various levels of complexity that constitute the web of human life invite a pluralism of methods of inquiry and analysis. Theologically, the diversity of disciplinary and methodological perspectives functions analogously to the many tongues of the Pentecost narrative. In what follows, I develop this two-pronged rationale by looking at the pentecostal phenomenon of glossolalia.[107] My claim is not only that our understanding of glossolalia can be fruitfully illuminated by the various scientific perspectives, but also that our understanding of God's action in the world need not be threatened by the diversity of scientific explanations.

From the standpoint of the sciences, the first two parts of this chapter

106. I say "at least" because that is all I have endeavored to discuss; for a more thorough presentation of a multileveled and dynamic theological anthropology, see Mark Graves, *Mind, Brain, and the Elusive Soul: Human Systems of Cognitive Science and Religion* (Burlington, VT, and Aldershot, UK: Ashgate, 2008).

107. It might be countered that I picked the "easy case" of glossolalia, which involves a high degree of human participation anyway. I think, however, that my supervenience account can also illuminate claims about miraculous healings, among other charismatic phenomena, as I hope to show in chapter 4.

have already shown that tongues speaking can be analyzed at many different levels. Let us summarize the preceding discussion, moving up the ladder of the sciences, so to speak. Technological advances in the cognitive sciences now allow us to observe neural and synaptic functions of those engaged in glossolalic prayer. Unsurprisingly, we note distinctive cerebral patterns as well as the activation of certain brain sites that can be compared and contrasted with what happens with people engaged in nonglossolalic but otherwise prayerful activity.[108] A reductionistic interpretation of such data might be tempted to eliminate the role of human mentality and thus "explain away" what happens in glossolalia as being no more than the epiphenomenal manifestation of various brain states. The argument might be that whatever else people might believe they are doing, the cognitive sciences tell us otherwise.

Yet while neuroscientists may be able to observe, from an outsider's point of view, the correlation between a person's brain functions and his or her conscious activity, this does not explain the insider's "first person" account of the same set of events. This argument of Murphy, Clayton, and others is not meant to demean the gains made in the cognitive sciences.[109] It only distinguishes much that can be illuminated by such studies, while also recognizing that outsider perspectives remain limited within the bigger scheme of things. This does not mean that the cognitive sciences are now in turn negligible since, as we have already noted, our embodiment constrains what can emerge and what happens after that. It means only that the neurophysiological, psychological, and psychosocial sciences are incomplete; put more strongly, apart from first-person accounts, we will not even be able to make the correlation between brain activities and mental states.

At these higher levels, we have already noted research suggesting that tongues speaking may be learned behavior or that glossolalists may fit certain psychological profiles. But gains certainly have been made, especially in overturning the earlier bias that identified glossolalia as pathological. More recent rigorous studies clearly indicate that tongues speakers are no

---

108. E.g., Andrew Newberg et al., "Cerebral Blood Flow during Meditative Prayer: Preliminary Findings and Methodological Issues," *Perceptual and Motor Skills* 97, no. 2 (2003): 625-30.

109. This is not only a theistic issue; Buddhist scholars also resist any reductionism that eliminates the first-person account of what is happening; see my essay "Mind and Life, Religion and Science: The Dalai Lama and the Buddhist-Christian-Science Trilogue," *Buddhist-Christian Studies* 28 (2008): 43-63.

more or less abnormal than non–tongues speakers. Instead, the former are less likely to experience depression, and they exhibit a less hostile personality type. On the whole, there may even be therapeutic benefits to consistent glossolalic practice.[110]

Still, pentecostal theologians, especially the more apologetically motivated, may be concerned about these psychological "findings." What if glossolalic profiling determines that only a small percentage of the human population is predisposed to speaking in tongues? Further, even if there is increasing evidence of the nonpathological nature of tongues speech, what about counterexamples, cases of genuinely pathological glossolalists, especially those snake handlers?[111] Last but certainly not least, if the psychological sciences are able to identify how the neurochemistry of tongues speaking functions therapeutically, does that not undermine the role and activity of the Holy Spirit as divine healing agent? To respond at least initially to the last question: If the Holy Spirit can heal through doctors and medicines, then why not through neurophysiological brain reactions? If embodiment is central to pentecostal spirituality,[112] then why wouldn't the work of the Spirit be mediated through human bodies and brains?

Similarly, we have seen that sociological analyses can also be illuminating. To be sure, such illumination can call attention to how glossolalia functions as a means of religious socialization (a relatively benign conclusion in some pentecostal circles, or one that is more amenable to those who view it as a sign or evidence of the Spirit's infilling), just as it can draw attention to the prevalence of glossolalia among more socially marginal-

110. See, e.g., John Donald Castelein, "Glossolalia and the Psychology of the Self and Narcissism," *Journal of Religion and Health* 23, no. 1 (1984): 47-62, and Steven A. Gritzmacher, Brian Bolton, and Richard H. Dana, "Psychological Characteristics of Pentecostals: A Literature Review and Psychodynamic Synthesis," *Journal of Psychology and Theology* 16, no. 3 (1988): 233-45.

111. Snake handling is a very limited phenomenon among global pentecostalism, reflecting, as much as anything else, the historical and cultural peculiarities of the Appalachian region. For a sympathetic yet illuminating discussion that does not pathologize serpent handlers, see Hood and Williamson, *Them That Believe* (n. 32 above). See also Thomas G. Burton, *Serpent-Handling Believers* (Knoxville: University of Tennessee Press, 1993), and Dennis Covington, *Salvation on Sand Mountain: Snake Handling and Redemption in Southern Appalachia* (Reading, MA: Addison-Wesley, 1995).

112. The centrality of the body to pentecostal and charismatic piety is documented by Thomas J. Csordas, *The Sacred Self: A Cultural Phenomenology of Charismatic Healing* (Berkeley: University of California Press, 1994), and *Body/Meaning/Healing* (New York: Palgrave Macmillan, 2002).

ized people groups (which may be less appealing for those in the upper classes). Parallel to this, as the research of Goodman and others has shown, cultural-anthropological perspectives have also documented how glosso-lalia serves as a semiotic marker among communities experiencing social upheaval in the transition from a premodern to a modern world. On the other hand, we also saw recent collaborative and multidisciplinary ap-proaches that revealed glossolalia flourishing among well-adjusted and upwardly mobile people groups too.

Predictably, polemicists have attempted to draw from selected scien-tific data to attack pentecostals personally or undermine pentecostal spiri-tuality and piety as a whole.[113] Such polemics are, however, inevitably reductionistic inasmuch as explanation provided at any one level — for example, neurobiology, psychology, or sociology — is thought to com-pletely account for the phenomenon in question. But this is an extrascientific conclusion that is smuggled in rather than derived from any individual data set. It also assumes either that a lower-level explanation exhaustively captures all there is to be known about what is under discus-sion or that the world itself is a closed system of causes and effects that ex-cludes a religious or theological dimension. The latter, of course, is a meta-physical assumption that is contested especially among those working at the theology and science interface.

My claim is that each level of scientific inquiry is important and help-ful for shedding light on the whole even as any adequate explanation of a religious phenomenon, including glossolalia, should also pay attention to the religious and theological explications of its practitioners. When this latter element is factored in, a genuine encounter between science and reli-gion would proceed in two directions. On the one hand, scientific view-points would complement and even enrich our religious and theological descriptions, rather than threaten them; on the other hand, religious and theological perspectives would also add depth to scientific accounts by providing "thick descriptions" of the phenomenon under investigation.[114]

---

113. E.g., Klemet Preus, "Tongues: An Evaluation from a Scientific Perspective," *Con-cordia Theological Quarterly* 46, no. 4 (1982): 277-93.

114. I provide such a "thick" account in my "'Tongues,' Theology, and the Social Sci-ences: A Pentecostal-Theological Reading of Geertz's Interpretive Theory of Religion," *Cyberjournal for Pentecostal/Charismatic Research* 1 (1997) (http://pctii.org/cyberj/cyber1 .html); see also Yong, "Tongues of Fire in the Pentecostal Imagination: The Truth of Glosso-lalia in Light of R. C. Neville's Theory of Religious Symbolism," *Journal of Pentecostal Theol-ogy* 12 (1998): 39-65.

So whereas a neurobiological, psychological, or sociological theory might be tempted to reduce tongues speaking to a single or lower-level variable, Malony and Lovekin's "transcendency deprivation" perspective would recognize each level of explanation as valid in its own way, yet seek a holistic viewpoint that includes the religious and theological dimensions involved in practitioner self-understandings.

In other words, to return momentarily to Murphy's supervenience hypothesis, the lines of causal explanation can be understood to flow in multiple directions, including a "top-down" role for human, and even divine, agency. So any particular glossolalic manifestation may be viewed from any number of disciplinary perspectives, each illuminating the phenomenon in its own way (neurobiologically according to certain brain functions, psychologically according to certain personality propensities, sociologically according to certain social deprivations, etc.). But this need not — indeed should not — displace the first-person account, one that may be testified to as having the character of a spiritual yearning, or, to put it in pentecostal terms, a "tarrying before the Lord."[115] In this case, the mental exertion put forth in tarrying for this or that blessing from God is constrained by and supervenes upon the existing or underlying neurobiological and psychological realities, but is not reducible to these lower levels without loss of the higher-level account. (Later in this book, I will reflect further on how such a supervenience account is applicable also to an understanding of other pentecostal phenomena like miracles and healings.)

Note, however, that we are here not arbitrarily making room for pentecostal interpretations. Rather, there is an increasing recognition that phenomena at each level up the hierarchy of sciences — for example, physics, chemistry, biology, neuropsychology, sociology — are in some way causally constituted by the lower level, but yet, once having emerged, add something to the explanation of the whole without which our understanding would be significantly impoverished.[116] So while lower-level explanations can illuminate observations at the next level to some degree, only a blatant reductionism would claim to provide an exhaustive account. At the same time, the emergentist hypothesis also recognizes the validity of the various

115. Daniel Castelo, "Tarrying on the Lord: Affections, Virtues and Theological Ethics in Pentecostal Perspective," *Journal of Pentecostal Theology* 13, no. 1 (2004): 31-56.

116. E.g., Philip Clayton and Paul Davies, eds., *The Re-emergence of Emergence: The Emergentist Hypothesis from Science to Religion* (Oxford: Oxford University Press, 2006), and Nancey Murphy and W. J. Stoeger, eds., *Evolution and Emergence: Systems, Organisms, Persons* (Oxford: Oxford University Press, 2007).

scientific discourses each at its own level — since the science at each level should be determined by the nature of the objects or things studied at that level — without negating the need for higher-level perspectives.[117]

The call for interdisciplinarity does not just seek to make room for theological perspectives. What is at stake is not just theology's "voice" but the integrity of each of the disciplines within and across the spectrum of the sciences. Anticipating here the defense in chapter 5 of a theology of evolutionary emergence, reductionism threatens not just theology but each science's investigation at higher or emergent levels. I insist on interdisciplinarity in order to preserve the relative autonomy of each of the scientific fields of inquiry.

The result is a scientific justification for methodological pluralism and interdisciplinarity that has a theological correlation. I am referring to an analogical interpretation of the many tongues of Pentecost. In my reading, the tongues of fire in the Acts narrative symbolize the many cultures, languages, and perspectives that constitute the human community, all of which combine, at least potentially if not actually, to declare the glory of God (Acts 2:11). Hence the many tongues of Pentecost serve metaphorically to suggest how many different linguistic and cultural perspectives can also be vehicles for declaring all truth as God's truth. By extension, in our contemporary world, I am suggesting that the many scientific disciplines and the diversity of viewpoints represented in the scientific enterprise constitute a multiplicity of modes of inquiry and discourses that also reveal how nature declares the glory of God (Ps. 19:1). Each speaks distinctively from its vantage point, illuminating the world in its own way, while complementing our knowledge of the whole. None can be eliminated without substantial loss, but simultaneously, none can presume to subsume all other explanations under its own rubric. Theology can therefore allow the various sciences to do their work, and need not fear (at least not in general) about the deliverances of the sciences. The two books — of nature and of Scripture — should not contradict one another, assuming they are

---

117. For an argument for multilevel or stratigraphic disciplinary analysis, see Alister E. McGrath, *The Science of God* (Grand Rapids: Eerdmans, 2004), chapter 5, and also McGrath, *A Scientific Theology*, vol. 2, *Reality* (Grand Rapids: Eerdmans; Edinburgh: T. & T. Clark, 2002), chapter 10 (who draws, in both cases, on the work of British philosopher Roy Bhasker). For an alternative argument against scientific reductionism, see Stuart A. Kauffman, *Reinventing the Sacred: A New View of Science, Reason, and Religion* (New York: Basic Books, 2008), although I'm less enthused about Kauffman's naturalistic theism that hearkens back to Spinoza's pantheism.

both being interpreted correctly.[118] Theology can learn from the sciences even while theology can also perhaps inform scientific inquiry.[119]

But we are missing one more element that has been percolating under our discussion throughout this chapter: the activity of God the Holy Spirit. Now for the record, I do *not* hold that God as spirit is also an emergent reality like human spirits. So since the preceding emergentist anthropology and interdisciplinary method open up space for human intentionality, made possible in terms of a supervening relationship between the mind and its environment (including the brain and the body), the question arises: What about divine intentionality? More precisely, how should we think about the person and workings of the Holy Spirit? How is science supposed to account for that?

This is not a moot question. In the glossolalic experience, many pentecostals will turn immediately to the biblical account, which states, "All of them were filled with the Holy Spirit and began to speak in other languages, as the Spirit gave them ability" (Acts 2:4). Quite apart from citing scriptural texts as explanations, pentecostal testimonies are pervasively infused with recognition of the Spirit's constant presence and activity in their lives. How can a pentecostal engagement with modern science register fairly this conviction about divine action? As we shall see from the argument of the next two chapters, I believe that pentecostal perspectives and emphases on the eschatological dimension of the Spirit's presence and activity can be understood as complementary to — even supervenient upon — the causal descriptions identified at the various levels of scientific inquiry.

118. See Yong, "Reading Scripture and Nature: Pentecostal Hermeneutics and Their Implications for the Contemporary Evangelical Theology and Science Conversation," *Perspectives on Science and Christian Faith* 63, no. 1 (2011): 1-13.

119. Robert John Russell, *Cosmology from Alpha to Omega: The Creative Mutual Interaction of Theology and Science* (Minneapolis: Fortress, 2008), pp. 9-24, suggests that theology can influence scientific work in at least the following ways: informing assumptions behind empirical research; providing models and analogies for imaginative interpretation of data; and suggesting criteria for choosing among rival interpretive theories.

3 The Spirit at Work in the World

A Pentecostal Perspective on the Divine Action Project

We now turn to focus especially on the challenges involved in talking about the activity of the Holy Spirit in the world of modern science. Of course, for materialistic and naturalistic skeptics there is no need to acknowledge any immaterial or spiritual realities, much less to find ways to talk about how such realities interface with or act within or upon the world. On the other side, most pentecostals talk extensively, in their testimonies and informal conversations, about the presence and activity of the Holy Spirit in their daily lives. Most theists involved in the theology and science dialogue can be understood as gingerly treading a *via media* between these two extremes: on the one hand, they wish to affirm at least the reality of God, even if they are not quite sure how such a God acts in the world; on the other hand, this reluctance to assert too much about divine action results in a fairly christologically constrained notion of divine action — at least for the theists who are also Christians — so that God is understood to act particularly in the life and ministry of Christ, but cannot be said to be doing too much more than that, at least not from a scientifically responsible point of view.

This chapter is the first of two to explore the possibilities of thinking about divine action in pneumatological terms, especially in light of the person and work of the Holy Spirit. The argument unfolds here in four parts. First, I show how the charismatic apocalypticism, miraculous supernaturalism, and divine interventionism of the pentecostal worldview are conflicted because it uncritically accepts certain modernistic assumptions about the nature of the world. Second, I assess the results of the Divine Action Project (DAP) organized conjointly by the Center for Theology and the Natural Sciences (Berkeley, California) and the Vatican Observatory. Third, I trace the proposals by some Project participants to rethink the idea of divine action within a wider christological framework that has included, via the doctrine of the resurrection, end-of-the-world or eschatological scenarios, and suggest that such christological and eschatological perspectives invite a more fully Trinitarian and pneumatological theology of divine action since they are all intimately related in the history of Christian theology to the person and work of the Holy Spirit. The fourth part, the longest section of this chapter, develops the contours of just such an eschatological-teleological theology of divine action in dialogue with pentecostal-charismatic practices, and then extrapolates from that toward a pneumatologically informed theory of God's action in the world.

The chapter suggests a unique pentecostal perspective on divine action as pneumatological (related to the Holy Spirit) and eschatological (anticipating the future) in dialogue with proposals from the Divine Action Project. Throughout, we will engage with contemporary scientific perspectives in two ways. First, we will seek to be constrained by the sciences in recognizing the limits about what can be said about divine action within the framework of modern science.[1] Second, however, we will also suggest how theological perspectives invite reconsideration of at least certain teleological notions that have been by and large excluded from contemporary scientific discussion. Our goal is to take a first step toward sketching the framework of what might be called a pneumatological and teleological theology of divine action from a pentecostal-charismatic perspective. The next chapter will argue more specifically about the coherence of such a model for understanding miracles in a world structured by the laws of nature.

Divine Action in Pentecostal-Charismatic Perspective: Challenges and Possibilities

Pentecostal piety and spirituality assume that God is present and active in the world. In this section, I elaborate on what it has meant historically for

---

1. Philip Clayton, *Adventures in the Spirit: God, World, Divine Action* (Minneapolis: Fortress, 2008), especially chapter 3, argues convincingly, in my opinion, about how theology's engagement with the sciences has to recognize just what can be said within scientific constraints. I take this as meaning not that science is supremely authoritative, but that when engaging specifically with the sciences, theologians need to understand that specific context and thus have to accommodate themselves, at least in part, to that field of discourse.

pentecostal theology to affirm divine action. I show that while pentecostal theology has always sought to ground its beliefs and practices in the apostolic witness of the New Testament, there are alternative readings of the canonical narratives that invite different understandings of divine action that may not be as conflicted in the world of modern science.

At the core of the pentecostal experience is a palpable, tangible, and kinesthetic encounter with the living God. This foundational conviction is most clearly manifest in the various spiritual or charismatic gifts of the Spirit prevalent in pentecostal worship: tongues and prophecies, healings, and miracles. In fact, in some pentecostal circles, the speaking in tongues (glossolalia) is considered an evidential sign of the speaker having received the gift or baptism of the Holy Spirit.[2] But more importantly, in almost all pentecostal contexts, God is believed to respond to the earnest intercessory prayers of the saints through the meeting of human needs, the healing of sick and diseased bodies, and the provision of timely and miraculous acts of wonder.[3]

Most pentecostal Christians expect God's ongoing intervention in the same manner as such divine action was displayed in the lives of the earliest Christians. In their fairly straightforward and literal reading of the New Testament narrative, God healed the sick, cleansed lepers, and raised the dead by the power of the Holy Spirit given on the Day of Pentecost — doing all this in response to the prayers and requests of God's people, and at their behest. As Jesus himself taught, "Ask, and it will be given to you; search, and you will find; knock, and the door will be opened for you" (Luke 11:9). Now of course God can and does also act sovereignly, before prayers are offered up, to reveal his power, goodness, and glory, and pentecostal Christians are grateful for this when they believe it occurs. However, pentecostal beliefs in an interventionist God are based on their sense of following in the footsteps of the early Christians as participants in an ongoing drama in which God is the major actor while they are the minor cast. In fact, it is precisely when human beings cry out to God in prayers and supplications in impossible situations that God's miraculous and timely interventions are most undeniable.

2. Gary B. McGee, ed., *Initial Evidence: Historical and Biblical Perspectives on the Pentecostal Doctrine of Spirit Baptism* (Peabody, MA: Hendrickson, 1991).

3. A recent survey confirmed that Pentecostals and charismatics are much more inclined to believe in miracles than are other Christians; see "Spirit and Power: A 10-Country Survey of Pentecostals" (Washington, DC: Pew Research Center 2006), 25 (available at http://pewforum.org/publications/surveys/pentecostals-06.pdf).

This evidentialist aspect of pentecostal theology of divine intervention needs further comment.[4] What counts evidentially for lay pentecostal believers is not what counts as evidence in formal argumentation. Rather, pentecostal piety recognizes divine presence and agency whenever things are otherwise inexplicable. On the one hand, this does open up to a sort of God-of-the-gaps faith that is problematic in the theology and science context. Alternatively, perhaps it can be said of pentecostals that theirs is a hermeneutics of charity: what is impossible for human beings can only be made possible if God intervenes.[5] In that sense, pentecostal Christians embrace a supernaturalist worldview in opposition to both the cessationism of much of fundamentalist Christianity on the right and the naturalism of some branches of liberal Protestantism on the left. These were the dominant theological options during the first half of the twentieth century against which early modern pentecostals reacted and with which many pentecostal Christians continue to wrestle in sorting out their theological commitments. Whereas cessationism limited the miraculous workings of the Holy Spirit to the apostolic age and therefore rejected pentecostal manifestations as spurious rather than religiously authentic, pentecostal spirituality insists that the charisms of the Spirit have never been revoked, and that in fact the Spirit's powerful workings have intensified in and through the modern pentecostal renewal.[6]

On the other side, the theological naturalism that emerged during the first half of the twentieth century spurred pentecostals to adopt a supernaturalistic view of divine action. Pentecostals resisted naturalistic definitions of what was possible (or not); they were interested, rather, in the God who could bring about what could not be accomplished by ordinary means. Insofar as many pentecostals, especially in the global South, come from the lower classes, they lack access to medical care, economic

4. The following distinguishes pentecostal evidentialism from what goes under that label in philosophy of religion circles, which insists that beliefs not sufficiently grounded in the available evidence are irrational; see, e.g., William Clifford, "The Ethics of Belief," in *The Philosophy of Religion: The Big Questions,* ed. Eleonore Stump and Michael J. Murray (Malden, MA: Blackwell, 1999), pp. 269-73.

5. Thus again, Jesus' words: "What is impossible for mortals is possible for God" (Luke 18:27); cf. also the declaration of the angel to Mary: "For nothing will be impossible with God" (Luke 1:37).

6. The definitive response to cessationism has been Jon Ruthven, *On the Cessation of the Charismata: The Protestant Polemic on Post-biblical Miracles* (Sheffield: Sheffield Academic Press, 1993).

means, social status, or political power — and in each of these respects, a God who is able to meet these day-to-day needs is more important than a God who can save only souls. Yet inasmuch as pentecostals in the global renewal also inhabit a modern world, their supernaturalism has not led them to question either the logical or the metaphysical underpinnings of the naturalistic paradigm.[7] I would go further to say that supernaturalism actually requires a fairly robust view of nature governed by physical laws to begin with since without this all-encompassing framework, divine signs, wonders, and miracles would not stand out from such laws and would thereby lose much of their capacity to evoke astonishment.

Ironically, it was this assumption regarding the laws of nature propounded within a naturalistic framework that secured the interventionist and supernaturalistic worldview of pentecostal-charismatic Christianity. After all, if the laws of nature dictated that things happen in this or that way, then only the supernatural intervention of God could cause events to turn out differently. Yet at the same time, it was also this unquestioning view of nature's mechanisms that renders pentecostal supernaturalism and interventionism increasingly problematic vis-à-vis developments in modern science.

Pentecostal Christians, for all their reliance on the apostolic witness to undergird their expectancy of miracles, have not usually noticed that the earliest Christians did not hold similar assumptions regarding a law-governed world. Whereas pentecostal supernaturalism and interventionism contest the naturalistic paradigm, early Christian miracles opposed not naturalism — an Enlightenment and post-Enlightenment phenomenon — but pagan magical practices.[8] In other words, God's power was not needed to overthrow strictly defined laws of nature (these had not yet been "discovered"), but to expose the futility of pagan magic. More importantly,

---

7. Things are slowly changing — e.g., see J. Kwabena Asamoah-Gyadu, "'God's Laws of Productivity': Creation in African Pentecostal Hermeneutics," in *The Spirit Renews the Face of the Earth: Pentecostal Forays in Science and Theology of Creation*, ed. Amos Yong (Eugene, OR: Pickwick, 2009), pp. 175-90.

8. E.g., Howard Clark Kee, *Medicine, Miracle, and Magic in New Testament Times* (Cambridge: Cambridge University Press, 1986); Jacob Neusner, "Science and Magic, Miracle and Magic in Formative Judaism: The System and the Difference," in *Religion, Science, and Magic: In Concert and in Conflict*, ed. Jacob Neusner, Ernest S. Frerichs, and Paul Virgil McCracken Flesher (New York and Oxford: Oxford University Press, 1989), pp. 61-81; and Andy M. Reimer, *Miracle and Magic: A Study in the Acts of the Apostles and the Life of Apollonius of Tyana*, Journal for the Study of the New Testament Supplement Series 235 (New York and London: Sheffield Academic Press, 2002).

divinely wrought miracles were evidential not to reveal God as more powerful than the laws of nature, but to highlight God's power vis-à-vis other
divine beings believed to populate the ancient world and to validate the
ministry of Jesus and produce faith in his announcement of the coming
kingdom.[9] Might it be that the pentecostal appeal to the canonical witness
heretofore has been selective, in a sense driven by contemporary apologetic interests shaped by popular understandings of how physical laws
work? And if so, how might a pentecostal reading of early Christianity and
the New Testament on its own terms rather than on those of modernity inform an alternative, although no less pentecostal or charismatic, view of
divine action particularly in the context of the contemporary theology and
science dialogue?

The Divine Action Project: Science in Search of the Causal Joint

The naturalistic assumptions undergirding the world of modern science
have evoked a wide range of responses by especially theists seeking to understand God's action in the world.[10] We will examine the more straight-
forwardly theological proposals in the next chapter, but here we focus specifically on a distinctive research project that has persisted over the last
twenty-plus years in attempting to reconsider the notion of divine action
in extensive and intensive dialogue with the sciences, especially the physical sciences. The Divine Action Project (DAP) was launched in the late
1980s and has involved both theologians and scientists throughout. It has
produced six major collections of papers.[11] In what follows, I identify the

9. This christological significance of the miraculous in especially the Lukan writings is
articulated by Marilyn McCord Adams, "The Role of Miracles in the Structure of Luke-
Acts," in *Hermes and Athena: Biblical Exegesis and Philosophical Theology,* ed. Eleanore
Stump and Thomas P. Flint, Notre Dame Studies in the Philosophy of Religion 7 (Notre
Dame, IN: University of Notre Dame Press, 1993), pp. 235-74, and Daniel Marguerat, "Magic
and Miracle in the Acts of the Apostles," in *Magic in the Biblical World: From the Rod of
Aaron to the Ring of Solomon,* ed. Todd E. Klutz (London and New York: T. & T. Clark, 2003),
pp. 100-124, especially 114.

10. I provide an overview of various models in my "How Does God Do What God
Does? Pentecostal-Charismatic Perspectives on Divine Action in Dialogue with Modern Science," in *Science and the Spirit: A Pentecostal Engagement with the Sciences,* ed. Amos Yong
and James K. A. Smith (Bloomington: Indiana University Press, 2010), pp. 50-71, especially
52-56.

11. The six volumes are: Robert John Russell, Nancey Murphy, and C. J. Isham, eds.,

main issues discussed by the DAP and summarize the major theories of divine action proposed by its participants.[12]

As the title of the first volume — *Quantum Cosmology and the Laws of Nature* — reveals, the DAP's attention has been focused on how to understand God's activity in a law-governed world. Other volumes have explored this question vis-à-vis chaos theory, evolutionary and molecular biology, neuroscience, and quantum mechanics. Throughout, DAP participants have assumed that the "laws of nature," however such might be understood scientifically, point at least theologically to the means through which the world is being sustained by God. Hence there has been little motivation to think of divine action as incompatible with the lawfully structured causal processes of the world.

But such compatibilism can take different shapes. A minority of DAP participants advocate various forms of what might be called "uniform divine action," which understands God to be "active" generally either in all events or in the world as a whole; without such general activity, creation would not be self-sustainable.[13] In this framework, those who take the further step of affirming "special" divine action understand that this characterizes not what God does but how human beings receive and interpret such events. Hence uniform or general divine action is special not in the

---

Quantum Cosmology and the Laws of Nature: Scientific Perspectives on Divine Action, 2nd ed. (Vatican City State: Vatican Observatory; Berkeley, CA: Center for Theology and the Natural Sciences, 1999); Robert John Russell, Nancey Murphy, and Arthur R. Peacocke, eds., *Chaos and Complexity: Scientific Perspectives on Divine Action* (Vatican City State: Vatican Observatory; Berkeley, CA: Center for Theology and the Natural Sciences, 1995); Robert John Russell, William R. Stoeger, and Francisco J. Ayala, eds., *Evolutionary and Molecular Biology: Scientific Perspectives on Divine Action* (Vatican City State: Vatican Observatory; Berkeley, CA: Center for Theology and the Natural Sciences, 1998); Robert John Russell et al., eds., *Neuroscience and the Person: Scientific Perspectives on Divine Action* (Vatican City State: Vatican Observatory; Berkeley, CA: Center for Theology and the Natural Sciences, 1999); Robert John Russell et al., eds., *Quantum Mechanics: Scientific Perspectives on Divine Action* (Vatican City State: Vatican Observatory; Berkeley, CA: Center for Theology and the Natural Sciences, 2001); and Robert J. Russell, Nancey C. Murphy, and William R. Stoeger, eds., *Scientific Perspectives on Divine Action: Twenty Years of Challenge and Progress* (Vatican City State: Vatican Observatory Publications; Berkeley, CA: Center for Theology and the Natural Sciences; and Notre Dame, IN: University of Notre Dame Press, 2008).

12. For another summary, see Wesley J. Wildman, "The Divine Action Project, 1988-2003," in Russell, Murphy, and Stoeger, *Scientific Perspectives on Divine Action,* pp. 133-76.

13. A representative voice in the DAP who is reluctant to affirm anything more than uniform or general divine action is Willem B. Drees, "Gaps for God?" in *Chaos and Complexity,* pp. 236-37.

ontological or objective sense but in an epistemological or subjective sense of revealing to human creatures something about the character and intentions of God.

Many DAP participants, however, think that a more robust account of God's action in the world is needed. The biblical narratives depict God as responding to and interacting with the world in ways that, absent this interaction, the world would be different. The traditional view would simply say that God intervenes on the world stage. Yet DAP participants are reluctant to embrace such interventionism for at least three reasons: (1) it seems to reduce God to being one among other actors in the world; (2) it assumes a literalistic and anthropomorphic hermeneutic of the Bible; and (3) it implies that God has to work against the divinely created laws of nature, and hence undermines the compatibilist idea already proposed. Hence what is needed is a middle way between the interventionism of traditional theology and the subjectivism of uniform or general divine action.

Unsurprisingly, the most creative and constructive proposals in the DAP seek what might be called noninterventionist objective (special) divine action (NIOSDA).[14] The question is how special divine action (SDA) might be both objective and yet noninterventionistic. DAP participants have thus been led to reexamine the nature of the world in quest of "open spaces" in and through which a causal joint can be found for God's acting in the world without having to overrule natural processes. Such open spaces in the causal nexus of the world — if they existed and could be identified — would serve as venues for NIOSDA that in principle would not be overturned through the ongoing march of science. The traditional God-of-the-gaps criticism is circumvented in this case since the gaps would be ontological rather than epistemological. DAP participants have suggested two domains in the natural world that might secure NIOSDA: quantum indeterminacy and chaos dynamical systems.

The possibility of God's action at the quantum mechanical level — quantum divine action (QDA) — is defended by a number of DAP members.[15] What is attractive about QDA is that, in the so-called Copenhagen

14. Robert John Russell's project, shaped by the DAP, has been to articulate a noninterventionist objective model of divine action; see, e.g., Russell, "Does 'the God Who Acts' Really Act? New Approaches to Divine Action in Light of Science," *Theology Today* 54, no. 1 (1997): 43-65.

15. E.g., Thomas F. Tracy, "Particular Providence and the God of the Gaps," in *Chaos and Complexity*, pp. 314-21, and Tracy, "Creation, Providence, and Quantum Chance," in *Quantum Mechanics*, pp. 250-51. See also Nancey Murphy, "Divine Action in the Natural Or-

interpretation of Niels Bohr (1885-1962) and Werner Heisenberg (1901-1976) — which is the view of the majority of physicists — the indeterminacy postulated at the quantum level derives essentially from the probabilistic nature of reality itself. Now while physicists warn that the quantum formalism should not be taken to depict literally the microscopic world, its repeated experimental successes suggest that it does provide an accurate statistical description of nature at its most fundamental level. Quantum systems are thus best described as probabilistic wave functions, but their outcomes — brought about by measurements of the system that are said to collapse the wave function — are essentially nondeterministic. This intrinsic unpredictability is suggestive of ontological "gaps" in the world that provide "openings" for divine action. In theory, God's activity at the quantum level could consist either of collapsing the wave function or influencing or picking out one of its many probabilities. Whereas some DAP members believe that God acts in all quantum events (e.g., Nancey Murphy), others postulate that God acts only in some (e.g., Thomas Tracy). A mediating view is that God acted in all quantum events prior to the emergence of human consciousness, and only in some since (Robert John Russell). For QDA proposals, then, God is thus the "hidden variable" at the quantum level, at the very least a necessary albeit insufficient cause of quantum events.

While most QDA proponents do not limit God's activity to the quantum level, other models of SDA subordinate, or question, its contribution to the discussion. For physicist-theologian John Polkinghorne,[16] QDA is questionable not only because the probability set is constrained if not predetermined by the wave function but also because it appears that God becomes a stopgap "hidden variable" inserted to solve the measurement problem. Instead of QDA, Polkinghorne suggests that the unpredictability of chaotic or nonlinear dynamic systems provides a more viable model for God's activity in the world.[17] Given the sensitivity of such chaotic systems

der: Buridan's Ass and Schrödinger's Cat," in *Chaos and Complexity*, pp. 339-44, and Robert John Russell, "Divine Action and Quantum Mechanics: A Fresh Assessment," in *Quantum Mechanics*, pp. 301-18.

16. The following derives primarily from John Polkinghorne, "The Metaphysics of Divine Action," in *Chaos and Complexity*, pp. 147-56.

17. John Jefferson Davis, *The Frontiers of Science and Faith: Examining Questions from the Big Bang to the End of the Universe* (Downers Grove, IL: InterVarsity, 2002), chapter 4, also thinks that chaotic unpredictability is helpful for theology, particularly in terms of replacing the determinism of the Newtonian and Laplacean paradigm; I am less sure, however,

to initial conditions, and given especially the vulnerability, openness, and interrelatedness of such dissipative systems with their environments (other systems), divine action can proceed through the input of what Polkinghorne calls "active information" that either adjusts the system's initial conditions and hence shifts (sometimes dramatically) its trajectory, or influences the evolution of the system through interaction with other systems in its environment. And if chaotic systems are drawn toward their futures by infinitely variable "strange attractors" that are not dictated by different energy states, then divine action can causally nudge the chaotic system in any direction without either "intervention" (since the system is ontologically gappy) or cost (since there is no added energy required to move the system in any direction).[18] While acknowledging that classical chaos theory is governed by deterministic equations, Polkinghorne says these might be "interpreted as downward emergent approximations to a more subtle and supple physical reality. They are valid only in the limiting and special cases where bits and pieces are effectively insulated from the effects of their environment."[19]

Biologist-theologian Arthur Peacocke is in basic agreement with Polkinghorne's chaos amplification approach, but Peacocke suggests distinctive adjustments based on top-down or downward causation considerations parallel to mind-brain models depicting human interaction with their bodies and with the world.[20] More so than Polkinghorne, Peacocke emphasizes how the behavior of whole systems influences their constituent parts, with evidence drawn from the biological sciences of evolutionary networks and patterns and from the psychological sciences focused on mental causation. A panentheistic model of the world as "within" God and of God as "exceeding" the world is suggestive for understanding how God acts superveniently on the world system as a whole. Peacocke is careful to avoid any implications of deism precisely through emphasizing the ongoing interaction between God and the world since the beginning of cre-

---

if Davis's views relate to human epistemic incapacities or are ontologically grounded in the nature of things.

18. The role of information in physics and biology is explored by the various essays in part II of Niels Henrik Gregersen, ed., *From Complexity to Life: On the Emergence of Life and Meaning* (New York: Oxford University Press, 2003).

19. Polkinghorne, "Metaphysics of Divine Action," p. 153.

20. Here I rely on Arthur Peacocke, "God's Interaction with the World: The Implications of Deterministic 'Chaos' and of Interconnected and Interdependent Complexity," in *Chaos and Complexity,* pp. 263-87.

ation. But given God's decision to create a world with its own autonomous integrity and intrinsically indeterminate causal processes, and assuming that the future lacks any ontological status, the doctrine of divine omniscience needs to be redefined to say that God knows the future definitively only insofar as it is predictable given God's infinite knowledge of present conditions and their related determining laws, and probabilistically for quantum-related entities.[21]

Responses to the DAP have ranged across a spectrum. While theologians like Wesley Wildman think that within the framework of the DAP "there are several viable possibilities for theories of SDA at the quantum level," others are not so optimistic.[22] If Peacocke's model is plagued by the inconclusive debates about the mind-body relation in the philosophy of mind and the neurocognitive sciences,[23] Polkinghorne's attempt to turn chaos theory from a deterministic to an indeterministic science is less than persuasive to DAP researchers.[24] QDA proposals are problematic not least because of various theological issues related to the measurement problem: even if God were to collapse the wave function, either God would then be dependent on the probabilistic outcome of the measurement (in which case, divine sovereignty would be threatened) or God would have to unilaterally determine the outcome, either by changing the wave function or by overriding the probability calculus (in which cases, the noninterventionist character of QDA is undermined). But even if these difficulties can be overcome, it takes too long, arguably, to get the desired macroscopic effects from divine agency enacted at the quantum level. One conclusion is that the search for a causal joint between God and the world is a failure: "all the existing claims for quantum SDA in relation to current under-

21. This revision of the doctrine of omniscience is now being increasingly embraced by process, relational, and open theists, among others; see, e.g., Paul R. Eddy and James K. Beilby, eds., *Divine Foreknowledge: Four Views* (Downers Grove, IL: InterVarsity, 2001).

22. Wesley J. Wildman, "The Divine Action Project, 1988-2003," *Theology and Science* 2, no. 1 (2004): 31-75, quotation from 63. Detractors are Nicholas T. Saunders, "Does God Cheat at Dice? Divine Action and Quantum Possibilities," *Zygon* 35, no. 3 (2000): 517-44; Jeffrey Koperski, "God, Chaos, and the Quantum Dice," *Zygon* 35, no. 3 (2000): 545-59; and Timothy Sansbury, "The False Promise of Quantum Mechanics," *Zygon* 42, no. 1 (2007): 111-21.

23. E.g., Joel B. Green and Stuart L. Palmer, eds., *In Search of the Soul: Four Views of the Mind-Body Problem* (Downers Grove, IL: InterVarsity, 2005).

24. In volume 2 of *Chaos and Complexity*, Polkinghorne's paper was the only one that explicitly suggested a chaos theoretical model for divine action, with a half-dozen other papers presenting alternative approaches.

standings of quantum theory fail," and "on the terms of our current understanding of quantum theory, incompatibilist non-interventionist quantum SDA is not theoretically possible."[25]

In response to these critical questions, Robert John Russell has continued to work to refine the notion of QDA.[26] He suggests that the God who works with the indeterministic probabilities of the wave function is not necessarily reducible to what is possible in nature's processes, but instead chooses to be revealed amidst especially the passibility and suffering of Christ. God's sovereignty is in this case revised away from traditional notions of divine power toward a more cruciform and Trinitarian conception. But yet, such views are complementary with QDA. With regard to how divine action can bring about macroscopic effects from quantum events, Russell points to superfluidity, superconductivity, and genetic mutations as examples of quantum mechanical processes that produce classical results.

I am sympathetic to Russell's efforts since he carefully avoids either identifying a causal joint that might compromise divine transcendence or creaturely autonomy (or both), or insisting on the observability and measurability of divine action that would then undermine the integrity of scientific explanation. Further, while he deftly engages the most recent advances in the sciences, he also works to take theology's commitments seriously. Yes, tough questions remain on both fronts, as well as at the intersection of theology and science,[27] but Russell's exploratory approach invites the collaboration of other researchers rather than forecloses the conversation. I am especially interested in seeing what kind of impact Russell's more theological insights might have on the DAP.

The Eschatological Horizon: Christological Implications for Divine Action

In this section I trace some of the ways that theology has played a more substantive role not only in the DAP but also in the wider discussion of di-

25. Nicholas Saunders, *Divine Action and Modern Science* (Cambridge: Cambridge University Press, 2002), pp. 170 and 172.

26. The following derives from Robert John Russell, *Cosmology from Alpha to Omega* (Minneapolis: Fortress, 2008), especially chapters 4–5. I am grateful to Russell for allowing me access to this manuscript before publication.

27. As I summarize also in my "Divining 'Divine Action' in Theology-and-Science: A Review Essay," *Zygon* 43, no. 1 (2008): 191-200.

vine action. We will see two noticeable shifts when theological commitments have been registered in this conversation: a more explicit focus on divine action in the incarnation, and hence, a more christological model of divine action, and a gradual but rather perceptible refocusing from God's action in nature and (past) history to explorations about divine action in the (far off) future.

In many respects the theological contribution to the discussion of divine action has turned repeatedly to the paradigmatic Christian claims related to God's revelation, incarnation, and action in the person of Jesus of Nazareth. For example, in his 1993 Gifford Lectures, Peacocke argued, "Jesus the Christ is the consummation both of the creative work of God in evolution and of the revelation of God made to the people Israel."[28] But can traditional Christian beliefs about Jesus be held without modification in a scientific age? Peacocke devotes two lengthy sections to wrestling with the virgin birth and the resurrection, two key christological events. The virginal conception is implausible on both biological and theological grounds: biologically because then the fully human character of Jesus' DNA profile would be unaccounted for, and theologically on the basis of the patristic principle that what Jesus has not fully assumed he has not redeemed.[29] And while Peacocke refuses to explain the resurrection merely as the psychological experiences of the disciples, he suggests that it may also not be a historical event on par with other historical events. Rather, the resurrection of Jesus appears to have "involved a transformation/re-creation of the dead Jesus to which the regularities and 'laws' of the natural sciences and ordinary experience do not in principle apply."[30] One would be forgiven for wondering why it is permissible to "suspend" the laws of nature in one case (the resurrection) but not in the other (the provision of a fully human DNA profile without a contributing sperm — this latter possibility being especially more real in light of recent developments in the technology of cloning).

John Polkinghorne has also repeatedly turned to Christology in thinking about divine action. What is distinctively characteristic of Polkinghorne's work, informed as it is by years of working as a physicist, is what he calls his "bottom-up" approach.[31] Carried over into theology, as we saw in

28. Arthur Peacocke, *Theology for a Scientific Age: Being and Becoming — Natural, Divine, and Human* (Minneapolis: Fortress, 1993), p. 336.

29. Peacocke, *Theology*, pp. 275-79.

30. Peacocke, *Theology*, p. 284.

31. John Polkinghorne, *The Faith of a Physicist: Reflections of a Bottom-Up Thinker* (Princeton: Princeton University Press, 1994).

the first chapter, Polkinghorne's emphasis has been on the concrete data and experiences of Christian life and practice. There is not only the centrality of the person and work of Christ as received through the apostolic witness but also the experience of the living Christ, for example in the eucharistic meal. Hence the theology and science discussion in general and the notion of divine action in particular should be informed by what Polkinghorne calls a "liturgy-assisted logic."[32] The liturgy not only transforms the habits of communicants so they are enabled to encounter the living Christ, but also nurtures "some anticipation, here and now, of the final eschatological reality of God's new creation."[33] Incarnational thinking in theology and science will thus focus on divine action not only in the past (in the life of Christ), but also in the present (in the eucharistic experience) and in the future (at the eschatological horizon).

But if it is difficult to provide a scientifically plausible account of divine action for past and present events, what might be said for events that have not yet occurred? The question is a legitimate one, Polkinghorne insists, because the science of cosmology is now able not only to peer back into the distant past but also to look ahead into the far-off future.[34] If the ultimate Christian hope for a new heaven and a new earth is a realistic rather than merely fideistic option, then Christian faith must confront the cosmological sciences that now anticipate two possible future scenarios, neither of which is amenable to Christian beliefs regarding the fate of the world. On the one hand, if the mass of the universe is above a certain critical threshold, the universe will eventually cease expanding and begin to collapse and contract on itself, leading to a final conflagration not too far from that described by the apostolic witness: "the heavens will pass away with a loud noise, and the elements will be dissolved with fire" (2 Pet. 3:10). On the other hand, if the mass of the universe is below that critical threshold, then the expansion of the universe will continue indefinitely, and in the process run down so that the stars, the universe's fuel, and life in all forms ultimately dissipate in the frozen cosmos.[35] In either case the escha-

---

32. John Polkinghorne, *Science and the Trinity: The Christian Encounter with Reality* (New Haven and London: Yale University Press, 2004), chapter 5.

33. Polkinghorne, *Science and the Trinity*, p. 134.

34. John Polkinghorne, *The God of Hope and the End of the World* (New Haven: Yale University Press, 2002).

35. For a succinct discussion of the various physical theories and their concomitant theological/religious interpretations, see Kate Grayson Boisvert, *Religion and the Physical Sciences* (Westport, CT, and London: Greenwood Press, 2008), chapter 8.

tological promises of the Bible would be frustrated. Polkinghorne thus suggests that human hope is possible only on the basis of the resurrection of Jesus Christ.[36]

This "fry or freeze" scenario also suggests to other DAP participants that just as the traffic between theology and science must in some way traverse the christological roadway, so also the key to connecting eschatology and science may be the event of the resurrection.[37] More crucially, Robert John Russell suggests that the perennial concern about the problem of evil in DAP discussion can be resolved only eschatologically because the doctrine of the resurrection not only concerns the person of Jesus but also anticipates God's final response to the human problems of sin and suffering.[38] Apart from the resurrection of Jesus, the hopelessness identified by the apostle Paul (1 Cor. 15:12-19) pertains not only to human beings but also to the fate of the cosmos as a whole. Accepting the resurrection, however, suggests that the future holds possibilities for humanity beyond death and for the cosmos beyond either frying or freezing. The eschatological end of the cosmos thus may unfold according to the resurrection paradigm of Jesus that transforms the universe as we know it. While we remain largely in the dark about the discontinuities between the present world and the one to come, Christian faith insists that "the future is already present and active in the present while remaining future, as exemplified by God's act in raising Jesus from the dead."[39]

Russell's understanding of the future's relationship to the present derives in part from the notion of prolepsis first introduced by theologian Wolfhart Pannenberg and subsequently elaborated by Ted Peters. For Pannenberg, the resurrection of Jesus is not only the ground of his unity with God, but it also validates — retroactively — the authority of his pre-Easter life and ministry.[40] But further, inasmuch as the resurrection of Je-

---

36. Polkinghorne, *Science and the Trinity*, pp. 166-68.

37. See Ted Peters, Robert John Russell, and Michael Welker, eds., *Resurrection: Theological and Scientific Assessments* (Grand Rapids and Cambridge: Eerdmans, 2002).

38. Russell, "Divine Action and Quantum Mechanics," in *Quantum Mechanics*, pp. 322-23; cf. Russell, "Sin, Salvation, and Scientific Cosmology: Is Christian Eschatology Credible Today?" in *Sin and Salvation: The Task of Theology Today III*, ed. Duncan Reid and Mark Worthing (Hindmarsh, Australia: ATF Press, 2003), pp. 130-53.

39. Robert John Russell, "Bodily Resurrection, Eschatology, and Scientific Cosmology," in *Resurrection*, p. 27.

40. Wolfhart Pannenberg, *Jesus — God and Man*, trans. Lewis L. Wilkins and Duane A. Priebe, 2nd ed. (Philadelphia: Westminster, 1977).

sus also is a promise of the future resurrection of all people, there is a proleptic or anticipatory element in Christian faith that simultaneously looks "backward" to the life, death, and resurrection of Christ and also "forward" to the resurrection of humankind and the re-creation of the world. The future both is revealed in and is the ground of the past (and present). Thus Pannenberg concludes, if the resurrection of Jesus has occurred, "then the end of the world has begun."[41] If Pannenberg is right, then divine action "works," unlike material or efficient causes proceeding from the past toward the present, proleptically (or teleologically, to use Aristotelian terms) in anticipation of the future.

The Lutheran theologian Peters has written an entire systematic theology based on this idea of prolepsis, "whereby the gospel is understood as announcing the preactualization of the future consummation of all things in Jesus Christ."[42] In his contribution to the DAP, Peters suggests that if the resurrection of Jesus on the first Easter "is the prototype that God promises to follow for our future resurrection,"[43] then the new creation must also be an eschatologically transformative act of God. Now as a divine act of God, is Jesus' resurrection a historical event susceptible to historical investigation? Alternatively, Peters suggests, "the resurrected body of Jesus as well as our resurrected bodies are not miracles within the existing natural order; rather, they are eschatological realities belonging to God's re-creation."[44] With Russell, Polkinghorne, Peacocke, and others involved in the DAP, then, Peters is concerned that specifically Christian ideas like incarnation and resurrection are closely rather than loosely tied into the wider debate on divine action.

It might seem that in turning to incarnation, resurrection, and the eschatological fate of the world we have moved far from the DAP. But I suggest that we have only shifted venues in our trajectories of inquiry. Whereas conventional discussion about divine action has usually focused on the origins of the universe or putative past or present acts of God, eschatological thinking looks ahead to the divine purposes regarding the end(s) of the world. Yet the problem for any scientific account of divine

41. Pannenberg, *Jesus — God and Man*, p. 67.

42. Ted Peters, *God — the World's Future: Systematic Theology for a New Era,* 2nd ed. (Minneapolis: Fortress, 2000), p. xi.

43. Ted Peters, "Resurrection of the Very Embodied Soul?" in *Neuroscience and the Person,* p. 323.

44. Ted Peters, "Resurrection: The Conceptual Challenge," in *Resurrection,* pp. 297-321, at 313.

action is that final causes were eclipsed during the Enlightenment when causality was reduced to the quantifiable terms of physical events (efficient causes). The result, arguably, is that teleological causation becomes empirically unmeasurable even as the associated modes of divine action became different kinds of explanations than that validated by science.[45] So can our understanding of divine action be transformed when considered in terms of proleptic anticipations rather than antecedent causes? I suggest in the remainder of this chapter that pentecostal-charismatic perspectives on God's action in and through the life of the church may open up possibilities for thinking eschatologically about divine action in relationship to modern science.

Toward a Pneumatological Theology of Eschatological Divine Action

In this final section of this chapter, I hope to advance the discussion of divine action from the perspective of pentecostal and pneumatological theology. My aim is to build on the groundwork already laid in the shift from origins to resurrection and eschatology,[46] but to reframe the issues in terms of the third article of the creed, which concerns the person and work of the Holy Spirit. We proceed programmatically in three steps. First, I specify why christological, resurrection, and eschatological discourses are best formulated in pneumatological terms. Second, I extend what Polkinghorne calls "bottom-up" perspectives to understand the eschatological work of the Spirit by seeing how a variant of his "liturgy-assisted logic" might illuminate the pentecostal-charismatic dynamics of SDA. Finally, I summarize my proposal to rethink proleptically the notion of divine action in thoroughly pneumatological terms. What emerges on the other side is a teleological perspective that identifies divine action only retroactively from a posture of faith, through the crite-

---

45. The issues are debated across the sciences in Neil Manson, ed., *God and Design: The Teleological Argument and Modern Science* (New York and London: Routledge, 2003).

46. Others have also suggested working along this venue — e.g., Zachary Hayes, O.F.M., *What Are They Saying about Creation?* (New York and Ramsey, NJ: Paulist, 1980), who, after discussing the disputes and difficult issues regarding human origins, shifts from the issues of monogenism and polygenism to proposing that human unity may lie not so much in its evolutionary history but in the eschatological destiny intended by God (p. 62).

rion of the coming kingdom that is manifest in the Son and illuminated by the Spirit.

Step 1: Resurrection and New Creation: Divine Action and the Holy Spirit

To talk about the resurrection of Jesus is to talk about the work of the Holy Spirit. The apostle Paul declared that Jesus "was declared to be Son of God with power according to the spirit of holiness by resurrection from the dead" (Rom. 1:4), and that "If the Spirit of him who raised Jesus from the dead dwells in you, he who raised Christ from the dead will give life to your mortal bodies also through his Spirit that dwells in you" (Rom. 8:11). The resurrection is thus a work not only of divine action in general but also of the Spirit of God in particular.

Yet it is not only that resurrection is a pneumatological event; rather, the Gospel writers tell us that the life and ministry of Jesus as a whole were empowered by the Holy Spirit. Jesus was conceived by the Holy Spirit (Luke 1:35; Matt. 1:18), and carried out his mission through the power of the Spirit. Saint Luke tells "how God anointed Jesus of Nazareth with the Holy Spirit and with power; how he went about doing good and healing all who were oppressed by the devil" (Acts 10:38). Hence his healings, exorcisms, raising the dead, and other miraculous actions were all accomplished through the Holy Spirit.

The Gospel narratives indicate that Jesus' works have eschatological significance. Jesus' announcement of his public ministry through quoting the prophet Isaiah makes an implicit connection with the coming kingdom of God:

"The Spirit of the Lord is upon me,
because he has anointed me
　to bring good news to the poor.
He has sent me to proclaim release to the captives
　and recovery of sight to the blind,
　　to let the oppressed go free,
to proclaim the year of the Lord's favor."
　　　　　　　　　　　(Luke 4:18-19, italics added; cf. Isa. 61:1-2)

This "year of the Lord's favor" was a reference to the Jubilee celebration, which over time had become connected to the messianic reign. Jesus' ministry thus involved ushering in a "realm of possibilities" related to the year of the Lord,[47] and his mighty works served as signs of and pronouncements regarding the coming kingdom.

I suggest then the following thesis: that the life, ministry, death, and resurrection of Jesus are pneumatologically constituted events that signify the coming era, proleptically announcing and providing a foretaste, in the past (and present), of the eschatological future of God. This connects with Saint Paul's statement (quoted above) about the Spirit's raising others from the dead according to the raising of Jesus. So when Paul definitively says, "But in fact Christ has been raised from the dead, the first fruits of those who have died" (1 Cor. 15:20), we can add that the Holy Spirit is the "nexus between Christ's resurrection and the future resurrection."[48] This view of the Spirit resonates with other Pauline claims regarding the charisms of the Spirit being the seal, deposit, or first installment of things to come (Rom. 8:23; 2 Cor. 1:22; Eph. 1:13-14).

When we shift back to the topic of divine action, we see that any discussion of "God's trinitarian self-communication in Jesus of Nazareth" is not exclusive but inclusive of "the mission and presence of the Holy Spirit."[49] So if there is a pneumatological aspect to the revelatory, redemptive, and eschatological works of God, then any discussion of SDA cannot ignore the work of the Spirit. The result, however, is that SDA understood as (miraculous) "interventions" in the world's processes should now be reformulated in both pneumatological and eschatological perspectives.

There are now two steps in this argument. First, if the resurrection of Jesus is God's final albeit proleptic response to sin, suffering, and death, then it stands as the ground for hope that the future is nonextrapolatable from the currently known laws of nature.[50] In this case, the resurrection suggests a third way beyond the freeze-or-fry alternatives posed by scientific cosmology, and any claim regarding "nomological universality" — that the "same laws of nature" govern the past and the far-off future — is unprovable and presumed only "on faith."[51] From a theological perspec-

47. See Ben Witherington III, *Jesus, Paul, and the End of the World: A Comparative Study in New Testament Eschatology* (Downers Grove, IL: InterVarsity, 1992), chapter 6.

48. Günter Thomas, "Resurrection to New Life: Pneumatological Implications of the Eschatological Transition," in *Resurrection*, pp. 255-76, quote from 267-68.

49. Denis Edwards, "The Discovery of Chaos and the Retrieval of the Trinity," in *Chaos and Complexity*, p. 171.

50. Jeffrey P. Schloss, "From Evolution to Eschatology," in *Resurrection*, p. 80.

51. Robert John Russell, "Eschatology and Physical Cosmology: A Preliminary Reflec-

tive, we might say that "miracles do not constitute an adjustment to creation, but an aspect of what the Apostle Paul calls the 'new' creation. Indeed, that a miracle violates natural law is itself a sign indicating the depths to which sin spoils the integrity of the created order, for in the wake of sin, God re-creates that order to its very roots, all the way down to the natural laws that for so long had operated without interference."[52] In sum, the resurrection gives us good reason to question nomological universality, at least in the far-off future, and grants us insights into God's intentions to restructure (re-create) the laws of nature infected by sin.

The second step in the argument toward a pneumatological and eschatological theology of divine action is to suggest that insofar as Jesus' life, death, and resurrection are pneumatologically constituted, to that same extent "the eschatological transformation of the fundamental conditions of nature" is also pneumatologically accomplished.[53] Such a pneumatological conception of divine action is already found in the theology and science discourse. For example, mathematical physicist-theologian George Ellis proposes that

> within the laws governing the behavior of matter, there is hidden another domain of response of matter to life than usually encountered: matter might respond directly to God-centered minds through laws of causal behavior, or there may be domains of response of matter encompassed in physical laws, but they are seldom tested because such God-centered minds are so seldom encountered; [in this case,] a new regime of behavior of matter (cf. a phase transition), where apparently different rules apply (e.g., true top-down action of mind on matter), *when the right "spiritual" conditions are fulfilled.* Thus the extraordinary would be incorporated within the regular behavior of matter, and neither the violation of the rights of matter nor the overriding of the chosen laws of nature would occur.[54]

---

tion," in *The Far-Future Universe: Eschatology from a Cosmic Perspective,* ed. George F. R. Ellis (Philadelphia and London: Templeton Foundation Press, 2002), pp. 266-315, especially 289-91.

52. Steven D. Crain, "Divine Action in a World of Chaos: An Evaluation of John Polkinghorne's Model of Special Divine Action," *Faith and Philosophy* 14, no. 1 (1997): 41-61, quotation from 57.

53. Robert John Russell, "Divine Action and Quantum Mechanics: A Fresh Assessment," in *Quantum Mechanics,* p. 323.

54. George F. R. Ellis, "Ordinary and Extraordinary Divine Action: The Nexus of Interaction," in *Chaos and Complexity,* p. 386, italics added.

In my view, Ellis is striving for language that is ultimately comprehensible only within an explicitly pneumatological frame of reference. The "right 'spiritual' conditions" were fulfilled first and foremost, but not only, in the life of Jesus Christ, the one anointed by the Holy Spirit.

Step 2: The Eschatological Agency of the Holy Spirit:
Pentecostal-Charismatic Perspectives

The "not only" in the preceding sentence is crucial to my argument not only because my confessional location is the pentecostal tradition but also because pentecostal and charismatic sensibilities regarding the ongoing presence and activity of the Spirit are arguably also at the heart of the Christian tradition, at least when understood on the terms established by the apostles (the New Testament writers). I thus now want to make connections between the pneumatological theology of divine action and the lived experience of Christians as a whole, through the pentecostal perspective more particularly. As Nancey Murphy rightly insists, any theory of divine action must not only be able to account for SDA, but must also preserve the presuppositions of Christian practice.[55] I suggest, following the bottom-up or liturgy-assisted logic of Polkinghorne, that the pentecostal experiences of the Holy Spirit provide historical, liturgical, experiential, and eschatological frames of reference to rethink fundamental notions of God's action in the world relative to the DAP.

From a pentecostal and apostolic perspective, I suggest that the charisms of the Spirit in the life of the church are extensions of the mighty acts of God manifest in the life of Christ. The Lukan narratives are clear that the power of the Spirit at work through Jesus (in the Gospel) is similarly at work through his followers (in Acts). Insofar as the miracles, healings, and exorcisms performed by Jesus through the power of the Spirit were signs heralding the coming kingdom, the outpouring of the Spirit on the Day of Pentecost also empowered the church to bear witness to the gospel "in the last days" (Acts 2:17). Hence the church is not only the body of Christ but also an end-time charismatic fellowship or communion of the Spirit (cf. 2 Cor. 13:13).

As such, I suggest that the basic elements of pentecostal piety and spir-

---

55. Nancey Murphy, "Divine Action in the Natural Order," in *Chaos and Complexity*, pp. 330-31.

ituality are deeply shaped by the charismatic works of the Spirit that signal the impending arrival of the eschatological kingdom.[56] In this framework, the gifts of tongues serve to announce the coming kingdom in cries and groans that cannot be contained by known languages. Other more conventional discourses that are nevertheless vehicles of the Spirit's pronouncements regarding the kingdom include the charisms of the interpretation of tongues, prophecy, and words of wisdom and knowledge, as well as the kerygmatic proclamation of the gospel. These gifts of the Spirit empower the witness to the gospel for the sake of the kingdom of God.

Similarly, other spiritual gifts operative in pentecostal circles such as healings, miracles, and discernment of spirits (cf. 1 Cor. 12:9-10) are also signs of the kingdom. Pentecostals embrace a restorationist or primitivist hermeneutic of "this is that,"[57] expecting that the gifts defined by the apostolic tradition remain available in every age of the church. But such pentecostal restorationism and primitivism are also eschatological trajectories of the gift of the Spirit that announce the end of this age even as they signal the coming of the new age.

This now-and-not-yet scenario makes it possible to talk about the ongoing work of the Spirit as fundamentally eschatological. In more recent work, Robert John Russell has suggested that cases of SDA include not only christological events like the incarnation and resurrection, but also other biblical events like the exodus and the miracles of the Gospels.[58] The pneumatological logic I am advocating recognizes such SDA as charismatic actions of the Spirit that are proleptic anticipations of the world to come. Each case of SDA, more or less miraculous, would be a sign of the new world that will be freed from the bondage of suffering and decay. But

56. Thus has eschatology been central to pentecostal piety from the beginning of the modern movement at the dawn of the twentieth century; see, e.g., Steven J. Land, *Pentecostal Spirituality: A Passion for the Kingdom* (Sheffield: Sheffield Academic Press, 1993); D. William Faupel, *The Everlasting Gospel: The Significance of Eschatology in the Development of Pentecostal Thought* (Sheffield: Sheffield Academic Press, 1996); and Matthew K. Thompson, *Kingdom Come: Revisioning Pentecostal Eschatology* (Blandford Forum, UK: Deo Publishing, 2010).

57. See Grant Wacker, "Playing for Keeps: The Primitivist Impulse in Early Pentecostalism," in *The American Quest for the Primitive Church*, ed. Richard T. Hughes (Urbana: University of Illinois Press, 1988), pp. 196-219. For more on the "this is that" hermeneutic, see Yong, "The 'Baptist Vision' of James William McClendon, Jr.: A Wesleyan-Pentecostal Response," *Wesleyan Theological Journal* 37, no. 2 (2002): 32-57, especially 44-51.

58. Robert John Russell, "An Appreciative Response to Niels Henrik Gregersen's JKR Research Conference Lecture," *Theology and Science* 4, no. 2 (2006): 129-35, especially 129.

from this perspective, the new age is not only future, but also present and on its way; hence, the proleptic aspect of the charismatic activity of the Spirit points not to some future understood in linear terms as being ahead of us, but to the qualitative in-breaking of God's "future" into "present" human (and natural) history. In this way, our move is not simply a shift from any causal "predeterminism" to a teleological "postdeterminism," nor is the future simply on par (symmetrically) with the past. Rather, the future that is announced by the outpouring of the Holy Spirit makes present the risen Christ and the hidden God, and thereby provides a foretaste of the transfiguration of the created order.[59]

There is, however, an important set of further issues in the pentecostal-charismatic account of divine action I am proposing that are related to the question of what analogies best serve our purposes for theorizing about divine action. First, while some instances of divine action such as Jesus' resurrection or his calming of the storm can be understood in terms of the unilateral work of the Spirit, in the vast majority of cases involving the charisms of the Spirit, human agency is involved. Thus SDA must not only be compatible with but must also preserve personal human agency in all its integrity.[60] If the charismatic activity of the Spirit involves free human agents, then any pneumatological theology of divine action must assume a more rather than less robust theory of creaturely freedom. I am attracted to a libertarian notion of freedom for at least five reasons: (1) it accounts for the freedom to do otherwise and hence preserves freedom at the level of the agent rather than relocating freedom to the level of creaturely desires (in the former case, antecedents are necessary but insufficient causes for agent decisions); (2) it provides some relief for the problem of evil in terms of placing responsibility in free creatures rather than in God; (3) it is able to secure the kind of human responsibility needed for the possibility of eschatological damnation; (4) it follows from the Christian doctrine of the *imago Dei* that human beings have libertarian freedom if they are cre-

---

59. On each of these points I have learned from F. LeRon Shults, who uses the language not just of "futurity" but of "absolute futurity" to call attention to the qualitative nature of the future-made-present; my contribution is toward a pneumatological and pentecostal reframing of these matters. See F. LeRon Shults, *Reforming the Doctrine of God* (Grand Rapids: Eerdmans, 2003), chapter 7.5.

60. This point is argued among DAP participants by William R. Stoeger, "Describing God's Action in the World in Light of Scientific Knowledge of Reality," and George Ellis, "Ordinary and Extraordinary Divine Action," both in *Chaos and Complexity*, pp. 258-60 and 379-82, respectively.

ated in God's image; and (5) it alone makes sense of the theory of mental or downward causation that is debated in contemporary philosophy of mind.

This last point leads to the second set of implications for our pentecostal-inspired theology of divine action: that the charismatic activity of the Spirit also proceeds from the "top down," and is somehow (as suggested by Peacocke) supervenient upon the activity of free human agents.[61] This means that the work of the Holy Spirit is constituted by yet not completely reducible to the actions of human agents. From a theological standpoint, this supervenience notion of SDA suggests that God's action as a noncorporeal being does not conflict in any a priori sense with the actions of psychosomatic creatures like us. From the scientific point of view, however, there is a need for a new view of causation that includes but is not limited to mechanistic causes, and that invites analysis of causal processes across the spectrum of the natural and human sciences. Hence the sciences can illuminate causal sequences from both synchronic and diachronic perspectives without recourse to theological explanations. However, since antecedent factors are necessary albeit insufficient causes for libertarian agency, charismatic SDA in particular, as well as general divine action, will remain "hidden" except to the eyes of faith.

Finally, it should be made explicit that libertarian freedom is neither arbitrary nor capricious but emergent from the intentions of free agents. So whereas compatibilist notions of freedom are shaped by preceding causal factors, libertarian choices are associated instead with final or teleological causation. To be sure, human agency is constrained by elements such as natural laws (on which more in the next chapter), yet libertarian freedom is by definition not predetermined by these antecedent factors. Similarly, we can say both that divine agency respects the integrity of creatures but is irreducible to creaturely agency (although in that sense it is constrained by creation), and that such a view of "double agency" may be coherent only if we think about the freedom of God as working proleptically in history prefiguring God's eschatological fu-

---

61. Among DAP participants, the following have advocated some form of divine action as supervenient upon human actions: Nancey Murphy, "Supervenience and the Downward Efficacy of the Mental: A Nonreductive Physicalist Account of Human Action," Theo C. Meyering, "Mind Matters: Physicalism and the Autonomy of the Person," and Philip Clayton, "Neuroscience, the Person, and God: An Emergentist Account," all in *Neuroscience and the Person*, pp. 147-64, 165-77, and 181-214, respectively. See also my brief discussion of supervenience in chapter 2 above.

ture.[62] In sum, I propose that God's activity supervenes upon human agency and does so proleptically according to the shape of the coming kingdom.

Step 3: The Work of the Spirit:
An Eschatological-Teleological Model

I have in this chapter summarized the DAP and assessed its outcomes. While the DAP produced promising insights, the results remained ambiguous: no consensus emerged about a scientifically plausible theory of SDA that at the same time preserved the essential theological features of divine action as described in the biblical narratives. What did emerge, however, was an eschatological horizon that left the end-of-the-world predictions of scientific cosmology side by side with the biblical promises regarding the resurrection and the new heavens and the new earth.

Yet from this conversation about divine action served up by engaging the idea of resurrection, I have proposed what might be called a pneumatological assist inspired by the pentecostal experience of the Spirit. Not only is the resurrection of Jesus brought about by the Spirit, but it is the first fruit of the Spirit's eschatological work that contributes to the inauguration of the world to come. This invites a pneumatological theology of divine action that is able to discern the mighty acts of God in the world precisely through the Spirit's illumination of the grand narrative culminating in the eschatological kingdom. Apart from such Spirit-given eyes of faith, the narrative of the natural history of the world can be, has been, and will be told from an increasing number of (natural scientific) disciplinary perspectives, perhaps always subject to conflicting interpretations. But when understood in faith from the redemptive-eschatological perspective of final theological causation, the story of the creation of the world comes alive with the breath of (the Spirit of) God, even as the many tongues of the various scientific disciplines can be seen to illuminate different facets of the Creator's artistic work.

We will unpack this pneumatological, eschatological, and teleological

---

62. In contrast to theories of "double agency" that think about God's preordination (in an Augustinian and Calvinist framework) of all things as being consistent (in a compatibilist sense) with human agency and responsibility — e.g., Vernon White, *The Fall of a Sparrow: A Concept of Special Divine Action* (Exeter, UK: Paternoster, 1985).

theory of divine action more in the rest of this book. In what remains of this chapter, however, I want to argue three points: that such a proposal is (1) consistent with the NIOSDA model of divine action we saw earlier in this chapter, with one qualification; (2) adequate to the eschatological framework that informs pentecostal (and Christian) spirituality; and (3) irreducible to a merely epistemological or subjective account of the Spirit's activity in the world.[63]

First, recall our earlier discussion about the quest for NIOSDA: noninterventionistic objective special divine action. Christian DAP participants said there needed to be a way to talk about divine action that was special (i.e., not merely general or not merely the affirmation that all things were caused ontologically by divine providence), objective (not merely subjective or epistemological), and yet noninterventionistic (since the quest for a causal joint has been unsuccessful, and, further, any insistence on interventionist divine action would undermine scientific inquiry that depends on repeatable experimental investigation based on isolated variables). DAP members could not agree about how to secure such a model of divine action: some advocated for God's activity at the quantum level; at least one (Polkinghorne) sought divine action amidst chaotic systems; others preferred to frame this in panentheistic or supervenience terms.

My claim is that a pneumatological-eschatological and teleological model of divine action understands God's activity in the world by faith according to the revelation of God in Christ. In other words, divine action can only be discerned proleptically from the perspective of Christ's inaugurating the kingdom, rather than protologically in advance. The lack of an ex-

---

63. As should be clear from what has been said so far, my teleological account is not only distinctively theological (in contrast to philosophical or scientific models like those of Henri Bergson, Samuel Alexander, and Alfred North Whitehead), but it is also uniquely pentecostal and charismatic in its fundamental intuitions and sensibilities. For an overview of the teleological ideas of these philosophers, see John D. Barrow and Frank J. Tipler, *The Anthropic Cosmological Principle* (New York: Oxford University Press; Oxford: Clarendon, 1986), chapter 3. The teleologist whose ideas most parallel mine in terms of methodology is Pierre Teilhard de Chardin (1881-1955), the Jesuit paleontologist and geologist, who combined his scientific work with a christocentric interpretation of the overall evolutionary trajectory of the cosmos. Teilhard's scientific knowledge certainly outpaces mine, although I think my proposal is theologically more robust, particularly in its Trinitarian (including pneumatological) character. See Russel B. Norris, "Creation, Cosmology, and the Cosmic Christ: Teleological Implications of the Anthropic Cosmological Principle," *Teilhard Studies* 31 (1995): 1-24.

perimentally identifiable causal joint, apart from theistic assumptions, means that there is no need to worry about scientifically locating divine intervention. Thus the hierarchy of the sciences can proceed to identify the cosmological causes in the world (all of which are measurable experimentally, as we discussed in chapter 2), leaving theology to provide, or at least to contribute to, a teleological account. In this framework, there is room for thinking about the Spirit's role of "inputting" information into the causal fabric of the world, not only in terms of how such information orders what happens in the world but also in terms of how we can understand the world and its various events in relationship to the coming kingdom.[64]

The one qualification to this theory I would suggest concerns the possibility of the Spirit's input of energy into the world. Ontologically, there is no reason why this cannot happen if we assume that the world as a whole is not causally closed to God's presence and activity. In terms of scientific inquiry, however, I agree that there is a problem methodologically if we were to constantly assume that God is an energetic "x" factor in any experiment. Further, the heretofore unsuccessful quest for a causal joint at the God-world interface should not encourage us to think that such will be identifiable any time soon; I actually think it is in principle impossible on scientific terms to conclusively identify such a causal joint.[65] However, following in the footsteps of Martin, Poloma, and other social scientists of pentecostalism (see chapter 2 above), I do think we can measure at least the consequences and effects of claims regarding divine action. In other words, we may not be able to identify the *how* of the Spirit's (energetic?) action in the world, so there is not much to be gained from insisting on such occurring; hence, the noninterventionist aspect of NIOSDA is preserved.[66] But we will still be able to specify, in faith, *that* the Spirit's action has made such and such a difference in the world (at least in terms of the input of information), and thus can affirm divine intervention in this eschatological sense.[67]

64. See also Sjoerd L. Bonting, "Spirit and Creation," *Zygon* 41, no. 3 (2006): 713-26, especially 719-21.

65. As Denis Edwards puts it, it may be impossible to locate a causal joint since "a dynamic relational presence of God in every quantum event, chaotic system, and free human act . . . suggests a presence and a causality that finally escapes comprehension" ("The Discovery of Chaos and the Retrieval of the Trinity," in *Chaos and Complexity*, p. 173).

66. Thus John Polkinghorne rightly speaks, in this sense, of "The Hidden Spirit and the Cosmos," in *The Work of the Spirit: Pneumatology and Pentecostalism,* ed. Michael Welker (Grand Rapids and Cambridge: Eerdmans, 2006), pp. 169-82.

67. Denis Edwards also insists on NIOSDA, but understands the "special" aspect of di-

Secondly, I also believe that such an account is consistent with the strong sense of divine action, not only of the type affirmed by pentecostal Christians on the basis of their own spirituality and experience, but also of the kind that should be embraced by all Christians for whom the apostolic witness of the New Testament is normative. In other words, I want to affirm the "special" aspect of NIOSDA, but not relegate that only to the life of Christ. Thus, for example, all Christians, not only those in the pentecostal tradition, should be able to affirm miraculous healing, the charismatic gifts of the Spirit, and divine answers to prayer within an eschatological frame-work. We will confront the hard questions about miracles in the next chapter, so I briefly unpack this claim with regard to the charismata and prayer.

With regard to the gifts of the Spirit, particularly the ones identified by Paul in 1 Corinthians 12:7-9, these can only be discerned ecclesially from a standpoint of faith. By this I don't mean that the gifts of the Spirit operate only within the church. Rather, I mean that we affirm certain expressions as charismatic gifts, whether occurring within or outside of the ecclesial people of God, only within a tradition of discernment — for example, one which assumes the reality of such a charism-giving Holy Spirit. The gifts, for example, are only for the edification of others. In other words, apart from such edification, we are not in any position to affirm that the Spirit has been active in the dispensing of the gifts. Thus it is only within a certain eschatological frame of reference, one that acknowledges the proleptic appearance of the coming kingdom, that we can, in faith, identify, operate in, and manifest the charismata of the Spirit.

Similarly, with regard to prayer, the Spirit's response can only be es-chatologically or teleologically identified. Our praying, after all, is itself a performance that enacts God's presence, at least in the illocutionary sense of our addressing God. More importantly, God's response is embedded, at least in part, in our praying and our own subsequent actions. Last but not least, then, there is no possibility of identifying God's answers to prayer in any neutral account. Without a causal joint, any miraculous answer, heal-

---

vine action in terms of the diverse mediations — since all events, divine actions as well, are mediated rather than direct (this is how Edwards avoids asserting divine intervention). But what emerges is that if all events are mediated in some way, so that what is "special" about any event is its distinctive mediations, then nothing is special about any event in the sense that all are mediated. The result is similar to classical notions of double agency that see a concordance between divine and creaturely actions. Readers will need to decide if our theories are complementary or not. See Edwards, *How God Acts: Creation, Redemption, and Special Divine Action* (Minneapolis: Fortress, 2010).

ing, or other evidence of God's response can only be affirmed within the bigger picture of the coming kingdom.

Thus healings anticipate the eschatological transformation of all things as signs of the kingdom.[68] They are empirically discernible as divine action only in faith. Even scientifically verified healings — that is, medical confirmation that previously diagnosed conditions are no longer present followed by the "expert" opinion that there are no natural causative mechanisms in play — however statistically improbable, are not arguments for divine action. Science cannot make those claims.[69] Of course, science can explain healings and miracles, etc., from its various disciplinary perspectives, although these explanations will not be exhaustive;[70] in turn, believers can make these assertions about God's role in the light of empirical data, although these will be theological rather than scientific affirmations.

Third, I must insist that the pneumatological-eschatological model of divine action I am proposing is not merely a subjectivistic or epistemological posture that only identifies God's activity *post facto*. There are at least three reasons why this account preserves the "objective" in NIOSDA. (1) I assume a kind of relational universe in which any strong demarcation between "objective" and "subjective" or between epistemology and ontology illegitimately bifurcates (usually based on modernist presuppositions) the participatory character of our being-in-the-world.[71] (2) From the per-

68. E.g., Howard M. Ervin, *Healing: Sign of the Kingdom* (Peabody, MA: Hendrickson, 2002).

69. Thus Harold G. Koenig, *The Healing Power of Faith: How Belief and Prayer Can Help You Triumph over Disease* (New York: Touchstone, 1999), p. 27, grants that while science cannot make religious or theological pronouncements about divine intervention in miraculous cures, "we can certainly explore and chart in a scientific manner the *effect* of religious faith and practice on physical and emotional health" (italics in original) — precisely what he does in his book. See also Larry Dossey, M.D., *Healing Words: The Power of Prayer and the Practice of Medicine* (New York: HarperSanFrancisco, 1993), and Reginald Cherry, M.D., *Healing Prayer: God's Divine Intervention in Medicine, Faith, and Prayer* (Nashville: Nelson, 1999), although the latter is not as nuanced with regard to what science can or cannot affirm.

70. For example, see the analyses of miracles from psychoimmunological, psychotherapeutical, neuropsychological, and neurophysiological perspectives in J. Harold Ellens, ed., *Miracles: God, Science, and Psychology in the Paranormal*, 3 vols. (London and Westport, CT: Praeger, 2008).

71. Elsewhere I have argued for a relational cosmology — e.g., *Spirit-Word-Community: Theological Hermeneutics in Trinitarian Perspective* (Aldershot, UK, and Burlington, VT: Ashgate; Eugene, OR: Wipf and Stock, 2002), chapter 3, and *The Spirit Poured Out on All Flesh: Pentecostalism and the Possibility of Global Theology* (Grand Rapids: Baker Academic, 2005), chapter 7.

spective of pentecostal piety in particular and of Christian experience more generally, our testimony is not only a descriptive explication of what God has done in the past, but a perlocutionary modality of our performative participation in the effective reality of the Spirit's action in human lives;[72] in other words, our testifying to God's activity in the world is part and parcel of, rather than incidental to, how the world is being transformed in anticipation of what is to come. (3) As we shall see in the next chapter, the objectivity of divine action I am proposing is located eschatologically (in view of the coming kingdom) or teleologically (with regard to God's final purposes for the world), not in terms of efficient or material causality.

None of this means that the ushering in of the kingdom is merely a human endeavor; that would relapse into the false vision of the world's endless progress into the eschaton. Instead, our pneumatological eschatology insists on the priority of the Spirit's redemptive work, even while holding forth the paradoxical claim that human agents can and do participate in that work, by the initiative and empowering of the Spirit.

In this proleptic and teleological framework, then, Ted Peters has suggested that Christianity "begins with the promise of the coming kingdom of God and the fulfillment of all creation that it will bring. It begins with the future and works back to the present."[73] In chapter 5 we will ask if the proposed pneumatological theology of divine action may enable our understanding not only of the eschaton but also of the origins of the world. Before doing that, however, we need to see if such an eschatological-teleological model of the Spirit's activity in the world can help us think further about pentecostal miracles in a world governed by nature and its divinely ordained laws.

---

72. As argued by Mark J. Cartledge, *Testimony in the Spirit: Rescripting Ordinary Pentecostal Theology* (Burlington, VT, and Aldershot, UK: Ashgate, 2010).

73. Peters, *God — the World's Future*, p. 378.

4 Natural Laws and Divine Redemption

Teleology, Eschatology, and the Activity of the Spirit

The previous chapter argued that a pentecostal perspective invites rethinking the notion of divine action in pneumatological and eschatological terms. By this I mean that God's action in a scientific and lawful world can be profitably illuminated when conceived in terms of the Holy Spirit, and that this suggests that divine activity occurs, in a sense, "from the future," especially in anticipation of the coming kingdom. Yet I also noted that at the popular level, much of pentecostal spirituality assumes the natural-supernatural distinction bequeathed by modernity. This cosmological or worldview assumption involves the idea that divine action proceeds only through intervening in, even trespassing upon, the laws of nature.

In this chapter, I want to reframe our understanding of nature's laws in both eschatological and teleological perspective. This reframing has four steps, correlating with the four sections of this chapter. First is a brief sketch of the history and then layout of a philosophical typology of the idea of natural laws, followed by a survey of how developments in modern science and philosophy have constrained theological reflection on miracles, prayer, and divine providential action. The third section reassesses the laws of nature as habitual, dynamic, and teleological generalities in dialogue with the American scientist-philosopher Charles Sanders Peirce.[1]

1. Peirce has been an ongoing dialogue partner for me over the years, e.g., my books *Spirit-Word-Community: Theological Hermeneutics in Trinitarian Perspective* (Aldershot, UK, and Burlington, VT: Ashgate, 2002), chapter 3, and *The Spirit Poured Out on All Flesh: Pentecostalism and the Possibility of Global Theology* (Grand Rapids: Baker Academic, 2005), chapter 7.

We conclude with a correlation of such a triadic view of the laws of nature with the pneumatological and eschatological sensibilities of the pentecostal-charismatic imagination. In the end, I hope to further discussion on divine action in a world "governed" by natural laws, while at the same time providing a more plausible and coherent account of the Holy Spirit's activity for Christian practice in the twenty-first century.

At one level, the argument presented in this chapter can be seen as the fulcrum upon which turns the overarching theological thesis in this book about a pneumatological contribution to theology and science. If such a revisioning of natural laws and divine action in teleological perspective is anywhere close to being successful, it will create theological space to reconsider the positivism and materialism that dominate the physical and natural sciences. This in turn will open up conceptual space for thinking about a theology of evolutionary emergence and a pneumatological cosmology in the next two chapters. This chapter suggests a pneumatological and teleological interpretation of nature's laws (regularities) that is consistent with the Christian conviction about a God who has created a world in order to redeem it in the end. Such a God acts, I suggest, in light of this future salvation, as revealed in the person and work of Christ, and as empowered through the pervasive work of the Holy Spirit in the world.

The Laws of Nature: Historical and Philosophical Perspectives

Our present understanding of the laws of nature is the result of discussions and debates going back over two thousand years.[2] In the following overview, we survey the major historical developments of the prescientific and scientific concepts and map out a basic typology of contemporary philosophical views. Having a clear comprehension of the issues will enable us to better appreciate the specifically theological challenges related to divine action.

While we should be wary of generalizations, it is fair to say the ancient Greeks and Hebrews had contrasting views of the way in which the world worked. Whereas the Greeks believed in a rationally ordered universe that

---

2. The most succinct history of the formulation and investigation of the laws of nature I have found is Mauro Dorato, *The Software of the Universe: An Introduction to the History and Philosophy of Laws of Nature* (Burlington, VT, and Aldershot, UK: Ashgate, 2005), chapter 1.

even the gods and their ideas were subjected to, the Hebrews affirmed instead an only God who created the world, established covenants with creatures, and made promises to the people of God — all of which implied that the world was under divine control. While Thomas Aquinas attempted to hold both views together — for example, through the doctrine of divine simplicity that fused the divine mind and the divine will — what emerged from the medieval discussions was a voluntarist theology in which the world and all its events are the result of the immutable decrees and dictates of an eternal and omnipotent God.[3] This theological universalism and determinism was transformed over the next few centuries into a mechanistic and law-governed universe.

This process of transformation was aided by the rise of modern science. The seventeenth century was a crucial period that saw the formulation of Kepler's geometrically and algebraically articulated laws of planetary motion, Galileo's principle of inertia, Boyle's laws of gases, Leibniz's law of conservation of kinetic energy, and Newton's three laws of motion and law of universal gravitation that were applicable not only to celestial but also to terrestrial bodies, among other scientific breakthroughs.[4] In keeping with these discoveries, philosopher-theologians like Descartes began to imagine a lawful and mechanistic universe, especially since the laws of nature could be mathematically quantified.[5] Continued advances along this front would produce claims such as those made by the French mathematician and astronomer Pierre-Simon Laplace (1749-1827), that if at any instant the positions, velocities, and accelerations of all things could be known, the entire future of the universe and all of its parts could be predicted.[6] Clearly by the eighteenth century, the regularities of the world once thought to be the product of the divine will were naturalized and dislodged from their theistic underpinnings. Developments in the nineteenth

3. Francis Oakley, *Natural Law, Laws of Nature, Natural Rights: Continuity and Discontinuity in the History of Ideas* (New York and London: Continuum, 2005), chapter 2; cf. Francis Oakley, *Omnipotence, Covenant, and Order: An Excursion in the History of Ideas from Abelard to Leibniz* (Ithaca, NY, and London: Cornell University Press, 1984).

4. Friedrich Steinle, "The Amalgamation of a Concept — Laws of Nature in the New Sciences," in *Laws of Nature: Essays on the Philosophical, Scientific, and Historical Dimensions,* ed. Friedel Weinert, Philosophie und Wissenschaft Transdisziplinäre Studien 8 (Berlin and New York: Walter de Gruyter, 1995), pp. 316-68.

5. René Descartes, *Principles of Philosophy,* trans. Valentine Rodger Miller and Reese P. Miller (Dordrecht, Boston, and London: D. Reidel, 1984), pp. 76-77 (II.64).

6. Richard Green, *The Thwarting of Laplace's Demon: Arguments against the Mechanistic World-View* (New York: St. Martin's Press, 1995), pp. 13-15.

and early twentieth centuries, especially Maxwell's discoveries regarding electromagnetism and Einstein's theories of relativity, further confirmed the view of the world as a lawfully organized space-time system of interconnected parts.

Yet such mechanistic laws of nature would undergo one more set of transformations in the twentieth century. The advent of quantum mechanics, while deterministic at the level of the Schrödinger equation for the wave function, has invited a rethinking of the laws of nature along three lines.[7] First, the superposition principle suggests that quantum realities, unlike macroscopic things that obey the laws of Newtonian physics, can be in multiple states or locations simultaneously, as long as they are not measured. But this raises, second, the measurement problem: that quantum "realities" are less actualities than they are potentialities (that include possibilities and probabilities), and that such only become actualities when observed or measured. This implies, again contrary to the objective world of classical physics, that the quantum world is a contingent and dynamic sea of potentialities dependent on interaction with conscious observers. Last but not least, as possibilities and probabilities, not only are quantum events indeterministic until measured, but also Heisenberg's uncertainty principle says it is impossible to simultaneously measure both the position and momentum of quantum particles.

The resulting picture is that there appear to be two sets of laws at work in the world: classical laws that govern the behavior of large objects or systems, and quantum potentialities that describe behaviors in the microscopic realm.[8] There have been attempts to unify both domains by suggesting that with regard to macroscopic phenomena the lower possibilities at both ends of the spectrum cancel out, leaving us with increasingly probable, stable, and predictable outcomes. Yet while this may resolve the prob-

---

7. For details, see the essays on the science of quantum mechanics in part I of Robert John Russell et al., eds., *Quantum Mechanics: Scientific Perspectives on Divine Action* (Vatican City State: Vatican Observatory; Berkeley, CA: Center for Theology and the Natural Sciences, 2001); cf. also Adrian Heathcote, "Of Crows and Quarks: Reflections on the Laws of Quantum Mechanics," and John Forge, "Laws and States in Quantum Mechanics," both in *Natural Kinds, Laws of Nature and Scientific Methodology,* ed. Peter J. Riggs, Australasian Studies in History and Philosophy of Science 12 (Dordrecht, Boston, and London: Kluwer Academic, 1996), pp. 145-61 and 163-85, respectively, for further discussion of the complexities related to laws of nature when we move from classical to quantum physics.

8. These two domains and their respective sets of natural laws are summarized by Roger Penrose in the first two chapters of Roger Penrose et al., *The Large, the Small, and the Human Mind,* ed. Malcolm Longair (Cambridge: Cambridge University Press, 1997).

lem of quantum indeterminism, it raises profound questions regarding creaturely freedom, even as it addresses neither the superposition principle nor the measurement problem.[9]

The preceding overview sheds light on why there is no consensus today about how to understand this notion of natural laws.[10] Because science does not prescribe any one view regarding the laws of nature, it has been left primarily to philosophers, including philosophers of science, to reflect on what the empirical data suggest. A number of theories have been suggested. In the following, I sketch only three general approaches to laws of nature, even among which there is some overlap: the necessitarian model, the regularist position, and the antirealist view.[11] There are some important nuances within each approach, but these will be mentioned only insofar as they concern our discussion about divine action and miracles.

The classical mechanical paradigm seems to have underwritten, in general, the necessitarian view regarding natural laws. Necessitarians say the laws of nature are relations among universals that actually *govern* the world so that the world's particularities "obey" its legal principles, and this governance enables us to project future developments and events.[12] Laws of nature are universal truths that are ontologically real and independent of our epistemic considerations. Hence they await our discovery, and tell us what must happen, not merely what has happened or what will happen under certain conditions. The advantages of the necessitarian account include its capacity to account for why things happen as they do, to explain

---

9. And it also leaves untouched the phenomenon of quantum nonlocality or entanglement, which suggests that communication at the quantum level is not constrained by the physics of relativity. I will leave this matter to one side as it does not relate directly to the question of how quantum theory suggests a revised understanding of the laws of nature as formulated by classical physics.

10. Cf. Rom Harré, *Laws of Nature* (London: Duckworth, 1993).

11. I do not discuss, for example, either the conventionalist or contextualist view since these are less important in contemporary discussion of the laws of nature; see, e.g., the editorial introduction to Jan Faye et al., eds., *Nature's Principles*, Logic, Epistemology, and the Unity of Science 4 (Dordrecht: Springer, 2005), pp. 35-41.

12. Necessitarianism goes by other names as well, including universal or immanent realism, as advocated by David Armstrong, *What Is a Law of Nature?* (Cambridge: Cambridge University Press, 1983); nomic realism, defended by John Carroll, *Laws of Nature* (Cambridge: Cambridge University Press, 1994); and nomic Platonism as propounded by Fred I. Dretske, "Laws of Nature," and Michael Tooley, "The Nature of Laws," both in *Readings on Laws of Nature*, ed. John W. Carroll (Pittsburgh: University of Pittsburgh Press, 2004), pp. 16-37 and 38-70, respectively.

how we can predict what will happen or why we can expect things to continue as they do, and to justify our claims about what happens under counterfactual conditions. Necessitarian advocates also point out that only this view helps us distinguish between nomological statements (which describe relations among universals that are inconsistent with their existential contradictories) and accidental but true generalizations (which describe facts about particulars that may be consistent with their existential contradictories).[13]

Regularists think that necessitarians are unsuccessful in making such a distinction between nomological statements (especially regarding counterfactuals that are never instantiated) and accidental but true generalizations (perhaps such a distinction should not and cannot be made). Further, regularists insist that necessitarians have to either overqualify their nomological statements (see the discussion of *Ceteris paribus* clauses below) to account for the many exceptions to the governance ascribed to natural laws, or, as is more often the case, end up taking leave of the empirical data in order to make their metaphysical claims about natural laws. Finally, regularists point out that necessitarian views are valid, if at all, only at the level of the physical sciences, and not across the social sciences where the element of creaturely freedom conspires against deterministic theories of how the world works. In contrast, regularity views are more empirical than metaphysical, apply across the entire spectrum of the physical and social sciences, and provide a better account of free agency.[14]

Put positively, regularists say the laws of nature are statements that *describe* what usually or regularly happens in the world, and such statements are contingent truths that are empirically determined. Rather than the laws of nature imposing themselves on us, we identify such laws in a sense retroactively, based on our experience and experimentation. So while the

13. So, in physics, "All uranium spheres are less than a mile in diameter" is a nomological statement because uranium's critical mass does not allow large uranium spheres to exist, while "All gold spheres are less than a mile in diameter" is an accidental generalization. In biology, "the heart pumps to circulate blood" tells us about the lawful functions of heart pumping, while "the heart pumps to make noise" tells us about an accidental side effect of heart pumping; see the introduction in Carroll, *Readings on Laws*, pp. 1-15, especially 2-3, and David J. Buller, "Introduction: Natural Teleology," in *Function, Selection, and Design*, ed. David J. Buller (Albany: State University of New York Press, 1999), pp. 1-27, especially 6-7.

14. See Norman Swartz, "A Neo-Humean Perspective: Laws as Regularities," in *Laws of Nature: Essays on the Philosophical, Scientific, and Historical Dimensions*, pp. 68-91, especially 86-88.

necessitarian says the world just has to be a certain way because of nature's laws, the regularist answers merely that the world just is this way, although it could have been otherwise. But since there is no necessity to the laws of nature, there is also no such thing as a violation of nature's laws. Now if in this account necessitarians wonder how predictions can be made so that scientific hypotheses can be tested, regularists respond that the laws of nature are empirically justified inferential rules of science that are reliable and accurate enough for scientific inquiry and practice.[15]

There are three variations of the regularity view, the first of which suggests that what we call the laws of nature are supervening descriptions of contingent and particular facts and events. Proponents of this variation, sometimes called "Humean supervenience," follow Hume's view that natural laws are no more than contingent generalizations drawn from, and hence descriptions overlaid upon, experience.[16] Supervenient accounts are, from the standpoint of the particular data, unnecessary; but, from a scientific perspective, such descriptive generalizations are helpful and even needed, so long as they are not illegitimately extended into metaphysical claims. Ironically, it may turn out that Hume was an "imperfect regularist" since his rejection of miracles assumed a necessitarian view of the laws of nature.[17] We will return momentarily to this issue.

The second variation to the regularity view also sees the laws of nature as being descriptive rather than prescriptive, but goes further to emphasize that nature's laws are approximate abstract formulations rather than completely isomorphic mappings of the world's regularities.[18] Physicist John

---

15. Marc Lange, *Natural Laws in Scientific Practice* (Oxford: Oxford University Press, 2000).

16. See David Lewis, "Humean Supervenience," *Philosophical Topics* 24 (1996): 101-27; cf. Barry Loewer, "Humean Supervenience," and Helen Beebee, "The Non-governing Conception of Laws of Nature," both in *Readings on Laws of Nature*, pp. 176-206 and 250-76, respectively.

17. See Norman Swartz, *The Concept of Physical Law* (Cambridge: Cambridge University Press, 1985), p. 107.

18. Interestingly, this view has been quite attractive to scientist-theologians — e.g., William R. Stoeger, "Contemporary Physics and the Ontological Status of the Laws of Nature," in *Quantum Cosmology and the Laws of Nature: Scientific Perspectives on Divine Action*, ed. Robert John Russell, Nancey Murphy, and C. J. Isham, 2nd ed. (Vatican City State: Vatican Observatory; Berkeley, CA: Center for Theology and the Natural Sciences, 1999), pp. 207-31, especially 209-19, and Niels Henrik Gregersen, "Divine Action, Compatibilism, and Coherence Theory: A Response to Russell, Clayton, and Murphy," *Theology and Science* 4, no. 3 (2006): 215-28, especially 221-22. Not coincidentally, I would add, natural scientist Robert

Polkinghorne, for example, suggests that laws of nature "can be interpreted verisimilitudinously, as the tightening grasp of an actual reality."[19] But Polkinghorne is not suggesting that such verisimilitude is due only to our epistemic limitations. Rather, the laws of nature appear as "asymptotic approximation[s] to a more subtle (and more supple) whole,"[20] because reality as revealed by the new sciences — for example, quantum mechanics and chaos theory — is loosely rather than rigidly structured. Such an approximationist position, however, does not merely degenerate into a constructivist position on natural laws; rather, laws are regularities operating according to a dynamic and interrelational manner that does not necessarily impose hard-and-fast constraints on the way the world is or should be.

A third regularist interpretation of natural laws has been called the statistical or probabilistic theory. From the physical sciences has emerged the notion of "statistical laws" — for example, "the half-life of radium is 1,600 years," meaning 50 percent of any sample of radium atoms will radioactively decay over the course of 1,600 years. Since the quantum revolution, the uncertainty principle has given further impetus to this view, especially with its probabilistic interpretation of quantum events. Probabilistic regularists believe their view can accommodate either the statistical or quantum interpretations, especially since neither prescribes how the world must work, precisely the weakness of the necessitarian model.

The antirealist position explicitly opposes necessitarianism, but also raises questions about and stretches the regularist views. Antirealists make their argument at two levels. First, there is the issue of the various qualifications usually attached to how, when, or where laws work. Known in Latin as *Ceteris paribus* — literally, "with other things [being] equal" — such qualifications or provisos are claimed by antirealists to undermine the ontological status of almost all identifiable natural laws.[21] Our formulations of laws do not seem to "work" unless we manipulate the equations, redefine (seemingly constantly) the terms and assumptions, specify the

---

Boyle (1627-1691) was one of the first to defend what is now called the regularity view because of his concern to protect God's freedom to decree how the world might or should otherwise be; see Dorato, *Software of the Universe*, p. 25.

19. John Polkinghorne, "The Laws of Nature and the Laws of Physics," in *Quantum Cosmology and the Laws of Nature*, pp. 429-40, quote from 429.

20. Polkinghorne, "The Laws of Nature," p. 431.

21. With the exception, perhaps, of the fundamental laws of physics, which are considered abstractions; see John Earman and John Roberts, "*Ceteris paribus,* There Is No Problem of Provisos," in *Readings on Laws of Nature,* pp. 207-49.

variables in our experiments, or even establish limits regarding the reach of what are considered universal laws.[22] Even Newton's first law of motion is stated explicitly as a contingency: every object in a state of uniform motion tends to remain in that state of motion *unless* an external force is applied to it. If the laws of nature each require provisos of various sorts — and this applies also in the regularity view of laws as approximations of reality (as presented above) — then antirealists argue that "it is impossible to fill in the proviso so as to make the resulting statement true without rendering it vacuous."[23]

Going beyond the *Ceteris paribus* issue, however, antirealists distinguish between laws of nature as models or simulacra that are applicable to our theories about the way the world works, and laws of nature as metaphysical realities that either describe literally or govern the world. The rejection of the latter is what earns the antirealist label, but some version of the former is what allows for scientific inquiry to proceed.[24] This reflects the empiricist bent of antirealist approaches, which insist that "the aim of science is not truth as such but only *empirical adequacy,* that is, truth with respect to the observable phenomena. . . . [The] criterion of success is not truth in every respect, but only truth with respect to what is actual and observable."[25]

Yet the challenges for antirealist approaches (and even for regularists) have to do with how to account for counterfactuals or inductive inferences (since both seem to assume natural laws), natural tendencies (for example, why do we expect rocks to remain solid?), and causation (why or how events are causally connected). It is especially difficult to be an antirealist about laws without being ad hoc about these and other nomic concepts. Precisely for this reason some philosophers have sought to develop theories about capacities or dispositions.[26] Even for those who retain the con-

22. Gerald James Holton and Stephen G. Brush, *Physics, the Human Adventure: From Copernicus to Einstein and Beyond,* 3rd ed. (New Brunswick, NJ: Rutgers University Press, 2001), pp. 195-96.

23. Ronald N. Giere, *Science without Laws* (Chicago and London: University of Chicago Press, 1994), p. 91.

24. This is the position of Giere, *Science without Laws,* an earlier version of which was argued in detail by Nancy Cartwright, *How the Laws of Physics Lie* (Oxford: Clarendon; New York: Oxford University Press, 1983).

25. Bas C. van Fraassen, *Laws and Symmetry* (Oxford: Clarendon, 1989), pp. 192-93, italics in original.

26. E.g., Nancy Cartwright, *Nature's Capacities and Their Measurement* (Oxford: Clarendon, 1989); George Molnar, *Powers: A Study in Metaphysics,* ed. Stephen Mumford (Oxford: Oxford University Press, 2003); and Stephen Mumford, *Dispositions* (Oxford: Oxford

cept of laws of nature, these are now understood as enduring tendencies. In fact, particular things are constituted by active properties like powers and propensities rather than passive qualities like size, shape, color, etc., and the former are irreducible to causal laws.[27] Capacities ground our expectations — for example, that aspirins cure headaches, that knives cut, that diamonds resist scratching. They enable us to make inferences, help us to explain counterfactuals, and contribute to a more dynamic, flexible, and interrelational account of how the world works. Unlike laws, which are often thought to provide a one-to-one correlation between causes and effects, capacities allow us to see how any event is actually a holistic nexus of many powers, dispositions, and tendencies.[28]

Hence while some capacity theorists such as Cartwright and Mumford are antirealists regarding the laws of nature, most agree that an ontological and metaphysical account of capacities or dispositions does all the work (and more) natural laws were supposed to have done when formalized in the seventeenth century, but without the liabilities of the latter.[29] The burden placed on natural laws to do more explanatory work than they were capable of may have derived from the legacy of early modern thinkers who assumed a mechanistic and inert natural world consisting of discrete things, and hence needed a metaphysical conception of natural laws to explain how things could move and interact.[30] But in this mechanistic universe, the laws of nature are caught on the horns of a dilemma: either such laws are external to things, in which case there has been so far no plausible account of how they interact with things, or they are internal to things, in which case they either lose their capacity to govern or degenerate into a mysterious vi-

---

University Press, 1998). While Stephen Mumford identifies himself as an antirealist regarding laws of nature understood as metaphysical realities, his metaphysical theory of powers and dispositions functions as a regularist account of the way the world works.

27. The one exception may be the second law of thermodynamics, but one exception does not by itself justify insistence on a class or category of laws of nature; see Stephen Mumford, *Laws in Nature* (London and New York: Routledge, 2004), p. 199.

28. E.g., Mumford, *Dispositions*, chapter 10. See also Alan Chalmers, "So the Laws of Physics Needn't Lie," *Australasian Journal of Philosophy* 71, no. 2 (1993): 196-205, and Chalmers, "Making Sense of Laws of Physics," in *Causation and the Laws of Nature*, ed. Howard Sankey, Australasian Studies in History and Philosophy of Science 14 (Dordrecht, Boston, and London: Kluwer Academic, 1999), pp. 3-16.

29. But see also other accounts that propose a metaphysics of powers related to rather than in place of laws of nature — e.g., Molnar, *Powers*, chapter 12, and Brian Ellis, "Causal Powers and Laws of Nature," in *Causation and the Laws of Nature*, pp. 19-35.

30. See Mumford, *Laws in Nature*, part I.

talism. A theory of capacities or dispositions, however, resolves the meta-physical question of how things change, explains how potentialities or ten-dencies can be unactualized yet remain real, and allows for a hierarchy of things or properties of greater or lesser range and influence. We will see momentarily how the regularity and capacities accounts of natural laws can be put to use in developing a theology of miraculous divine action that is compatible with the NIOSDA model discussed in chapter 3.

Miracles, Prayer, and Providence: Natural Laws and the Problem of Divine Action in Modern Theology

With this scientific and philosophical background in place, I now want to trace the developments in thinking about miracles especially since the early modern period. We begin with the response of Hume's meditation "Of Miracles," proceed to discuss the place of miracles in modern liberal theology, and then lay out a spectrum of contemporary views on miracles. Our objective is to locate pentecostal and charismatic thinking about divine action and miracles more securely on the historical and theological landscape.

Hume held an early version of what is now called the regularity view of the laws of nature. Hume's regularism derived from his empiricist epis-temology. In his *Enquiry concerning Human Understanding,* Hume sug-gested that our experiences generate habits and customs whose regularities are appropriately generalized in lawful terms.[31] But such generalized asso-ciations of ideas then often illegitimately mutate into propositions about metaphysical necessities (such as cause and effect). The reason why the general descriptions are allowed but not the metaphysical extensions is that our previous experiences can never guarantee future experiences, at least not at the demonstrable level,[32] and all it takes is one exception to fal-sify claims regarding metaphysical necessity.

31. Here Hume builds on the empiricist tradition of Locke, who had earlier argued that the laws of morality, which Locke also called laws of nature, were accessible not because they were Platonically inscribed into the minds and hearts of human beings, but because they are attained through sense experience; see Mark Goldie, ed., "Essays on the Laws of Nature," in *Locke: Political Essays* (Cambridge: Cambridge University Press, 1997), pp. 79-133, especially 97-106.

32. See David Hume, *An Enquiry concerning Human Understanding,* ed. L. A. Selby-Bigge (Chicago: Encyclopedia Britannica, 1952), 4.29; references to this volume will be made parenthetically in the text as *Enq,* followed by book and paragraph numbers.

What is interesting, however, is that (as noted above) when he discussed miracles in the tenth book of the *Enquiry*, Hume appears to have switched to a necessitarian view of the laws of nature. A miracle was defined there as "a transgression of a law of nature by a particular volition of the Deity, or by the interposition of some invisible agent" (*Enq* 10.90 n. 1). This led to Hume's a priori argument against miracles: "A miracle is a violation of the laws of nature; and as a firm and unalterable experience has established these laws, the proof against a miracle, from the very nature of the fact, is as entire as any argument from experience can possibly be imagined" (*Enq* 10.90). In addition, Hume also provided a number of a posteriori arguments against miracles (*Enq* 10.92-95): (1) that miraculous claims often originate from undependable eyewitnesses; (2) that the perpetuation of miracles is often accomplished through human gullibility; (3) that the current absence of miracles also speaks against their past occurrences; and (4) that the religious ideologies that utilize miracles apologetically often contradict one another (e.g., Jewish, Christian, and Muslim views regarding the miraculous). But the problem, simply put, is if the laws of nature are no more than regularities, then the presence of irregularities by themselves would never amount to the kind of violation of natural laws mentioned in Hume's definition;[33] on the other hand, under the necessitarian form of the laws of nature implicit in Hume's definition, there is already an a priori impossibility of miracles considered as transgressions of such law.[34] I suggest that popular pentecostal piety, like Hume,

33. Thus Mary Hesse states in her response to Hume, "in the absence of any clear idea what 'laws of nature' would look like . . . , it is impossible to know what a 'violation' would look like either"; see Hesse, "Miracles and the Laws of Nature," in *Miracles: Cambridge Studies in Their Philosophy and History*, ed. C. F. D. Moule (New York: Morehouse-Barlow; London: A. R. Mowbray, 1965), pp. 33-42, especially 39. Put alternatively, "An outright miracle by definition is an inexplicable event, and insofar as it is inexplicable it is under no law and violates no law"; see Albert W. J. Harper, *Studies in the Interrelationship between Miracles and the Laws of Nature* (San Francisco: Edwin Mellen, 1993), p. 8.

34. These and other arguments have been marshaled against Hume's criticism of miracles by David Johnson, *Hume, Holism, and Miracles* (Ithaca, NY, and London: Cornell University Press, 1999), and John Earman, *Hume's Abject Failure: The Argument against Miracles* (Oxford: Oxford University Press, 2000), among many others. But see also Robert J. Fogelin, *A Defense of Hume on Miracles* (Princeton and Oxford: Princeton University Press, 2003), who argues that Hume's case rests first on the criteria he establishes that miracle claims must meet in order to be considered viable, and second on his insistence that no testimonies to miracles have actually met such criteria. I think the Humean hermeneutics of suspicion should be tempered (not replaced) with a hermeneutics of charity based on a posture of critical faith, and attempt to present just such an approach here.

uncritically assumes a necessitarian position on laws of nature, even though regularism is more coherent scientifically and vis-à-vis both pentecostal sensibilities and Christian commitments.

In many respects, Hume's skepticism regarding miracles understood as (literal) historical events has carried the day for over two hundred years, especially in the tradition of liberal Protestantism running from Schleiermacher through Strauss and Renan to Bultmann.[35] Two related questions gave impetus to these developments: the issue of divine action in general, particularly as impinging on theistic notions of providence and prayer, and the problem of suffering and evil. With regard to the former, the idea of a world governed by natural laws led first to a deistic theology and then, later, to a reinterpretation of the classic doctrines of providence and prayer that downplayed notions of divine intervention and emphasized instead prayer's functional character. Prayer, for example, does not really induce divine action; rather, prayer results in the transformation of those who pray, produces psychological wholeness, and enables a sense of solidarity with others and an existential connection with the divine.[36] If miracles were considered violations of a law-governed world, then divine intervention in response to creaturely supplications would be impossible. The problem of evil is implicated in liberal Protestant views regarding prayer, providence, and miracles. In fact, defending the plausibility of miracles within a scientific framework brings challenging questions to the fore: If God could intervene in response to prayer or to prevent evil, why is there gratuitous evil in the world?[37]

This is not to say there were no moderate Protestant voices that attempted to salvage the concept of miracle in response to liberal trends. C. S. Lewis defended the idea of miracles but did so by relocating them from the modernist framework back into the religious domain.[38] Miracles

---

35. See J. Houston, *Reported Miracles: A Critique of Hume* (Cambridge and New York: Cambridge University Press, 1994), especially chapters 5–6 and 12.

36. See William Adams Brown, *Life of Prayer in a World of Science* (New York: Charles Scribner's, 1927); cf. Rick Ostrander, *The Life of Prayer in a World of Science: Protestants, Prayer, and American Culture, 1870-1930* (Oxford: Oxford University Press, 2000), especially chapter 7.

37. David Basinger and Randall Basinger, *Philosophy and Miracle: The Contemporary Debate*, Problems in Contemporary Philosophy 2 (Lewiston, NY, and Queenston, Ontario: Edwin Mellen, 1986).

38. C. S. Lewis, *Miracles: A Preliminary Study* (New York: Macmillan, 1947); cf. Colin Brown, *Miracles and the Critical Mind* (Grand Rapids: Eerdmans; Exeter, UK: Paternoster, 1984).

cannot be abstracted from the milieu within which they are claimed; and with regard to the miracles of specific religious traditions (in Lewis's case, Christianity), they must be considered within their wider theistic world-view. Similarly, claims regarding divine answers to prayer have to be understood within the broader context of how theists interact and interrelate with the divine, and how they view God's relationship with the world in general and with God's people in particular.[39] In short, an approach like Hume's will naturally generate skepticism regarding miracles; on the other hand, a faith-informed approach will resist reducing miraculous events and testimonies of such.[40] While Lewis and most conservative Protestants seek to defend the plausibility of biblical accounts of miraculous divine interventions in history, pentecostal Christians are more interested in the miracles they believe God continues to do in the present.

Yet there is no doubt the faith-seeking-understanding approach of Lewis and others has been deeply influential in contemporary attempts to defend the idea of miracles from the Humean and skeptical critique. In the remainder of this section, I summarize three general types of apologetic approaches to miracles that draw respectively from philosophical, scientific, and theological resources. But in each case there is an unquestioned assumption of a necessitarian philosophy of nature motivating the specific moves that are made.

First, when an entire worldview is factored into the equation, two philosophical approaches come to the fore. One, a hermeneutical approach, correlates with contemporary supervenience models in suggesting that miracles are only interpretations overlaid on events. In this view, miracles are always interpreted events, informed by specific presuppositions, shaped by varying expectations, and designed to explain life's twists and turns. Most importantly, miracles are perceived by faith, and provide for meaningful explanations for life's events. Hence there are the "outer facts"

---

39. H. H. Farmer, *The World and God: A Study of Prayer, Providence, and Miracle in Christian Experience,* 2nd ed. (London: Nisbet and Co., 1948).

40. In fact, "Miracles and all unique events, with their 'surprise and wonder,' are anathema to explanation because explanation explains by undoing the unique, by specifying a genus, individualizing a universal, particularizing the general, engaging a dialectic (or by taking the reverse direction, since explanation is both synthetic and analytic), or, temporarily, by re-presenting to consciousness"; Richard A. Cohen, "The Miracle of Miracles: More Ancient Than Knowledge," in *Divine Intervention and Miracles in Jewish Theology,* ed. Dan Cohn-Sherbok, Jewish Studies 16 (Lewiston, NY, Queenston, Ontario, and Lampeter, UK: Edwin Mellen, 1996), pp. 75-98, quote from 96.

of what happened and which can be confirmed as such by anyone, but these can also be seen and understood from different "insider" viewpoints. To the eyes of faith, miracles are "inner meanings" or explanations of common events where retelling is designed to move the audience (or) readers to greater and deeper faith.[41] This hermeneutical analysis risks, of course, viewing miracles in epistemological rather than ontological terms. Instead of miracles denoting actual (historical) events, they become subjective interpretations supervened upon objective facts. This is why I have sought to think, beyond a supervenience account, about divine action teleologically as well.

Alongside the hermeneutical approach to miracles is a philosophical interpretation of miracles understood as noncausal divine actions. This view assumes miracles are special acts of God that are beneficial, marvelous, and religiously significant, but goes on to articulate how they are also not violations of the laws of nature. Resources are mined from contemporary philosophy of action based on theories of intention rather than on theories of causation. When we say, for example, "I raise my arm," there is no need to explicate the causal joints activated in the raising of the arm. Rather, such are "basic actions" that tell us not *how* but *that* they happened. "Analogously, if we think of miracles as basic divine actions, we do not have to think of a miracle as coming about through the operation of some kind of occult force."[42] If laws of nature are not transgressed when free agents bring about events, why would such violations occur when God acts? But then a major question arises about how miracles are identified. Linking back to the hermeneutic approach, miracles through divine basic actions are events that evoke thanksgiving, praise, and worship. On the one hand, this view of miracles as basic divine actions provides a plausible alternative to the causal theories dominating the discussion. On the other hand, it also may evacuate the notion of miracles in a nonsupernaturalist and even noninterventionist interpretation that privileges a governance view of the laws of nature. Is this a problem for a pentecostal theology of miracles?

A third scientific theory of divine action suggests a kind of interventionist God who works miracles either by destroying or by creating mass/

41. Jeffrey John, *The Meaning in the Miracles* (Grand Rapids: Eerdmans, 2004).

42. David Corner, *The Philosophy of Miracles* (London and New York: Continuum, 2007), p. 3; cf. Mark Corner, *Signs of God: Miracles and Their Interpretation* (Aldershot, UK, and Burlington, VT: Ashgate, 2005), chapter 3.

energy units in the world. Hence, similar to how the world was originally created, miracles happen because God changes "the material conditions to which the laws of nature apply."[43] This interventionist proposal, however, has been largely ignored in the science and theology discussion. Yet it, along with the quantum and chaos divine action theories, still presumes that the laws of nature constrain divine action in some way and thus need to be made more flexible if miracles are to occur. Pentecostal believers (along with other Christians) would simply make the opposite assumption: it is the existence and activity of God that sustain the laws of nature, rather than the other way around.

This leads to the explicitly theological defense not only of miracles, but also of the laws of nature. Rather than discounting either the philosophical or scientific arguments, a theological approach assumes the kind of worldview recommended by Lewis, and goes further to argue both that only theism can adequately account for the laws of nature,[44] and that in any theistic account, natural laws do not govern the universe on their own. Instead, God has created the world and its laws so as to accomplish God's goals, and as Creator of nature's laws, God is also free to supersede, alleviate, or interact with such laws as befits God's purposes.[45] In some respects, such a forthrightly theological approach is most in tune with pentecostal sensibilities. Further, when extrapolated, such views have been featured in conservative evangelical apologetics regarding miracles in ways that resonate with pentecostal commitments.[46] But note also that such overtly the-

43. Robert A. H. Larmer, *Water into Wine? An Investigation of the Concept of Miracle* (Kingston, NY, and Montreal: McGill-Queen's University Press, 1988), p. 20. A parallel attempt to show how the laws of nature can be understood as accommodating miracles is Werner Schaaff's apologetic for Jesus' resurrection based on the new physics of materiality and radiation; see Schaaff, *Theology, Physics, and Miracles*, trans. Richard L. Renfield (Washington, DC: Canon Press, 1974), pp. 87-93.

44. E.g., John Foster, *The Divine Lawmaker: Lectures on Induction, Laws of Nature, and the Existence of God* (Oxford: Clarendon, 2004).

45. See Richard Swinburne, *The Concept of Miracle* (London: Macmillan and St. Martin's Press, 1970); R. L. Purtill, "Defining Miracles," in *In Defense of Miracles: A Comprehensive Case for God's Action in History*, ed. R. Douglas Geivett and Gary R. Habermas (Downers Grove, IL: InterVarsity, 1997), pp. 61-72; and Loren Haarsma, "Does Science Exclude God? Natural Law, Chance, Miracles, and Scientific Practice," in *Perspectives on an Evolving Creation*, ed. Keith B. Miller (Grand Rapids and Cambridge: Eerdmans, 2003), pp. 72-94.

46. Hence C. John Collins argues for a supernaturalistic and interventionistic theology of miracles: "God is also free to 'inject' special operations of his power into this web at any time, e.g., by adding objects, directly causing events, enabling an agent to do what its own

istic assumptions neither interrogate the necessitarian model of laws of nature nor seem to have much use for the spectrum of regularity views.

Rethinking the Laws of Nature: A Dialogue with C. S. Peirce

Given the various regularity and even antirealist theories of natural laws surveyed above, why do theological discussions of miracles and the laws of nature still seem, for the most part, to presuppose necessitarianism? I suspect the ghost of Hume continues to make his presence felt whenever the necessitarian head surfaces even though this is only one side of Hume's (inconsistent) position. But is theology beholden to the (conflicted) Humean account, and if not, what metaphysical alternatives are available for consideration?

I turn now to the thought of Charles Sanders Peirce (1839-1914), an American scientist and perhaps its most original philosopher, for help with how to rethink the laws of nature. I am convinced that Peirce's triadic and evolutionary metaphysics can assist pentecostal theologians with the task of developing a coherent and scientifically plausible account of miraculous divine action vis-à-vis the laws of nature. I will sketch the issues that shaped and informed Peirce's metaphysical project before presenting his understanding of the laws of nature as habitual, dynamic, and general but yet real tendencies. Our goal is to lay the metaphysical ground for a pentecostal theology of miracles to be proposed in the last section.

Peirce is a complex thinker, and we have neither the time nor the space to adequately discuss the entirety of his scientific metaphysics.[47] Two basic points, however, should be kept in view. Foremost, Peirce's basic metaphysical categories of Firstness (quality, immediacy, or potentiality — the *hows* of things), Secondness (fact, opposition/resistance, or actuality — the *whats* of things), and Thirdness (law, intelligibility, or possibility — the *whence/whithers* of things) can be seen as responses to the inadequacies, as he understood them, of the categorical systems of his predecessors. Whereas Plato's dualism promoted a static worldview in which time is only

---

natural properties would never have made it capable of, and by imposing organization, according to his purposes"; see Collins, *The God of Miracles: An Exegetical Examination of God's Action in the World* (Wheaton, IL: Crossway, 2000), p. 128.

47. For an overview of Peirce's philosophy, including his basic categories, see Yong, "The Demise of Foundationalism and the Retention of Truth: What Evangelicals Can Learn from C. S. Peirce," *Christian Scholar's Review* 29, no. 3 (Spring 2000): 563-88.

the moving image of eternity, and Aristotle's substance metaphysics asserted but could not account for genuinely changing things, Peirce's Thirdness articulated how potencies could be transformed into actualities — through lawful possibilities. Against the medieval nominalism that denied the reality of abstract entities (reducing universals to mere concepts) and insisted that only individuals exist, Peirce argued that universals were lawful and real tendencies or habits — not eternal or Platonic essences — that effected qualities and perpetuated facts. Finally, if Kant's critical philosophy promoted no more than a phenomenological metaphysics and Hegel's Geist sublated history, Peirce's triadic metaphysics neither succumbed to Kant's skepticism (since reality is now triadically related rather than dyadically divided between phenomenon and noumena) nor lost sight of real history (since Secondness is now interrelated with Thirdness rather than subordinated to and overcome by it).[48] This is not to say Peirce's triadic metaphysics neatly resolves these major disputes in the history of philosophy, but it is to say the Peircean construct is at least suggestive of an alternative to the reigning philosophical paradigms.

But this leads, second, to the more fundamental backdrop against which Peirce's triadic metaphysics emerged: Darwin's evolutionary hypothesis.[49] Peirce approved in general of Darwin's theory of evolution through "fortuitous variation" (6.296 passim).[50] Yet he questioned — rightly in hindsight of developments in evolutionary biology — whether Darwinian natural selection could account in full for evolutionary progress. But Peirce also rejected any form of metaphysical determinism since

48. Peirce was not a systematic writer, but he discusses his categories in depth in Charles Sanders Peirce, *Pragmatism as a Principle and Method of Right Thinking: The 1903 Harvard Lectures on Pragmatism,* ed. Patricia Ann Turrisi (Albany: State University of New York Press, 1997). For more also on Peirce vis-à-vis his dominant predecessors in the Western philosophical tradition, see Rosa Maria Perez-Teran Mayorga, *From Realism to "Realicism": The Metaphysics of Charles Sanders Peirce* (Lanham, MD: Lexington, 2007).

49. See Philip P. Wiener, *Evolution and the Founders of Pragmatism* (New York: Harper Torchbooks, 1965), chapter 4; Joseph L. Esposito, *Evolutionary Metaphysics: The Development of Peirce's Theory of Categories* (Athens: Ohio University Press, 1980); Carl R. Hausman, *Charles S. Peirce's Evolutionary Philosophy* (Cambridge: Cambridge University Press, 1993); and Andrew Reynolds, *Peirce's Scientific Metaphysics: The Philosophy of Chance, Law, and Evolution* (Nashville: Vanderbilt University Press, 2002).

50. Unless otherwise noted, all citations from Peirce will follow conventional Peirce scholarship in referring to *The Collected Papers of Charles Sanders Peirce,* ed. Charles Hartshorne, Paul Weiss, and Arthur W. Burks, 8 vols. (Cambridge, MA: Harvard University Press, Belknap Press, 1965-1966), and be noted in the text by volume and paragraph numbers.

that did not square with the statistical theories then emerging not only in the biological but also in the chemical, mechanical, and sociological sciences. What was needed was a kind of final cause to draw the evolutionary process forward, one that was neither random nor mechanistic but sufficiently open-ended so as to allow for the emergence of novelty. Part of the answer Peirce proposed was encapsulated in his category of Thirdness: law considered as habitual, dynamic, and general but yet real tendencies. Let us examine each of these features in turn.

What does it mean to say, as Peirce does, that laws are habits and that reality consists of "effete mind, inveterate habits becoming physical laws" (6.25)?[51] There are at least three aspects to this claim. First, the basic analogy is human habit-taking and habit-changing defined as "a modification of a person's tendencies toward action, resulting from previous experiences or from previous exertions of his will or acts, or from a complexus of both kinds of causes" (5.476). Note here that habits span the spectrum of instinctive physiological reactions to consciously developed tendencies and general behaviors, all of which combine in turn to shape future actions. From this, second, we observe that scientific inquiry is itself a specific form of habitual action involving a recurrent process of hypothesis formation, prediction, testing, and revision.[52] If habitual creatures come to determine the laws of nature through habitual processes, then, third, Peirce surmises (or hypothesizes), nature itself is habitual. He writes: "diversification is the vestige of chance spontaneity; and wherever diversity is increasing, there chance must be operative. On the other hand, wherever uniformity is increasing, habit must be operative. . . . [M]echanical laws are nothing but acquired habits, like all the regularities of mind, including the tendency to take habits, itself; and . . . this action of habit is nothing but generalization" (6.267 and 6.268). To say that natural laws are habits is to say that nature unfolds or behaves in rulelike ways.

Peirce assumes that the rhythms of nature vacillate between chance and irregularity on the one hand and uniformity and regularity on the other. In the Peircean ontology, habits or tendencies are what bring the latter out of the former. Hence they parallel the powers, properties, and dis-

51. The notion of habit plays an important role in Peirce's philosophy; for introductory studies, see Sandra Rosenthal, "Meaning as Habit: Some Systematic Implications of Peirce's Pragmatism," *Monist* 65 (1982): 230-45, and Gary Shapiro, "Habit and Meaning in Peirce's Pragmatism," *Transactions of the Charles S. Peirce Society* 9 (1973): 24-40.

52. Cathy Legg, "Real Law in Peirce's 'Pragmaticism' (Or: How Scholastic Realism Met the Scientific Method)," in *Causation and the Laws of Nature*, pp. 125-42.

positions suggested by some of the contemporary theorists discussed above.[53] As important, however, Peirce's habits are real dispositions or legal tendencies (against medieval nominalism) that function as final causes. Menno Hulswit suggests: "Final causes are basically habits: they ('habitually') direct processes toward an end state. Like human habits, habits of nature (laws of nature) are final causes because they display tendencies toward an end state. . . . Moreover, habits are not static entities, for they may evolve in the course of time. Peirce called the possible evolution of final causes 'developmental teleology.'"[54]

But if the laws of nature are habits that function teleologically, then two concerns immediately arise: that introducing teleology undermines the possibility of developing a coherent naturalistic account of the laws of nature, and that it provides a "back door" (or "front door," in this case) for the reintroduction of God as the final and determining cause of nature's events. I suggest, however, that built into Peirce's triadic metaphysics are two further notions that satisfactorily meet both of these potential objections. We look first at the evolutionary character of Peirce's notions of habit and law before turning to a discussion of how habitual laws function through generalities rather than as an established blueprint for future events.

What does it mean to say, with Peirce, that laws are not static, and that they are evolutionary, developmental, and dynamic? Peirce put it this way: "conformity with law is a fact requiring to be explained; and since law in general cannot be explained by any law in particular, the explanation must consist in showing how law is developed out of pure chance, irregularity, and indeterminacy" (1.407; cf. 6.46). In fact, chance is needed to explain growth and evolving complexity. From this, Peirce reasoned, "Now the only possible way of accounting for the laws of nature and for uniformity in general is to suppose them results of evolution. This supposes them not to be absolute, not to be obeyed precisely. It makes an element of indeterminacy, spontaneity, or absolute chance in nature" (6.13). Evolution cannot be guided merely by mechanical principles (as suggested by social Darwinists like Herbert Spencer) because law itself is a result of evolution, and because exact law cannot produce heterogeneity (6.14). But this means,

53. Shapiro, "Habit and Meaning," p. 36, reminds us that habits are general albeit indeterminate powers in the Peircean ontology. To my knowledge, however, Peirce is not mentioned in the work of Cartwright, Molnar, or Mumford.

54. Menno Hulswit, "Peirce's Teleological Approach to Natural Classes," *Transactions of the Charles S. Peirce Society* 33, no. 3 (1997): 722-72, quote from 742-43.

then, that even laws of nature "have naturally grown up. . . . In the original chaos, where there was no regularity, there was no existence" (1.175). More precisely,

> uniformities in the modes of action of things have come about by their taking habits. At present, the course of events is approximately determined by law. In the past that approximation was less perfect; in the future it will be more perfect. The tendency to obey laws has always been and always will be growing. . . . Moreover, all things have a tendency to take habits. . . . This tendency itself constitutes a regularity, and is continually on the increase. . . . According to this, three elements are active in the world: first, chance; second, law; and third, habit-taking. (1.409)[55]

So, to recapitulate, for Peirce, laws derive from chance developments and indeterminacies in the evolutionary process and also continue to evolve. This locates Peirce squarely in the regularity camp, fully consistent with the probability model of quantum physics. Yet even his suggestion that the laws of nature have evolved and continue to evolve is not bizarre. Contemporary physicists and philosophers of science have pondered the implications of the measurement problem in quantum mechanics for understanding how natural laws are interrelated with consciousness. They have also suggested that the higher temperatures closer to the big bang may not have operated under the same laws as lower temperatures, and wondered whether or not it makes sense to talk about biological laws prior to the emergence of life.[56] These considerations have led some to conclude that "As the universe evolved, the circumstances created their own laws," and to "concede that as the universe evolves, so new laws emerge."[57] The point is both that Peirce's proposals are not as outlandish as they may seem

55. Elsewhere, Peirce wrote: "if the laws of nature are still in process of evolution from a state of things in the infinitely distant past in which there were no laws, it must be that events are not even now absolutely regulated by law" (7.514; cf. 6.101).

56. As suggested by João Magueijo, *Faster Than the Speed of Light: The Story of a Scientific Speculation* (New York: Penguin, 2004).

57. Quotations respectively from Walter Thirring, "Do the Laws of Nature Evolve?" in *What Is Life? The Next Fifty Years — Speculations on the Future of Biology*, ed. Michael P. Murphy and Luke A. J. O'Neill (Cambridge: Cambridge University Press, 1995), pp. 131-36, at 135, and Paul Davies, "Algorithmic Compressibility, Fundamental and Phenomenological Laws," in *Laws of Nature: Essays on the Philosophical, Scientific, and Historical Dimensions*, pp. 248-67, at 267.

on first sight, and that his teleological intuitions are nevertheless natural-
istically grounded in the evolutionary history of the world.

But if laws are teleological habits that are dynamic (evolving), then
what is their final destination? Classic teleology in the tradition of natural
theology insisted the final cause existed in the divine mind and thus carried the creation onward toward its fulfillment (usually articulated in theistic terms). For Peirce, however, the evolutionary or developmental teleology did not include any blueprint for how things must turn out, much less
a divinely orchestrated consummation; rather, the habitual laws of nature
evolved only according to *general* tendencies. A law or habit is nothing less
than "a tendency to strengthen itself. Evidently it must be a tendency toward generalization, — a generalizing tendency. . . . Now the generalizing
tendency is the great law of mind, the law of association, the law of habit
taking. Hence I was led to the hypothesis that the laws of the universe have
been formed under a universal tendency of all things toward generalization and habit-taking" (7.515). Now Peirce associated law and generalization with mind, thus accounting for consciousness under his category of
Thirdness.[58] What is more important for our purposes is that this law of
habit-taking functions only in a vague and general way rather than in fully
determinate terms. Peirce puts it this way:

> all causation divides into two grand branches, the efficient, or forceful;
> and the ideal, or final. If we are to conserve the truth of that statement,
> we must understand by final causation that mode of bringing facts
> about according to which a general description of the result is made to
> come about, quite irrespective of any compulsion for it to come about
> in this or that particular way; although the means may be adapted to the
> end. The general result may be brought about at one time in one way,
> and at another time in another way. Final causation does not determine
> in what particular way it is to be brought about, but only that the result
> shall have a certain general character. (1.211; cf. 6.63)[59]

Peirce's point is twofold: that rather than being precise blueprints for
development, laws considered as evolving habits are general pathways con-

58. Thus Peirce equates psychical causation with final causation; see 1.250, 1.266, and
1.269.

59. Put alternatively, "a disposition or habit as a rule of generation is something whose
possibilities of determination no multitude of actually generated instances can exhaust"
(Rosenthal, "Meaning as Habit," p. 235).

stituted in part by chance or fortuitous events and that natural laws exist not as determining actualities but as indeterminate possibilities.[60] If mechanical behaviors are predetermined and irreversible, final causes are creative, unpredictable, and irreducible to preexisting causes, parts, or antecedents. Because habitual laws as final causes provide only general guidelines for development, end states can be reached in different ways. Precisely for the same reason, in the Peircean system "final causes cannot specify exact results."[61]

It should now also be clear why Peirce's final cause does not invoke God or supernatural blueprints.[62] Such may be theological addendums motivated by the posture of faith, but they are not essential to Peirce's teleology. In fact, Peirce's project may actually be seen as an attempt to chart a middle way between Emerson's romanticist divinization of nature on the one hand, and William James's pragmatist pluralization of nature on the other.[63] Peirce's triadic metaphysics left room for God, but they attempted a fully naturalistic account through retrieval and rethinking of Aristotle's final causes. Where Aristotle presupposed fixed and immutable essences, Peirce suggests *finious* processes tending toward general final states (7.471).

In sum, for Peirce the laws of nature are habitual tendencies that function teleologically like final causes. However, such laws have emerged out of the fortuitous variations of the evolutionary process, even as they provide general (rather than specific) pathways for nature's evolution. Interestingly, however, Peirce did not apply his theory of laws of nature to his thinking about miracles. Rather, while he accepted the possibility of mira-

60. Demetra Sfendoni-Mentzou, "Peirce on Continuity and the Laws of Nature," *Transactions of the Charles S. Peirce Society* 33, no. 3 (1997): 646-78, notes: "laws for Peirce are those which are neither instantiated [Aristotle] nor uninstantiated [Plato] but those which are instantiatable" (p. 665).

61. Menno Hulswit, "Teleology: A Peircean Critique of Ernst Mayr's Theory," *Transactions of the Charles S. Peirce Society* 32, no. 2 (1996): 182-214, quote from 195.

62. So even if the constants of nature have been finely tuned, to use the rhetoric of advocates of the anthropic principle, even to the point of providing a blueprint for the evolution of the world — e.g., as suggested by John D. Barrow, *The Cosmic Blueprint* (New York: Simon and Schuster, 1988) — chaos theoretical models indicate that initial fluctuations can still result in a wide range of possible outcomes. In other words, a blueprint for creation, even if such were to be theologically affirmed, would not necessarily mean a deterministic world, thus securing the generalist teleology that I am arguing for here.

63. Vincent Colapietro, "C. S. Peirce's Reclamation of Teleology," in *Nature in American Philosophy*, ed. Jean De Greet, Studies in Philosophy and the History of Philosophy 42 (Washington, DC: Catholic University of America Press, 2004), pp. 88-108.

cles, he also approached miracles almost in typically Humean fashion, saying: "I do not see how we can ascertain *a priori* whether *miracles* (be they violations of the laws of nature or not) and special providences take place or not. . . . Miracles . . . are always *sui generis.* . . . The isolatedness of the miracle is really no argument against its reality . . . , but it effectively prevents our ever having sufficient evidence of them" (6.515).[64] I think the question is not so much about evidence as about how we understand the laws of nature, and on this point, Peirce has much more to offer than has been previously mined toward a scientifically informed and theologically coherent account of divine action.

Miracles, the Laws of Nature, and the Eschaton: A Pneumatological and Teleological View of Divine Action

Attempts to retrieve Peirce's triadic metaphysics for a theology of nature and of evolution have already begun to appear.[65] In this concluding section of the chapter, I draw the threads of the preceding discussions together in order to reengage the questions about divine action in a world of natural laws. I suggest that Peirce's triadic metaphysics and theory of natural laws as habitual, dynamic, and general are helpful for those attempting to formulate a theology of divine action in dialogue with contemporary science. Hence Peirce is helpful in extending the hypothesis proposed in the previous chapter so that what emerges is a pneumatological and charismatic view of divine action that sees the Holy Spirit as working in and through nature and its laws, but also proleptically and continually transforming such in anticipation of the general shape of the coming kingdom.

Theologically, recall that the basis of our pneumatological model of

64. In an essay (ca. 1901) titled "Hume on Miracles" (6.522-6.547), Peirce mainly focused on Hume's views on inferences drawn from empirical observation, especially challenging Hume's confusion regarding the logic of abduction or retroduction. It is this capacity correlated with the elasticity of habit that allows for scientific inquiry to proceed rather than predetermines the outcomes of the scientific enterprise. Yet while accepting the possibility of miracles, Peirce did not think there can be modern proofs for Christianity or of the divinity of Christ since "all the evidence which can now be presented for them is quite insufficient, unless the general divinity of the Christian religion be assumed" (6.538).

65. E.g., Andrew J. Robinson, "C. S. Peirce as Resource for a Theology of Evolution: Continuity, Naturalism, and Contingency — a Theology of Evolution Drawing on the Semiotics of C. S. Peirce and Trinitarian Thought," *Zygon* 39, no. 1 (2004): 111-36.

divine action is the work of the Holy Spirit as seen especially in the life of Christ, the anointed one. But the life of Christ is itself an announcement of the coming kingdom of God. In fact, the miracles of Jesus are themselves signals of his messianic anointing through which the eschatological presence of God is pronounced.[66] Most importantly, Jesus was raised from the dead by the Holy Spirit (Rom. 1:4), who is the power of the coming age (Rom. 8:23; 2 Cor. 1:22; Eph. 1:13-14). In the life, death, and resurrection of Christ, then, the Spirit of God proleptically announces the arrival of the coming kingdom of God.

This christological and pneumatological starting point leads, then, to the claim (suggested in chapter 4) that the life of Christ in general and the resurrection in particular could be a prototype, perhaps "the first instance of the kind of transformation that awaits the entire cosmos."[67] This is first and foremost a theological claim derived from the Trinitarian narrative of God acting proleptically in Christ by the Holy Spirit.[68] At the same time, given the theory of natural laws as evolutionary and developmental, I suggested that the events of the incarnation and Pentecost manifest the "emergence of new laws" that constitute the ways of the world to come.[69] Robert John Russell has gone so far as to suggest that the principle of nomological universality — the claim that the "same laws of nature" govern the past and the far-off future — is unproven, unprovable, and presuppositional.[70] Now

66. See Graham H. Twelftree, *Jesus the Miracle Worker: A Historical and Theological Study* (Downers Grove, IL: InterVarsity, 1999), chapter 10.

67. George F. R. Ellis, "Ordinary and Extraordinary Divine Action: The Nexus of Interaction," in *Chaos and Complexity: Scientific Perspectives on Divine Action,* ed. Robert John Russell, Nancey Murphy, and Arthur R. Peacocke (Vatican City State: Vatican Observatory; Berkeley, CA: Center for Theology and the Natural Sciences, 1995), pp. 359-95, quote from 387; cf. Ted Peters, "Resurrection of the Very Embodied Soul?" in *Neuroscience and the Person: Scientific Perspectives on Divine Action,* ed. Robert John Russell et al. (Vatican City State: Vatican Observatory; Berkeley, CA: Center for Theology and the Natural Sciences, 1999), pp. 305-26, especially 323-26.

68. This proleptic principle — that the Christ event instantiates the future kingdom of God at the center of human history — was articulated first by Wolfhart Pannenberg, *Jesus — God and Man,* trans. Lewis L. Wilkins and Duane A. Priebe, 2nd ed. (Philadelphia: Westminster, 1977), pp. 53-66, and has been expanded on since by others (many of whom are cited here).

69. See Robert John Russell, "An Appreciative Response to Niels Henrik Gregersen's JKR Research Conference Lecture," *Theology and Science* 4, no. 2 (2006): 129-35, especially 131.

70. Robert John Russell, "Eschatology and Physical Cosmology: A Preliminary Reflection," in *The Far-Future Universe: Eschatology from a Cosmic Perspective,* ed. George F. R. Ellis (Philadelphia and London: Templeton Foundation Press, 2002), pp. 266-315, especially 289-91.

of course, within a necessitarian framework, no new laws could appear. However, if Peirce and others cited above are right, then the laws of nature do not function as rigid governors in a mechanical system. As theologian Keith Ward writes: "the laws of physics we are able to formulate do not, and cannot ever, provide us with a totally comprehensive, exhaustive and accurate picture of the real physical world. . . . If the universe is an open, emergent and interconnected system, and scientific laws are ideal models for understanding regular and quantifiable connections within it, there will always be some features of the physical universe that laws of nature cannot capture."[71] Religiously understood miracles could thereby be seen as basic divine actions that work within a regulatory system established by God rather than as violations of a strictly mechanistic created order.

What I am proposing is consistent with the modified uniformitarian view of the laws of nature proposed by Paul Davies.[72] In Davies' view, God establishes laws that not only allow for genuine chance events but also enable the emergence of creativity and complexity in nature. This is not as far-fetched as it might sound, since Niels Henrik Gregersen has also suggested that while nomological universality may be retained at the level of fundamental physics, a richer conception of explanatory models is needed in other disciplines for emergent levels of reality that simultaneously presuppose different conceptual schemes.[73] I am sympathetic to this idea, although I think that nomological universality even at the level of fundamental physics, while methodologically acceptable, is problematic either

71. Keith Ward, *God, Faith, and the New Millennium: Christian Belief in an Age of Science* (Oxford: Oneworld, 1998), p. 98. See also Keith Ward, *Divine Action* (London: Collins, 1991).

72. See Paul Davies, "Teleology without Teleology: Purpose through Emergent Complexity," in *Evolutionary and Molecular Biology: Scientific Perspectives on Divine Action,* ed. Robert John Russell, William R. Stoeger, S.J., and Francisco J. Ayala (Vatican City State: Vatican Observatory Publications; Berkeley, CA: Center for Theology and the Natural Sciences, 1998), pp. 151-62.

73. See Niels Henrik Gregersen, "Special Divine Action and the Quilt of Laws: Why the Distinction between Special and General Divine Action Cannot Be Maintained," in *Scientific Perspectives on Divine Action: Twenty Years of Challenge and Progress,* ed. Robert J. Russell, Nancey C. Murphy, and William R. Stoeger (Vatican City State: Vatican Observatory Publications; Berkeley, CA: Center for Theology and the Natural Sciences; and Notre Dame, IN: University of Notre Dame Press, 2008), pp. 179-99, especially 195-99. I agree with Gregersen in his argument reflected in the subtitle of his paper, that the distinction between general and special divine action is problematic, but my reasons are a bit different: I think the whole general/special categories are infected with modernist presuppositions, and are therefore unsustainable, just as are the notions general and special revelation or natural versus supernatural.

scientifically going back toward the big bang singularity or theologically going forward to the far-off future. In other words, in the end, I still propose a theological conception of teleology, one that exploits the teleological trajectories opened up in the various scientific disciplines, but that finally depends on philosophical and theological assessments instead.[74]

My theological framework suggests a view of divine action that is charismatically accomplished in anticipation of the coming kingdom. In the Hebrew Bible, the emergent laws of nature can be seen to represent the basic commitments of a covenant-making God that presume human response and divine counterresponse.[75] But God's covenants are never deterministic grids into which free agents must fit.[76] Rather, they constitute God's general, albeit eschatological, intentions, suggested to human creatures, yet whose final shape and realization depend, at least in part, on creaturely response. However, the fallenness of human beings means most free agents are not amenable to cooperating with God or acting according to God's general intentions for the world. What we need is not more freedom, but divine empowerment and enablement so the kingdom can emerge.

It is here that the pentecostal perspective registers itself most palpably. Extrapolating from C. S. Lewis's suggestion that the miracles of the new creation are glimpses of the coming kingdom when the relations between the world and God as S/spirit will have been transformed,[77] I suggest that the charismatic gifts and miracles as recorded in the New Testament and witnessed to by pentecostal piety and practice are proleptic signs of the world to come. After all, if the Holy Spirit is the "nexus between Christ's resurrection and the future resurrection,"[78] so also does the Spirit bring

74. Thus heeding the warnings of both Wesley J. Wildman, "Evaluating the Teleological Argument for Divine Action," and William R. Stoeger, "The Immanent Directionality of the Evolutionary Process, and Its Relationship to Teleology," both in *Evolutionary and Molecular Biology*, pp. 117-50 and 163-90, respectively.

75. Tim Morris and Don Petcher, *Science and Grace: God's Reign in the Natural Sciences* (Wheaton, IL: Crossway, 2006), pp. 139-46.

76. This is the weakness of the medieval notion of divine omnipotence in relationship to a covenant-making God; see Francis Oakley, *Omnipotence and Promise: The Legacy of the Scholastic Distinction of Powers,* Etienne Gilson Series 23 (Toronto: Pontifical Institute of Mediaeval Studies, 2002).

77. Lewis, *Miracles*, pp. 141-56.

78. Günter Thomas, "Resurrection to New Life: Pneumatological Implications of the Eschatological Transition," in *Resurrection: Theological and Scientific Assessments*, ed. Ted Peters, Robert John Russell, and Michael Welker (Grand Rapids and Cambridge: Eerdmans, 2002), pp. 267-68.

about our new participation in God's eternal life in the here and now. More to the point, Christian life in the Spirit suggests our capacity in this world to walk according to the "laws" of the coming kingdom. The current "laws of nature" can now be understood as habitual, dynamic, and general but nevertheless real tendencies through which the Holy Spirit invites and empowers free creatures to inhabit the eschatological presence of God. In this charismatic intersubjectivity, wherein human creatures come to know, seek out, and embody the living presence and activity of God, we are periodically given foretastes of the emergence of what George Ellis calls "a new regime of behavior of matter (cf. a phase transition), where apparently different rules apply (e.g., true top-down action of mind on matter). . . . Thus the extraordinary would be incorporated within the regular behavior of matter, and neither the violation of the rights of matter nor the overriding of the chosen laws of nature would occur."[79]

Such a pneumatic, charismatic, and eschatological approach correlates well with a theology of miraculous divine action that does not violate the laws of nature. In this view, charismatic manifestations in general and authentic miracles in particular are interruptions of habitual events that in turn open up the possibility of the emergence of new habits precisely because their full meaning can only be proleptically discerned in light of the coming kingdom.[80] Hence there is, as we have already noted at the end of the last chapter, a hermeneutical aspect to the reality of miracles that is intrinsically connected to how interpreters understand larger issues. In the Christian case, these issues are related to God's purposes of validating the person of Jesus through his resurrection and ascension, legitimating the activity of the apostolic believers, and, most important for pentecostal purposes, fostering faith in the Christian community in anticipation of the culmination of salvation history.[81] Hence, as an extension of C. S. Lewis's

---

79. Ellis, "Ordinary and Extraordinary," p. 386.

80. Keith Ward writes: "It is better to construe miracles as such transformations of the physical to disclose its spiritual foundation and goal than to think of them as violations of inflexible and purposeless laws of nature"; see Ward, "God as a Principle of Cosmological Explanation," in *Physics, Philosophy, and Theology: A Common Quest for Understanding,* ed. Robert John Russell, William R. Stoeger, S.J., and George V. Coyne, S.J. (Vatican City State: Vatican Observatory, 1988), pp. 247-61, quote from 260-61.

81. Matti Myllykoski, "Being There: The Function of the Supernatural in Acts 1–12," in *Wonders Never Cease: The Purpose of Narrating Miracle Stories in the New Testament and Its Religious Environment,* ed. Michael Labahn and Bert Jan Lietaert Peerbolte, European Studies on Christian Origins 288 (London and New York: T. & T. Clark, 2006), pp. 146-79.

reminder, miracles make sense only within the wider teleological framework of Christian eschatology.

Further, however, miracles are never merely just a claim about nature on its own or even about nature's laws; rather, miracles involve free agents: their actions and reactions in relationship to God. This locates divine action most meaningfully in the interpersonal and intersubjective sphere: firstly in the intra-Trinitarian life of God, and secondly in the divine-human interchange.[82] Hence, the charism of miracles points not so much to a "supernaturalistic" aspect that overcomes the laws of nature, but rather to the interrelational domain within which human beings live and move in response to God's covenantal initiative. Here the evolutionary or developmental aspect of Peirce's theory of natural laws allows for the proleptic interruption of the coming kingdom in the here and now, even while we await the teleological transformation of creation as a whole into the eschatological rule of God.

But such transformation, as Peirce's rule of generality would caution us, involves a genuine interaction between God and the world so that what is coming is the kingdom, but not any specific form of it other than that which has been generally and proleptically revealed in the Trinitarian narrative of God. Just as even the probabilistic and statistical laws of nature allow for chance developments,[83] so also the coming reign of God will be unpredictably shaped by the agency of free creatures in the present world. Hence the eschatological future of the world and of its various creatures is open, conceivable only in general terms because what is to appear remains indeterminate in important respects. This does not mean that God's intentions might be thwarted, or that what has been revealed in Christ by the power of the Spirit will not be recognizable. It only means that we know in part both because we see only in part (as the apostle Paul says in 1 Corinthians 13:12) and because the future consists of real (and indeed miraculous!) tendencies and possibilities rather than only of predetermined actualities.[84]

---

82. William R. Stoeger, "Describing God's Action in the World in Light of Scientific Knowledge of Reality," in *Chaos and Complexity*, pp. 239-61, especially 259-60.

83. See David J. Bartholomew, *God of Chance* (London: SCM, 1984), and *God, Chance, and Purpose: Can God Have It Both Ways?* (Cambridge: Cambridge University Press, 2008), especially chapter 8, and passim. Of course, Bartholomew's answer to the question in the title of his more recent book is yes.

84. This is the reason why I am sympathetic to open theism but in the end do not consider myself an open theist. The openness position still relies on protological thinking rather than having an eschatological orientation. Within the protological framework, the question

In sum, the last two chapters have been motivated by the intuition that the pentecostal imagination has unique perspectives, sensibilities, and commitments that present both challenges and opportunities for pentecostal scholars who seek to approach the science and religion (or science and theology) dialogue table. The main challenge we have engaged in the preceding pages has been how to make sense of the pentecostal conviction regarding a miracle-working God amidst a world governed by natural law and defined by modern science. In fact, it has been precisely the pentecostal commitment to a robust theology of divine action that has motivated our laborious explorations of the concept of natural law from scientific, philosophical, and theological perspectives. At the same time, the pentecostal perspective has also urged an eschatological focus on what God intends to bring about, rather than a backward-oriented view toward creation and origins that has exercised others.

With help from the triadic metaphysics of Charles Sanders Peirce, I have suggested that the pentecostal-charismatic imagination invites a rethinking of the laws of nature and divine action within what might be called a pneumato-eschatological framework. My proposal is that while the laws of nature should be defined in habitual, dynamic, and general rather than in necessitarian terms, they are nonetheless real possibilities and tendencies through which the Holy Spirit is bringing about the coming kingdom. Hence the laws of nature are amenable to the basic actions of God and sufficiently flexible so that they can be miraculously redeemed to usher in the patterns and habits of the coming world. This results in a somewhat unique pentecostal contribution to a theology of miraculous divine action that is consistent with the laws of nature as understood by

---

inevitably arises about whether or not the future is open or closed vis-à-vis God's predetermining will. An eschatological perspective, on the other hand, need not say anymore than that it is the work of the triune God to bring about the kingdom in accordance with what has been revealed in the life of Christ by the power of the Spirit. From this, then, I can agree with open theists in affirming the important role that creatures play in responding to the kingdom initiatives of the eschatological God. For my discussion of open theism in relationship to the doctrine of creation, see my "Possibility and Actuality: The Doctrine of Creation and Its Implications for Divine Omniscience," *Wesleyan Philosophical Society Online Journal* 1, no. 1 (2001) (http://home.snu.edu/~brint/wpsjnl/v1n1.htm). For my analysis of the claims of open theism in relationship to other options, see my essays "Divine Knowledge and Future Contingents: Weighing the Presuppositional Issues in the Contemporary Debate," *Evangelical Review of Theology* 26, no. 3 (2002): 240-64, and "Divine Knowledge and Relation to Time," in *Philosophy of Religion: Introductory Essays,* ed. Thomas Jay Oord (Kansas City, MO: Beacon Hill Press/Nazarene Publishing House, 2003), pp. 136-52.

modern science on the one hand, but that also preserves fundamental Christian commitments about God's redemptive presence and activity in the world on the other. In the process, perhaps this pentecostal insight may also help other theists with similar religious intuitions to think through and respond to these matters in dialogue with the sciences.

5 *Ruach* over the Primordial Waters

A Pneumatological Theology of Emergence

So far in this book I have made two basic arguments: a methodological one regarding the need for many scientific disciplines to investigate the many kinds of emergent realities that make up this world, and a theological one regarding how the person and work of the Holy Spirit can illuminate the theology and science dialogue. Of course, even the methodological claim has been defended theologically, so that we have a theological rather than merely pragmatic justification for interdisciplinarity and for the acceptance of the conclusions of science, however provisional. Of the specifically theological argument, I have suggested that focusing on the work of the Spirit provides us with an eschatological framework for understanding divine action and hence invites a teleological orientation that is guided by a general vision of the kingdom as revealed in the life of Christ. This eschatological and teleological compass is distinct from the emphasis on origins that has been debated almost *ad nauseam* especially by those across the spectrum of conservative Christianity.[1] But with such a pentecostally in-

---

1. This is not to say that pentecostals have not been concerned at all with the doctrine of creation or with understanding the origins of the world; it is to say that much of what pentecostals have done so far has been established on the theological framework of their conservative evangelical or even fundamentalist Christian alliances — e.g., Michael Tenneson and Steve Badger, "Teaching Origins to Pentecostal Students," in *The Spirit Renews the Face of the Earth: Pentecostal Forays into Science and Theology of Creation*, ed. Amos Yong (Eugene, OR: Pickwick, 2009), pp. 210-31, especially 221-25 — rather than based on their own hermeneutical sensibilities or overarching theological instincts. It is the latter that I intend to develop in this chapter.

formed eschatological and teleological framework in place, it is now time for us to see if this might make a difference for understanding the origins and cosmic "history" of the world.[2]

This chapter thus attempts to develop a theology of evolutionary emergence. My aim is to understand the origins of the world in light of the Christian doctrine of salvation and the eschaton, rather than the other way around.[3] I thus intend to fill in the theology of emergence begun in chapter 2, which I believe is compatible with the eschatological orientation of the pentecostal-charismatic imagination; I also believe both can be mutually illuminating. If we are successful, the result will be a theology of emergence that assumes the interdisciplinarity required to explore the plurality of emergent realities and that complements the pneumato-eschatological theology of divine action proposed in the preceding two chapters of this book.

The argument here will proceed from science to philosophy to exegesis to theology. The first section sketches the standard scientific account of the history of the world, paying particular attention to emergentist themes and perspectives. Next, I provide an exposition of Philip Clayton's philosophy of emergence, motivated by the conviction that it provides a helpful bridge between the evolutionary sciences and eschatological theology. This is followed by a rereading of the creation narratives from what I call a canonical-pneumatological perspective, wherein I suggest resonances between the ancient biblical text and the contemporary sciences of emergence. The concluding fourth section shows how our pneumatological views regarding divine action not only augment Clayton's metaphysical hypothesis toward a theology of emergence, but also provide theological justification for his concerns — which, as I have shown in chapter 2, are also my own — about the integrity of science and its various descriptions about the natural world.

---

2. I put "history" in quote marks because "history," technically, belongs to the story of humanity, a fairly late arrival on the cosmic scene.

3. Pentecostals by and large have followed the theological tradition by focusing on origins and the doctrine of creation under the rubric of the first article of the creed — e.g., Timothy Munyon, "The Creation of the Universe and Humankind," in *Systematic Theology: A Pentecostal Perspective,* ed. Stanley M. Horton (Springfield, MO: Logion Press, 1994), pp. 215-53. My approach is to begin with the third article, and thus work toward a pneumatological theology of creation instead.

The Cosmic Story: The Standard Account
in Emergentist Perspective

I am not a scientist, so table 1 on page 136 represents my summary intended
to accomplish the following objectives. First, I have attempted to gain a synoptic view of what we might call the "cosmic story" — the "history" of the
universe and of humanity's place in it. For this, I have relied on numerous
other sources,[4] but most of what appears in the table should not be disputed
by the scientific establishment. Second, I have also attempted to map the
"history of emergence" onto the cosmic narrative. Given my own sympa-
thies with the emergentist framework, I have tried to locate the development
of complexity from out of their underlying levels of organization. Here, I
have drawn upon Harold Morowitz's discussion of twenty-eight levels of
emergence, in order to identify some of the emergence phenomena that are
dependent upon yet explanatorily irreducible to their constitutive parts.[5]
Finally, my interests in interdisciplinarity and in the integrity of each discipline motivate me to identify just some of the major fields of inquiry associated with each emergent level. This précis therefore provides a frame of ref-

---

4. Helpful for me, precisely because of the Christian commitments of the authors, have
been Keith B. Miller, ed., *Perspectives on an Evolving Creation* (Grand Rapids and Cam-
bridge: Eerdmans, 2003), especially the essays in part II; Darrel R. Falk, *Coming to Peace with
Science: Bridging the Worlds between Faith and Biology* (Downers Grove, IL: InterVarsity,
2004); Stephen J. Godfrey and Christopher R. Smith, *Paradigms on Pilgrimage: Creationism,
Paleontology, and Biblical Interpretation* (Toronto: Clements Publishing, 2005); and Davis A.
Young and Ralph F. Stearley, *The Bible, Rocks, and Time: Geological Evidence for the Age of the
Earth* (Downers Grove, IL: IVP Academic, 2008). Otherwise, one can also consult standard
texts like Trinh Xuan Thuan, *The Secret Melody: And Man Created the Universe,* trans. Storm
Dunlop (Oxford: Oxford University Press, 1995; reprint, Philadelphia and London:
Templeton Foundation Press, 2005), in cosmology; G. Brent Dalrymple, *Ancient Earth, An-
cient Skies: The Age of the Earth and Its Cosmic Surroundings* (Stanford: Stanford University
Press, 2004), in geology; Roger Lewin, *The Origin of Modern Humans* (New York: Scientific
American Library, and W. H. Freeman, 1993), and Donald C. Johanson and Blake Edgar,
From Lucy to Language, rev. ed. (New York: Simon and Schuster, 2006), in anthropology; and
J. Wentzel van Huyssteen, *Alone in the World? Human Uniqueness in Science and Theology —
the Gifford Lectures, 2004* (Grand Rapids and Cambridge: Eerdmans, 2006), for the rise of
human culture. A succinct overview is Kate Grayson Boisvert, *Religion and the Physical Sciences* (Westport, CT, and London: Greenwood Press, 2008), pp. 102-12.

5. See Harold Morowitz, *The Emergence of Everything: How the World Became Complex*
(New York: Oxford University Press, 2002). The details with regard to many of Morowitz's
levels of emergence continue to be contested, especially in terms of their explanation at the
lower level. I mention some of these later in this chapter.

Table 1 Natural History: The Standard Account[a]

Time Period[b]	Major Events & Periodization[c]	Emergent Levels of Complexity[d]	Representative Disciplines[e]
13-15 BYA 300 million years later	Big bang singularity Formation of matter out of cooling-off radiation from hydrogen and helium atoms	Four forces, protons, neutrons, electrons, and radiation Nucleosynthesis resulting in	Cosmology Physics Chemistry Astrophysics
12 BYA 4.6 BYA	Formation of galaxies Formation of our sun	elements, periodic table, stars, solar systems, galaxies & planetary structures	Astronomy
4 BYA	Formation of earth through gravitational forces, heat exchanges, gas transformations, and comet bombardment	Earth's geospheres, atmospheres, and biosphere	Geology Geophysics Paleontology
3.8–3.5 BYA	Archean era	Simple cell bacteria (prokaryotes), metabolic processes	Zoology Cell biology
2.7 BYA	Proterozoic era	Cells with chromosomes (eukaryotes), energy-producing mitochondria	
635-550 MYA	Ediacaran period	Multicellular organisms	
550-500 MYA	Cambrian period	Neurons, sea life, invertebrates, chordates	Anatomy
445-415 MYA	Silurian period	Land plants	Botany
415-360 MYA	Devonian period	Deuterostomes, vertebrates, cephalization, amphibians	Genomics
300-250 MYA	Permian period	Reptiles, insects	
248-208 MYA	Triassic period	Arboreal mammals	
206-144 MYA	Jurassic period	Mammals, dinosaurs	
144-65 MYA	Cretaceous period	Birds	
65 MYA	Paleocene period	Pongids, primates, apes	
8-5 MYA	Late Miocene period	Hominids (*Australopithecines*), tool use	Paleoanthropology
2 MYA	Lower Paleolithic period	Neanderthal species Stone tools	Anthropology Cognitive sciences
300,000–30,000 YA	Middle Paleolithic period	*Homo sapiens* Art/symbolic language/culture	Cultural anthropology Psychology
40,000-10,000 YA	Upper Paleolithic period	Agriculture	Sociology Philosophy
3,000 YA	Bronze Age	Technology Philosophy & religion	Religious Studies Theology

a. By "standard account," I mean no more than that this is the consensus that one currently reads about in most science textbooks. Of course, I am not unaware of the controversy in science education, but that is something that the science establishment has to negotiate, just as theologians have to adjudicate controversies in that field.

b. BYA = Billion years ago; MYA = million years ago; YA = years ago. These numbers are very general approximations, especially as we go back further and further in time.

c. Various disciplines use different labels like *eras, epochs,* or *periods;* I default to the most relevant for my purposes in each case.

d. Here I follow Morowitz, in general, although I do not identify all twenty-eight of his levels of emergence.

e. There are certainly overlaps in the following scheme; the scientific disciplines are by no means watertight compartments or areas of inquiry.

erence for understanding the scientific consensus about the origins and history of the world, and for our own theological ruminations that follow.

I will make a few comments on how I am processing this consensus in mainstream science. As we work through this chapter and the rest of the book, I will be inviting readers to conceptualize this "data" in eschatological and even teleological perspective. In other words, every scientific account — or in this case, the accumulation of various scientific accounts — invites theological signification, which I am attempting to provide in this volume as a whole.

First, I am increasingly convinced that this standard account makes good sense. Most scientific, technological, and medical advances our generation is privileged to experience — from electronic media and communicative technologies to cures for cancer to transportation achievements (i.e., placing human beings on the moon) — are based on the same methods that have generated "the standard account." I do not think it plausible for us to enjoy the benefits of contemporary technology, medicine, and other applications of modern science and then summarily dismiss their overarching explanatory framework.[6]

Second, cosmologically, the world, of which we inhabit only a small corner, is truly a bedazzling "place." It is not easy to imagine that we live in a universe that is literally billions of light-years across (remember that this measurement is based on the speed of light, which travels at 186,000 miles per second!). More unfathomable is that there are more than 170 billion galaxies in the observable universe, with each galaxy having from 10 million stars (dwarf galaxies) to 1 trillion stars (giant galaxies). Our sun is one of 200-400 billion stars in the Milky Way galaxy,[7] with the neighboring Andromeda galaxy containing about 1 trillion stars.

Third, the evolution of our star, solar system, and planets is itself a remarkable sequence that lasted over a billion years.[8] The constants of nature, as well as the chance events that contributed to the formation of the sun, the interstellar dust and nebular and gaseous disks, the planetesimals

6. For a panoramic but no less kaleidoscopic overview of the achievements of science, see Patricia Fara, *Science: A Four Thousand Year History* (Oxford: Oxford University Press, 2009).

7. The uncertainty is due to the number of low-mass stars that are difficult to identify because of low luminosity; see A. H. Delsemme, *Our Cosmic Origins: From the Big Bang to the Emergence of Life and Intelligence* (Cambridge and New York: Cambridge University Press, 1998), p. 56.

8. Delsemme, *Our Cosmic Origins*, chapter 4, provides a brief but fascinating account.

(tiny objects that were ancestors of the asteroids, comets, and, now, the moons around the various planets), the giant planets, and later the terrestrial planets, and the moons of the planets, etc. — each of these emerged out of the whirlwind of our solar system as it developed within its environment in the Milky Way galaxy. The earth itself has been variously shaped by the sun and larger planets' gravitational fields; an extended period of cometary, asteroid, and meteoroid bombardment; and its lunar relations, among other factors, all of which have contributed to the formation of its atmosphere, geosphere, oceans, and landmasses.

Within this matrix, fourth, the natural history of this planet unfolded, along with the evolutionary scope of life that stretches back almost 4 billion years.[9] Comparatively, we have known human (recorded) history only in about the last few thousand years. In other words, the arrival of humankind, even if we include all members of the *Homo* species, accounts for only a small fraction of evolutionary or geologic time. Across the broad scope of natural history, literally millions of species have come and gone. If

---

9. As Michael Roberts, *Evangelicals and Science* (Westport, CT, and London: Greenwood Press, 2008), shows, evangelicals have in many circles come to make peace with an old earth since the early nineteenth century, with the debate revolving primarily, although not exclusively, around the questions of the origins of life and of human origins. The three most prominent attempts that have been proposed to reconcile the Genesis account with the age of the earth have been the gap, day-age, and progressive creation theories. The first, dependent on a primeval fall of angels between Gen. 1:1 and 2, has never seemed to me to make sense of the rest of the creation narrative (see further my comments on Stephen Webb's neo-gap-theory proposal in the next chapter). The day-age account seems plausible, although it presumes a concordist approach to Genesis and modern science that isn't necessary — as argued persuasively by Denis O. Lamoureux, *Evolutionary Creation: A Christian Approach to Evolution* (Eugene, OR: Wipf and Stock, 2008), especially chapters 5–7. Progressive creationism, most widely defended in evangelical circles by astronomer Hugh Ross, especially his *Creation and Time: A Biblical and Scientific Perspective on the Creation-Date Controversy* (Colorado Springs: NavPress, 1994), and, with Fazale Rana, *Origins of Life: Biblical and Evolutionary Models Face Off* (Colorado Springs: NavPress, 2004), is appealing to some evangelicals since it accepts all of geologic and evolutionary time yet holds that God created each kind of animal as well as *Homo sapiens* directly. Many contemporary progressive creationists also embrace the notion of intelligent design (on which, see below, n. 18). Some might see parallels between this special creationism and the various levels of emergence, except that the latter does not posit any ontological discontinuity in the history of life (only the unpredictable appearance of complexity that once manifest is irreducible to its ancestors) and is concerned not just with animal life but also with the development of the cosmos as a whole. My pneumatological framework developed in chapters 3–4 above does not require rejection of the interventionism of progressive creation, although I prefer an eschatological and teleological interpretation of divine action instead.

we are to take the standard account seriously, we must acknowledge many more evolutionary dead ends than living species to testify to life's journey on our planet.

Fifth, biologically, the question persists about the mechanism of evolutionary change, as that is often referred to in the field. The neo-Darwinian synthesis involves random mutations at the genomic level with evolutionary adaptation of populations via the process of natural selection.[10] The reigning ideas here include the common descent of all life from a single source, even if that does not mean that evolutionary paths have proceeded only in linear fashion. This is also not to say that there are no debates, for example, about the origins of life; transitionary forms (with regard to the functions of intermediary structures); biological functions; the tempo, mode, and specific role of natural selection; the Cambrian explosion; macroevolutionary processes; speciation; the classification of species; sexual selection; self-organization and complexity of dynamical systems; evolutionary sociobiology, as well as the biology of morality (altruism) and religiosity.[11] It may even be that some of these issues will never attain adequate scientific/biological resolution. My suggestion is to allow scientists to continue to do their work since it is the nature of science to pursue the existing questions until either answers are found or a new way to form the questions — a new paradigm — emerges.

Within the reigning biological paradigm, four related developments propel the emergence hypothesis. The first is the theory of spontaneous, even if law-governed, self-organizing adaptations in far from equilibrium or dissipative (chaotic) systems interacting with their environments that result in order and complexity.[12] Self-organizing systems often derive from

10. Ernst Mayr, *What Evolution Is* (New York: Basic Books, 2001); Douglas J. Futuyma, *Evolution,* 2nd ed. (Sunderland, MA: Sinauer Associates, 2009); and Douglas Palmer, *Evolution: The Story of Life* (Berkeley: University of California Press, 2009), are now the standard texts. See also Peter J. Bowler, *Evolution: The History of an Idea,* 3rd ed. (Berkeley: University of California Press, 2003).

11. An informative discussion of the still-debated issues is provided by Michael Ruse, *The Evolution Wars: A Guide to the Debates,* 2nd ed. (Millerton, NY: Grey House, 2009), especially throughout part II. I also like David L. Wilcox, *God and Evolution: A Faith-Based Understanding* (Valley Forge, PA: Judson, 2004), who is very honest about the contested questions, although not to the point of being skeptical about the "standard account."

12. This has been popularized by Stuart A. Kauffman, *The Origins of Order: Self-Organization and Selection in Evolution* (Oxford: Oxford University Press, 1993). For a biological interpretation, see Brian Goodwin, *How the Leopard Changed Its Spots: The Evolution of Complexity,* 2nd ed. (Princeton: Princeton University Press, 2001).

the interactions of their lower-level components, even as these interactions are influenced if not determined by the wider surroundings, and result in or exhibit emergent properties. Those advocating application of this theory, less contested in physics and the physical sciences, to biology argue that natural selection on its own is incapable of fully accounting for the continuous evolution of life on earth.

Another theory is evolutionary convergence.[13] The argument here is that under the classical mechanistic model, the pathways of life are probabilistically too minute to be chanced upon. But what if evolutionary adaptations were inevitable in terms of general types? In other words, what if distinct evolutionary lineages led, in effect, to general destinations such as those that enabled certain functional capacities like vision/sight, locomotion, flight, etc., or those that resulted in specific species like photosynthesizing plants, mammalian animals, or bipedal hominids, etc.? In other words, the theory of convergent evolution says there are optimal biological forms and general functions that evolutionary adaptations inevitably stumble upon, even if such are developed from different environmental niches. If this is true, then if the tape of life were replayed on this planet, at least in some instances things would take a very similar, rather than drastically different, course.[14]

The idea of convergent evolution, of course, raises questions about the anthropic principle and the finely tuned constants of nature — the physics of the cosmos as a whole, not to mention the fitness of the terrestrial and chemical environment on our planet — that have allowed human life to evolve in this part of the universe.[15] I understand why scientists are gener-

13. See Simon Conway Morris, *Life's Solution: Inevitable Humans in a Lonely Universe* (Cambridge: Cambridge University Press, 2004), and Conway Morris, ed., *The Deep Structure of Biology: Is Convergence Sufficiently Ubiquitous to Give a Directional Signal?* (West Conshohocken, PA: Templeton Foundation Press, 2008).

14. As opposed to the idea that even after replaying the evolutionary tape of history "a million times," there is no reason to believe "that anything like *Homo sapiens* would ever evolve again" — as famously asserted by Stephen J. Gould, *Wonderful Life: The Burgess Shale and the Nature of History* (New York and London: Norton, 1989), p. 289.

15. The literature is voluminous since the first major proposal: John D. Barrow and Frank J. Tipler, *The Anthropic Cosmological Principle* (New York: Oxford University Press; Oxford: Clarendon, 1986). See also Errol J. Harris, *Cosmos and Anthropos: A Philosophical Interpretation of the Anthropic Cosmological Principle* (Atlantic Highlands, NJ: Humanities Press International, 1991). For a more recent overview, see John D. Barrow et al., eds., *Fitness of the Cosmos for Life: Biochemistry and Fine-Tuning* (Cambridge: Cambridge University Press, 2008).

ally reluctant to embrace any such notions in their work since I agree that to make such moves inevitably lands us in metaphysical or philosophical — even worse: theological! — territory. Yet physicists themselves have suggested a cosmological theory of natural selection such that universes are born out of black holes and, depending on their initial parameters (constraints), will produce (or not) various types of worlds, one of which, of course, is ours.[16] Once a universe with the constraints that happen to characterize ours materializes, then evolutionary convergence itself becomes plausible. While I would see my teleological interpretation of science to be consistent with — even complementary to — the main lines of discussion presented by anthropic principle advocates, my approach remains resolutely theological.

Still, the theory of convergent evolution and the anthropic principle both separately and together raise the contentious issue of function and design in the contemporary biological sciences. The biological literature is staggering, with many resisting any teleological language, some advocating for a redefined notion of teleology, and others introducing alternative concepts like teleonomy and teleomaticity in order to distinguish biological functions from earlier concepts of design operative in natural philosophy.[17] This situation is potentially confusing given my own teleological model of divine action that has been proposed in this book. Let me reiterate that my proposal is thoroughly theological, and I am certainly not attempting to smuggle the concept of final causation into the biological sciences (much less into the cosmological sciences, in terms of debates about the anthropic principle). Yet as a theologian, I should also note that I am

16. See the discussion of Lee Smolin, *The Life of the Cosmos* (Oxford: Oxford University Press, 1997), although at times his ruminations about the natural selection of baby universes with various physical parameters and constants from out of black hole inflationary expansions verges on science fiction (at least to one like me who lacks the astrophysical background to follow through all the argument).

17. For a discussion of these issues, see Stephen Pope and Anthony T. Annunziato, "The Old Teleology and the New: An Experiment in Conversation," in *The Dialogue between Science and Religion: What We Have Learned from One Another,* ed. Patrick H. Byrne (Scranton, PA: University of Scranton Press, 2005), pp. 47-82, and André Ariew, "Teleology," in *The Cambridge Companion to the Philosophy of Biology,* ed. David L. Hull and Michael Ruse (Cambridge: Cambridge University Press, 2007), pp. 160-81. On teleonomic and teleomatic functions — goal-directed processes or behaviors influenced by an evolved program and end-directed processes shaped by natural laws, respectively — see Ernst Mayr, *What Makes Biology Unique? Considerations on the Autonomy of a Scientific Discipline* (Cambridge and New York: Cambridge University Press, 2004), pp. 49-56.

not surprised that the concept of teleology has persisted in the field of biology to the present, not to mention in the cosmological sciences, even as I think it will resist being expunged from the debate in the future.[18]

My goal is not to resolve any of the preceding issues at their scientific levels — in fact, to be true to my methodological commitments, none of them are for me to resolve because they lie beyond my domain of expertise as a theologian.[19] My point with the preceding set of reflections is only to suggest that ours is an emerging universe, with each level of (self-organized) complexity inviting, even demanding, its own methods for study and analysis. Ours is thus also a dynamic world, not requiring any fundamentally ontological dualism at any point, but yet, perhaps paradoxically, suggesting an ontological pluralism in terms of the various levels of emergent complexities and their study.[20]

18. It is here that I should note my sympathy with intelligent design (ID) theorists who insist that teleological factors must be factored into mainstream science (especially biology): the complexity of certain biological forms, structures, and functions, for example, cannot have evolved via random mutation and natural selection — they must have been designed as such (hence ID being a version, a much more sophisticated one no less, of progressive creationism). The difference is that my position is set forth as a strictly theological account, albeit one not without scientific implications. Further, I'm wary of ID's interventionism since it comes off as too much of a God-of-the-gaps account for explaining complexity, a strategy that risks undermining itself with the ongoing march of science. In part for this reason, they will not be able to convince the scientific community that their notion of "design" functions scientifically rather than religiously, try as they may. For more on what I have thought about ID so far, see my essays "The Spirit and Creation: Possibilities and Challenges for a Dialogue between Pentecostal Theology and the Sciences," *Journal of the European Pentecostal Theological Association* 25 (2005): 82-110, especially 92-94, and "God and the Evangelical Laboratory: Recent Conservative Protestant Perspectives on the Interface between Theology and Science," *Theology & Science* 5, no. 2 (2007): 203-21, especially 208-12. For a historical perspective on ID as a creationist model, see Ronald L. Numbers, *The Creationists: From Scientific Creationism to Intelligent Design,* rev. and expanded ed. (Cambridge, MA, and London: Harvard University Press, 2006), chapter 17, and on the scientific status of the ID program, consult part III of Robert T. Pennock and Michael Ruse, eds., *But Is It Science? The Philosophical Question in the Creation/Evolution Controversy,* updated ed. (Amherst, NY: Prometheus Books, 2009).

19. I am happy here to refer readers to the arguments for an evolutionary theism by Christians who are also first-rate scientists such as the neurochemist Denis R. Alexander, *Creation or Evolution: Do We Have to Choose?* (Oxford and Grand Rapids: Monarch Books, 2008); of course, his answer to the question in the title is no.

20. See Philip Clayton and Paul Davies, eds., *The Re-emergence of Emergence: The Emergentist Hypothesis from Science to Religion* (Oxford: Oxford University Press, 2006); Nancey Murphy and W. J. Stoeger, eds., *Evolution and Emergence: Systems, Organisms, Persons* (Oxford: Oxford University Press, 2007); and Mark Bedau and Paul Humphreys, eds.,

It is in part for this reason that I prefer to talk methodologically about theology and science as being complementary rather than convergent. Here, of course, we must not confuse biological convergence (as discussed a few paragraphs ago) with methodological convergence. The latter might suggest that theology and science are actually talking about and agreeing on the same thing — that is, converging across their disagreements. I am reluctant to make such a claim when even *within* the sciences, many disciplines are talking not about the same thing but about different things. Thus I prefer to talk about theology and science as being complementary instead.[21] By saying this, I am affirming that the two sets of discourses — with the plurality of discourses even within each category — do not necessarily need to contradict one another, that it is likely that they can be complementarily illuminating about different aspects of the one world in which we live, and that in some instances they may even be mutually supportive.

But do these notions of self-organizing order, convergent evolution, and emergent complexity revive the vitalism long ago rejected by especially the evolutionary sciences?[22] The philosophy of vitalism has been despised by the scientific community both because of its dualistic underpinnings — which distinguished vital forces from their material manifestations — and because it suggests that there were hidden life forces directing the course of the history of evolution toward predetermined ends, so the rejection of vitalism was simultaneously the rejection of final causes, or teleology, in biology in particular and in the sciences in general. Does not our dependence on teleological language (in chapters 3–4) reintroduce final causes once again into scientific discussion?

My short answer is no, and for at least the following two, related reasons. First, as I hope has been clear, mine is an eschatological and therefore theological reading of science, proposed not for scientists per se but for

---

Emergence: Contemporary Readings in Philosophy and Science (Cambridge, MA: MIT Press, 2008). I return to this notion of ontological pluralism momentarily in my discussion of Clayton's philosophy of emergence.

21. As does Terence L. Nichols, *The Sacred Cosmos: Christian Faith and the Challenge of Naturalism* (Grand Rapids: Brazos, 2003), especially in his chapter 9.

22. E.g., Timothy Lenoir, *The Strategy of Life: Teleology and Mechanics in Nineteenth-Century German Biology* (Dordrecht: D. Reidel; Boston: Kluwer, 1982), and Marjorie Grene and David Depew, *The Philosophy of Biology: An Episodic History* (Cambridge: Cambridge University Press, 2004), especially chapter 10. For an overview, however, of vitalism's persistence, seen in its continuously generating staunch resistance from many scientific quarters, see Monica Greco's "On the Vitality of Vitalism," in *Inventive Life: Approaches to the New Vitalism,* ed. Mariam Fraser, Sarah Kember, and Celia Lury (London: Sage, 2006), pp. 14-27.

those working at the interface of theology and science. If scientists think teleological notions need to be recovered in their work, that is for them to discuss and debate (and I would certainly welcome such an interpretation within the scientific community). My motivation is that I think a teleological interpretation of divine action and the God-world relationship makes good theological sense of the scientific data. But more importantly, second, as I have argued in the previous chapter, my eschatological teleology is generalizable only in vague terms, according to the Trinitarian shape of God's proleptic work in the incarnational and pentecostal events of salvation history. Thus not only is there no possibility of arguing for any backward or retro-causation from the future since the future is, after all, only generally known according to the pattern of the kingdom rather than specifically predetermined. Besides, while final and ultimate causes that provide theological meaning and significance are connected in some respects with penultimate causes that invite functional analyses of natural realities, they are nevertheless still distinct and should not be conflated. In the rest of this chapter, I will try to follow through on this theological intuition vis-à-vis the standard account as presented above, and do so philosophically, exegetically, and theologically.

Philip Clayton's Philosophy of Emergence

Philosophically, I propose to develop my argument in conversation with Philip Clayton's theory of emergence, presented in one of his recent books, *Mind and Emergence.*[23] Clayton is an ideal dialogue partner in part because of his long-standing interest and participation in the theology and science conversation,[24] but also because of his attempts over the last few years to wrestle with what he has called the "emergence of spirit."[25] As a philosophical theologian working in the philosophy of science, Clayton's theory of emergence is presented as a metaphysical hypothesis that he be-

23. Philip Clayton, *Mind and Emergence: From Quantum to Consciousness* (Oxford: Oxford University Press, 2004).

24. For Clayton's previous book-length forays into the theology and science conversation, see his *Explanation from Physics to Theology: An Essay in Rationality and Religion* (New Haven: Yale University Press, 1989), and *God and Contemporary Science* (Grand Rapids: Eerdmans, 1997).

25. See Clayton, "The Emergence of Spirit," *CTNS Bulletin* 20, no. 4 (2000): 3-20, and "Emerging God," *Christian Century* 121, no. 1 (January 13, 2004): 26-30.

lieves not only provides a more coherent explanatory framework for the disparate data of many scientific disciplines, but also contributes to framing future research programs that may, in turn, either confirm or falsify the emergence thesis. Given this concern for the integrity of science and scientific methods, Clayton is cautious about the kinds of theological claims he makes. While I appreciate Clayton's discretion on this and also see his philosophical framework as serving a mediating function between the scientific and theological enterprises, I am convinced that pneumatology can contribute to his project at both levels: that of reinforcing his metaphysical hypothesis with an analogous theological vision, and that of further clarifying his concerns about the distinctiveness and yet relatedness of theological and scientific methodologies.

To be clear, emergence is a philosophical or metaphysical hypothesis rather than a theological doctrine or scientific datum.[26] Yet the theory of emergence, Clayton suggests, identifies patterns of developments in the natural history of the cosmos as understood through the findings of the various scientific disciplines. That the theory is sufficiently comprehensive to have implications for an account of the God-world relationship is an added benefit, although not a central concern in his volume. Hence, emergence theory is a large-scale theoretical framework derived primarily from our engagement across the spectrum of the natural sciences and answerable chiefly to them. For our purposes, the best way to grasp the scope of Clayton's theory is to identify what he considers to be its eight primary characteristics, and to fill in the details as we go.

First, emergence theory presumes that the world in all its complexity is nevertheless made out of one kind of stuff. Here, Clayton is advocating a kind of *monism* over and against any kind of Cartesian or substance dualism on the one side and a crass materialism on the other. Instead, emergentist monism provides a coherent theoretical framework to explain the differentiated but ultimate unity between, for example, consciousness and the material substrate of the world.[27]

26. Hence Clayton's proposals should be read within the context of the wider discussion of emergence especially in the philosophy of science — e.g., Mark A. Bedau and Paul Humphreys, eds., *Emergence: Contemporary Readings in Philosophy and Science* (London and Cambridge, MA: Bradford/MIT Press, 2008).

27. Clayton acknowledges here his acceptance of the label "emergentist monism" from fellow science-and-religion scholar Arthur Peacocke; see Peacocke, "The Sound of Sheer Silence: How Does God Communicate with Humanity," in *Neuroscience and the Person*, ed. Robert John Russell et al. (Vatican City: Vatican Observatory Publications, 1999), pp. 214-47.

Second, emergence theory is able to account for the *hierarchical complexity* of the world. By this, Clayton is calling attention to the "ontological pluralism" of the world manifest, for example, in human creatures who are physical, biological, psychological, and even (Clayton suggests) spiritual realities.[28] Each of these levels or domains emerges from the previous one, but once emergent, is sufficiently distinct to require different kinds of explanations. To proceed along these lines assumes that emergent levels of reality are neither merely aggregates of sublevel entities nor reducible to those parts.

This leads, *third,* to the recognition of the *temporal* dimension of emergentist monism. Whether understood through neo-Darwinian theory or otherwise, increasingly levels of complexity are structured and have evolved over time. With this, Clayton insists that new elements appear in the world that are dependent upon previous configurations of things (hence monism) but are irreducible not only epistemologically and ontologically but also temporally to their parts. With this latter claim, the processes of emergence are unpredictable. Novelty's evolutionary trail can be recognized in retrospect, but not predetermined in advance.

Fourth, emergence theory is sufficiently comprehensive to recognize that there is *no monolithic law of emergence* that can account for the disparate processes occurring at each level of complexity. This needs a bit of unpacking, so let us briefly digress to distinguish between what happens at the level of physics and chemistry and what happens at that of biology. (I will comment later on how Clayton conceives of the laws operative at the level of consciousness.)

At the level of physics, emergence calls attention to "the development of complex physical and chemical systems which, though verifiable through observation, cannot be derived from fundamental physical principles."[29] Examples Clayton gives, with references to scientific literature, are conductivity that cannot be reduced to the study of electrons; fluid dynamics that cannot be deduced from the motion of individual particles; and ordered patterns such as snowflakes, snow crystals, and other ice phenomena that cannot be predicted from their chemical structures.[30] At this

28. Clayton, *Mind and Emergence,* p. 148.

29. Clayton, *Mind and Emergence,* p. 66.

30. Here, I will not bog down my summary by reproducing Clayton's references. Clayton is careful to cite his scientific sources since he is writing primarily to convince scientists. As a theologian, I will have to defer to scientists about the legitimacy of his culling these sources for the purposes of formulating the emergence theory.

level, Clayton recognizes that some physicists and chemists would admit only that our current state of knowledge cannot adequately account for these emergent phenomena, but not that we cannot in principle do so given further inquiry. Hence, Clayton is willing to label these examples of *weak emergence* given the possibility that future discoveries will enable an explanation in terms of their constitutive parts.

Stronger forms of emergence, however, can be identified at the biological level. Four kinds of emergent processes govern interactions at this level.[31] First, there are differences in scale such that what happens at the level of cells, molecules, and neurons is different from what happens at the level of the central nervous system or the organism as a whole; microstructures and microorganisms act and react differently than macrostructures and macroorganisms. Second, biochemical processes are sustained in part through feedback loops: cells interact with other cells, plants with their environment, etc. Beyond the horizontal relationships that constitute feedback loops are more vertically organized relationships that comprise local-global interactions, for example, plants-and-animals-in-their-environment affecting the larger ecosystem, which in turn influences the behavior of the individuals. Finally, there are nested hierarchies wherein complex systems survive and perpetuate as they incorporate other discrete subsystems. Clayton's point is that different laws of emergence characterize what happens at the level of physics and chemistry on the one hand, and at the level of biology on the other. Even within the biological domain, there are weaker or stronger forms of emergence across the spectrum, depending on whether we're talking about the emergence of microphysical cell states or of macrophysical organisms.

Hence, *fifth*, the emergence hypothesis links together disparate processes of complexity in natural history via broadly similar patterns of creativity. Clayton proposes that observations across the sciences reveal a family resemblance of shared traits that characterize the pattern of emergence across levels. Level 2 emerges from level 1, he suggests, if L_1 is chronologically and historically prior to L_2 and L_2 *both* does not exist apart from L_1 but emerges unpredictably (in terms of the rules governing what emerges and in terms of the qualities or properties of the emergent level) from "a sufficient degree of complexity in L_1," *and* is finally irreducible causally, explanatorily, metaphysically, or ontologically to L_1.[32] Insofar as

31. Clayton, *Mind and Emergence*, pp. 80-84.
32. Clayton, *Mind and Emergence*, p. 61.

this is empirically derivative from scientific data, "emergence is just that pattern that recurs across a wide range of scientific (and non-scientific) fields."[33]

Sixth, downward causation is exercised by higher levels on lower levels. As discussed in chapter 2, the clearest evidence for this is found at the level of biological creatures, especially in the emergent properties of entities that exercise sentient agency in various levels. Now Clayton does recognize the debates taking place at this level among cognitive neuroscientists. There are, of course, materialists or reductive physicalists who treat mind or consciousness epiphenomenally, as explicable finally in terms of brain states. There are also nonreductive physicalists who may advocate a theory of the mind as *strongly supervenient* upon brain states: in this case, while admitting that mental states do constrain brain activity, they believe that mental states are finally determined by the physical or neural substrate, resulting in the real explanation being provided by the processes that characterize the subvenient level of brain functions. Alternatively, there is the *weak supervenience* theory that Clayton himself (and others) subscribes to: in this case, the mind is dependent on but irreducible to the neurobiological processes of the brain-body, even while the mind not only constrains but also exercises causal agency that affects brain and body activity.[34] Note here that those who favor *strong supervenience* are like those who advocate *weak emergence:* both groups are likely to suggest that explanation is in principle reducible to the lower level, given further scientific discovery. By contrast, Clayton favors (with others) *weak supervenience* together with *strong emergence,* arguing that mind and higher-level properties are in principle irreducible to brain and lower-level parts because the former concern qualitatively and ontologically distinct realities. The difference, then, is that strong supervenience finally allows only for "upward causation" wherein brain states affect mind states, whereas weak supervenience accounts for "downward causation" as well.

Seventh is what Clayton calls *emergentist pluralism.* This combines the hierarchical complexity and ontological pluralism of his second thesis

---

33. Clayton, *Mind and Emergence,* p. 49.

34. The cognitive sciences are increasingly confirming the plasticity of the brain, its susceptibility to be transformed as a result of mental activity; see, e.g., Sharon Begley, *Train Your Mind, Change Your Brain: How a New Science Reveals Our Extraordinary Potential to Transform Ourselves* (New York: Ballantine Books, 2007), and Michael S. Gazzaniga, ed., *The Cognitive Neurosciences,* 4th ed. (Cambridge, MA: MIT Press, 2009), especially the essays in part II.

with the temporal and emergent monism of his third thesis, resulting in the claim that new levels of ontologically primitive realities appear over time that are not just aggregates of lower-level entities and cannot be reduced to them. Further, Clayton also wishes to emphasize the pluralism of levels spanning the entirety of natural history (to date) and the broad spectrum of the scientific disciplines. If there were only two levels — that is, physical and mental — then Clayton's emergence theory would collapse to a dualist metaphysics. However, if there are three or more levels — and Clayton often refers to Harold Morowitz's aforementioned study — then identification of similar patterns of activity across these multiple levels sustains a more comprehensive philosophy of emergence that goes beyond reductionistic materialism or dualism.

Finally, Clayton proposes to understand *mind as emergent.* More accurately, rather than claiming to understand "mind" fully, Clayton prefers to talk about "mental properties" as dependent upon, interactive with, and irreducible to physical properties.[35] The driving force behind Clayton's theory of mind is the "hard problem of consciousness": self-conscious and personal states of experience.[36] The options, generally speaking, remain: (1) materialism or epiphenomenalism; (2) dualism; (3) strong supervenience/weak emergence; or (4) weak supervenience/strong emergence. (1) fails to account for either the hard problem or human moral agency; (2) fails to account for the neuroscientific data that shows mental states to be dependent upon brain states; and (3) is finally reductionist, allowing "upward causation" but not the reverse. Only (4) preserves human agency, acknowledges that the mind is dependent on but irreducible to the brain, and provides an account of consciousness that can deal with the hard problem. Mind as emergent is therefore a way between reductionism on the one side and dualism on the other. Generalizing from the neuroscientific data toward an ontology of part-whole relations (with neither being reducible to the other) and a theory of downward causation leads Clayton to his theory of emergence.

Clayton recognizes that the perspective of science will endorse the weak emergence thesis if attracted to emergence theory at all. This is be-

35. E.g., Clayton, *Mind and Emergence,* p. 169.
36. Clayton, *Mind and Emergence,* pp. 120-23. We have already discussed this briefly in chapter 2; for Clayton's book-length reflections on just this matter, see his *In Quest of Freedom: The Emergence of Spirit in the Natural World,* Religion Theologie und Naturwissenschaft/Religion Theology and Natural Science 13 (Göttingen: Vandenhoeck & Ruprecht, 2009).

cause the weak emergence thesis privileges the physical domain and presupposes a kind of ontological closure to the world that not only enables its final reductionistic move but also fits with the strict demands of empirical science. In this sense, Clayton acknowledges that weak emergence is the position to beat.[37] On the other hand, Clayton advocates the strong emergence thesis — as defined by the preceding eight characteristics — because of its greater explanatory power, especially with regard to human consciousness and causation. Further, insofar as emergence theory passes initial plausibility conditions, it provides a theoretical framework for a scientific research program that can invigorate scientific inquiry. Finally, inasmuch as emergence is presented as a metaphysical hypothesis, it is in principle falsifiable by the empirical data that is culled from such a wide-ranging scientific research program. In any case, throughout, Clayton attempts to find a *via media* between attention to empirical detail and philosophical generalization (in terms of scientific and philosophical method), between physicalism and dualism (with regard to the neurology and philosophy of mind), and between reductionism and supernaturalistic emergence (with regard to naturalism and materialism versus supernaturalistic theism).[38]

I have not so far said anything about where theism fits into Clayton's hypothesis. While Clayton's discussion of theism occupies only part of the final chapter of his book, some comments need to be made in light of what follows. That Clayton is led to theism seems to follow naturally from his working to find a more complete metaphysical account that goes beyond simply rejecting physicalism, postulating "persons as self-conscious agents,"[39] advocating for the causal openness of the world (against weak emergentists), and presuming an inexplicable rationality to the world. Clayton's suggestion to "conceive mind (or spirit or deity) not merely as an emergent quality of the natural world, but also as a source of agency in its own right," signals his shift from an immanentist theism to a transcendent divine mind.[40] As a fairly traditional theist who rejects the idea that God is dependent upon the world, Clayton recognizes that he is trading in the

37. Clayton, *Mind and Emergence*, p. 32.

38. To appreciate the deftness needed to navigate between the Scylla and Charybdis of these various poles, see the essay by Michael Silberstein, "Reduction, Emergence, and Explanation," in Peter Machamer and Michael Silberstein, *The Blackwell Guide to the Philosophy of Science* (Malden, MA, and Oxford: Blackwell, 2002), pp. 80-107.

39. Clayton, *Mind and Emergence*, p. 175.

40. Clayton, *Mind and Emergence*, p. 182.

mind-body dualism for "theological dualism."[41] By this, of course, he is referring to his commitment to a monism about the world of minds, bodies, etc., as consisting of one kind of stuff, in contrast to his confession of God who transcends this world. So while Clayton can talk about the emergence of mind or consciousness and, in that sense, about the emergence of spirit, he does not talk about the emergence of the divine Spirit within these same processes of natural and biological history; doing so would compromise the otherness of God.

What then does Clayton think about the God-world relation? While God may be at work at the quantum level, this is empirically untestable. Further, surely God can influence human minds even as human beings influence one another, but we need to be wary lest the divine mind be anthropomorphized and reduced to just another consciousness at work in the world. In the end, Clayton generalizes from the human experience of personal and purposeful activity to the conclusion that divine activity is similarly personal and purposeful. The cost, of course, is that divine activity is not amenable to scientific investigation even as the language of purpose, intention, and desire we know at the human level escapes the scope of scientific inquiry. Yet this theistic account, Clayton suggests, is not incompatible with the data of science, and in fact adds substantially to a more complete metaphysical vision.[42]

A Canonical-Pneumatological Reading of the Creation Narratives

At this point I provide what I would call a "pneumatological assist" to Clayton's project through a rereading of the creation narratives. As a theologian I am interested in further securing the theological credentials of emergence theory without undercutting its appeal to the sciences. I am optimistic that a pneumatological reading of the creation narratives will contribute to a more robust theological vision both in terms of illuminating aspects of emergence theory with the biblical witness and in terms of the cross-fertilization that I believe can occur between a metaphysic of emergence and a pneumatological theology. In the next, concluding, section I

41. Clayton, *Mind and Emergence*, pp. 185-87.

42. The preceding is consistent with the theistic account elaborated upon by Clayton in a later book, *Adventures in the Spirit: God, World, Divine Action* (Minneapolis: Fortress, 2008).

will also briefly suggest reasons why the following pneumatological theology of creation also sustains rather than undermines the standard account of the origins and history of the world.

At this point, however, the question arises: Why Genesis 1–2? This is not unimportant since few biblical scholars and theology-and-science researchers today would be willing to read these chapters as contributing to a scientific understanding of the world. From a strictly exegetical and historical perspective, I believe that the authors of the Priestly and Yahwist portrayals were intent on combating ancient Near Eastern cosmogonies rather than either the big bang theory or neo-Darwinism, just to name two contemporary scientific orthodoxies.[43] From a canonical-pneumatological perspective, however, I suggest that the creation narratives not only contain key insights that would complement and even enrich the (rather anemic) theological component of Clayton's emergence metaphysic as presented in *Mind and Emergence,* but also that they make sense best according to the teleological and eschatological theological framework being developed in this book. By "canonical-pneumatological," I am referring to the broader biblical witness and its thematic contributions to a Christian understanding of the Holy Spirit.[44]

Having made this claim, however, I would also insist that there is a twofold basis within the creation narratives that justifies such a pneumatological interpretation. First, the Priestly account of the *ruach Elohim* ("breath," "wind," even "storm of God") that "swept over the face of the waters" (Gen. 1:2)[45] continues with the breath *(nephesh)* given to *all*

43. Hence a literary-theological interpretation of Gen. 1–2 would emphasize its contrasts with other ancient Near Eastern cosmogonies, the biblical account being less, if not completely, nonpolitical, noncultic, and nonmythological. For developed arguments, see Nahum M. Sarna, *Understanding Genesis: The Heritage of Biblical Israel* (1966; New York: Schocken Books, 1970), especially chapter 1; Henri Blocher, *In the Beginning: The Opening Chapters of Genesis,* trans. David G. Preston (Leicester, UK, and Downers Grove, IL: InterVarsity, 1984); Susan Niditch, *Chaos to Cosmos: Studies in Biblical Patterns of Creation,* Scholars Press Studies in the Humanities 6 (Chico, CA: Scholars, 1985); and Bruce K. Waltke, with Cathi J. Fredricks, *Genesis: A Commentary* (Grand Rapids: Zondervan, 2001), pp. 55-78.

44. Hence I see what I am doing in the rest of this chapter as providing, in dialogue with the sciences, a complementary reading of the Genesis narrative to that which Warren Austin Gage provides in terms of reading the creation narratives soteriologically according to the broad scope of the biblical canon; see Gage, *The Gospel of Genesis: Studies in Protology and Eschatology* (Winona Lake, IN: Carpenter Books, 1984).

45. "Swept over" has also been translated "hovering over" (NIV) or "moved upon" (KJV), and is from the Hebrew *merachephet 'al,* which means, literally, flutter, flap, or shake. More lit-

living creatures (1:30). The Yahwist account also adds that the Lord
breathed *(yiphach)* specifically into *ha'adam* "the breath [*nishmat*] of life"
(Gen. 2:7). I suggest that references to the wind and breath of God at the
beginning and end of the Priestly narrative — not to mention the further
specification in the Yahwist text — together serve as "bookends" of an account regarding divine creativity that not only allows but also solicits a
more specifically pneumatological understanding.[46] From this, second, a
canonical reading of the creation narrative justifies connecting the breath
given to all creatures in general and to *ha'adam* in particular with the
ruach Elohim especially in light of Qohelet's affirmation that "the dust returns to the earth as it was, and the spirit [*ruach*] returns to God who gave
it" (Eccles. 12:7). There is no need to read the divine *ruach* here as referring
to the third person of the Trinity since that would certainly be an anachro-
nistic imposition upon this text. At the same time, given the Christian testament witness to God as spirit (cf. John 4:24), a pneumatological rereading of Genesis 1–2 can proceed at least on this basis. I thus agree with Jay
McDaniel that creation can be understood to be "en-spirited by God."[47]
Not only does God create all things through Word — "Let there be . . ." —
by the Spirit, but all things are creations of God precisely because they
originate in the divine Word spoken and uttered by the *ruach Elohim*.[48]

But what about those who would reject readings of the creation as the
work of the divine breath? Gerhard von Rad claims that Genesis 1:2 and its

---

erally, *ruach Elohim . . . merachephet 'al* could read "the wind of God . . . shook. . . ." Yet the
word occurs elsewhere only in Deut. 32:11 to denote a bird brooding over its young, retaining
some of the connotations of the Syriac root, *rahep,* literally, to brood, incubate, shake, or protect; see Ludwig Koehler and Walter Baumgartner et al., *The Hebrew and Aramaic Lexicon of
the Old Testament,* trans. and ed. M. E. J. Richardson, 2 vols. (Leiden, Boston, and Cologne:
Brill, 2001), 2:1219-20. For this reason, I present a pneumatological-*canonical* perspective on
the creation narrative, since the warrant to see *ruach Elohim* as referring to the Spirit of God
comes not explicitly from the Priestly account but can be derived implicitly from the text if
read within the broader biblical framework. My thanks to Gary A. Long for pointing me to the
Syriac background.

46. For another attempt to read the creation narratives from a pneumatological vantage point, see D. Lyle Dabney, "The Nature of the Spirit: Creation as a Premonition of God,"
in *Starting with the Spirit: Task of Theology Today II,* ed. Gordon Preece and Stephen Pickard
(Adelaide: Australia Theological Forum and Openbook Publishers, 2001), pp. 83-110.

47. See Jay McDaniel, "'Where Is the Holy Spirit Anyway?' Response to a Sceptic Envi-
ronmentalist," *Ecumenical Review* 42, no. 2 (1990): 162-74.

48. See Wolfhart Pannenberg's discussion in "Cooperation of Son and Spirit in the
Work of Creation," in his *Systematic Theology,* vol. 2, trans. Geoffrey W. Bromiley (Grand
Rapids: Eerdmans, 1994), pp. 109-15.

reference to the divine breath stands on its own concerning God's activity over the chaotic elements, and that the Spirit "takes no more active part in creation."[49] In response, while verse 1 certainly introduces the entire creation narrative, it is equally certain that verse 2 also belongs to the activities of God on the first day.[50] But, further, from a canonical perspective, the psalmist also warrants a pneumatological reading of the creation story:

> By the word of the LORD the heavens were made,
>   and all their host by the breath of his mouth. (Ps. 33:6)

> When you hide your face, they [the animals] are dismayed;
>   when you take away their breath, they die
>   and return to their dust.
> When you send forth your spirit, they are created;
>   and you renew the face of the ground. (Ps. 104:29-30)

Again, of course, this pneumato-theological account should then be understood not primarily as a scientific treatise about the history of creation (notice the creation of light, day, and night and the appearance of terrestrial vegetation before the calling forth of the sun and moon, which certainly is at odds with the standard scientific account), but rather as a statement against polytheism, astrological practices, and the pantheistic worship of nature in its variations, all prevalent in the surrounding ancient Near Eastern cultures.[51] Note then the following movements of the Spirit vis-à-vis the creation, which I will present summarily rather than through a verse-by-verse exposition, and intersperse comments related to Clayton's hypothesis.

First, creation in all its complexity flows from *ruach Elohim* brooding

---

49. Von Rad continues, "The Old Testament nowhere knows of such a cosmological significance for the concept of the spirit of God"; Gerhard von Rad, *Genesis: A Commentary*, trans. John H. Marks, rev. ed. (Philadelphia: Westminster, 1972), pp. 49-50.

50. Umberto Cassuto, *A Commentary on the Book of Genesis, Part I: From Adam to Noah, Genesis I–VI8*, trans. Israel Abrahams (1961; reprint, Jerusalem: Magnes Press, Hebrew University, 1989), pp. 19-20, and Claus Westermann, *Genesis 1–11: A Commentary*, trans. John J. Scullion, S.J. (Minneapolis: Augsburg, 1984), pp. 94-97 and 102-10.

51. Thus, the Priestly writer's insistence on the creaturely status of the sun and even light itself reflects his concern with the ancient worship of the sun. Later biblical writers, however, would equate light with the divine itself; cf. 1 John 1:5; 1 Tim. 6:16; James 1:17; and Ps. 104:1-2, with Westermann, *Genesis 1–11*, p. 114.

over or moving upon the primeval watery chaos *(tohu wabhohu)*.[52] For good reason, then, the rabbis since at least the time of Philo have understood the spirit of God as "the element of creative fire, or the divine intellect that gives form to matter."[53] In this case, not only does the *ruach Elohim* restrain and reshape the primeval chaos, but this chaos is itself neither a messy something-or-other nor a literal void. Of course, some who affirm the doctrine of *creatio ex nihilo* would understand the void to be purely chaotic and, hence, indeterminate and in that sense indistinguishable from nothing.[54] Yet the Priestly author indicates that the *ruach Elohim* hovered not over pure nothing, but over the waters *(mayim)*.[55] On the one hand, then, some have understood the primeval chaos as "a state of maximal plenitude, in which all things are churning, boiling, but without the discrete unities and form that enable the stuff of this world to obey laws and enter into networks of relationship."[56] Others, however, suggest that this is to spin the *tohu wabhohu* too positively since current cosmological findings view the initial singularity state (at $t = 0$) as a matter-less chaotic vacuum (entropy near infinity) and the big bang explosion as a quantum fluctuation in this vacuum.[57] Taking both viewpoints together, I propose that

52. If verse 1 is understood as introductory to the entire narrative, then any speculation about a primeval fall of angels, etc., between the first two verses is just that: speculation read into the text rather than emergent from the text; see von Rad, *Genesis*, pp. 50-51.

53. Peter Ochs, "Genesis 1–2: Creation as Evolution," *Living Pulpit* 9, no. 2 (April-June 2000): 8-10, quote from 9. Cp. Max Pulver, "The Experience of the *Pneuma* in Philo," in *Spirit and Nature: Papers from the Eranos Yearbooks*, ed. Joseph Campbell, Bollingen Series 30.1, trans. Ralph Manheim (1954; reprint, Princeton: Princeton University Press, 1982), pp. 107-21, who discusses Philo's view of the *pneuma* as an intelligent cosmic principle.

54. For this view, see Robert Cummings Neville, *God the Creator: On the Transcendence and Presence of God* (Albany: SUNY Press, 1992). For a more traditional creation-out-of-nothing reading of Gen. 1, see Paul Copan and William Lane Craig, *Creation out of Nothing: A Biblical, Philosophical, and Scientific Exploration* (Grand Rapids: Baker Academic, 2004).

55. I agree with Westermann, *Genesis 1–11*, pp. 109-10, when he says that the debate between *creatio ex nihilo* and creation out of chaos cannot be settled from Gen. 1–2. The Priestly writer intended neither of these ideas that arose in Judaism much later when it wrestled with Greek thought during the intertestamental period.

56. See Ochs, "Genesis 1–2," p. 8; cf. Archie Lee Chi-Chung, "Creation Narratives and the Movement of the Spirit," in *Doing Theology with the Spirit's Movement in Asia*, ed. John C. England and Alan J. Torrance, ATESEA Occasional Papers 11 (Singapore: ATESEA, 1991), pp. 15-26, and for full-length theological argumentation, James E. Huchingson, *Pandemonium Tremendum: Chaos and Mystery in the Life of God* (Cleveland: Pilgrim Press, 2001), especially chapters 5–6.

57. These would be spontaneous disappearances of a pair of antiparticles, producing a

the link between *tohu wabhohu* and *mayim* is suggestive of both the chaos of disorder and randomness (the vacuum) and also the primordial plenitude (or *plenum*), arguably consistent with the modern scientific notion of chaos and its unpredictable and nonlinear movement from simple perturbations of potentialities and possibilities to complex outcomes.[58] The *ruach Elohim* is here shown to be both transcendent over and also implicated in the stirrings of the primeval chaos.[59]

From this, second, the working of the *ruach Elohim* proceeds to order or divide light from darkness, evening and morning, on the first day (vv. 4-5), and separate the upper and lower waters, and the waters and the dry land, on the second day (vv. 6-7). We therefore see the creation emerging pneumatologically from the primordial chaos through processes of division, distinction, differentiation, and particularization, beginning with the separation of light from darkness and continuing with the separating out of species of plants and types of animals, each in its own or after its own kind (1:11, 12, 21, 24, 25).[60] These primordial divisions have not only onto-

----

large amount of energy, which can form another pair of antiparticles, and so on. I am grateful to Sjoerd L. Bonting for (electronic) conversations helping me to formulate this point. For explication, see Bonting, *Chaos Theology: A Revised Creation Theology* (Ottawa: Novalis and St. Paul University Press; Mystic, CT: Twenty-Third Publications, 2002).

58. See Trinh Xuan Thuan, *Chaos and Harmony: Perspectives on Scientific Revolutions of the Twentieth Century*, trans. Alex Reisinger (Oxford: Oxford University Press, 2001), chapter 3 on chaos. I say "consistent with" so as not to claim too much regarding any alleged harmonization between Gen. 1 and contemporary science; I am asserting only that there is no contradiction between what the ancient author wrote and present understandings in the science of chaos.

59. Besides Bonting, others who also argue that Gen. 1:2 supports a creation out of chaos instead of the traditional *creatio ex nihilo* include Bernhard Anderson, *Creation versus Chaos: The Reinterpretation of Mythical Symbolism in the Bible* (New York: Association Press, 1967); Jon D. Levenson, *Creation and the Persistence of Evil: The Jewish Drama of Divine Omnipotence* (New York: Harper and Row, 1987); Robert K. Gnuse, *The Old Testament and Process Theology* (St. Louis: Chalice Press, 2000), especially chapter 8; and Catherine Keller, *Face of the Deep: A Theology of Becoming* (New York: Routledge, 2003). Each of these authors, however, understands the primordial chaos differently. From a scientific perspective, my own view most closely approximates Bonting's, even if this should not be understood to signal Bonting's agreement with my pneumatological reading of Gen. 1.

60. Leon R. Kass, "Evolution and the Bible: Genesis 1 Revisited," *Commentary* 86 (1988): 29-39. For more on pneumatology and the particularity of created things, see George Hendry, *Theology of Nature* (Philadelphia: Westminster, 1980), pp. 169-70, and Colin Gunton, *The One, the Three, and the Many: God, Creation, and the Culture of Modernity* (Cambridge: Cambridge University Press, 1993), pp. 180-209.

logical significance, but also epistemological and linguistic implications, thus providing for the possibility of thought (the Logos) and of language (the naming of things and the animals; cf. Gen. 2:19).[61] At this point, we want to stop short of saying that the processes of differentiation in the Priestly narrative are equivalent to Clayton's hierarchical, temporal, and emergent pluralism theses; rather, better to suggest that the ancient biblical witness is not incompatible with such a hypothesis, provided that the order of "emergent" levels in the biblical narrative is not taken chronologically as referring to natural history.

Before moving on, it is important to note that in Clayton's emergence hypothesis, the earlier stages of cosmic evolution — for example, chemistry and physics, especially — reflect not the intentional and purposive character of God's intervention but rather the autonomic aspect of God's sustaining the world. Is this aspect of the emergence theory compatible with a pneumatological theology of creation derived from the Priestly narrative? At least two options are available in response. *Either* we say that emergence is compatible with the Spirit's working not personally in the creative process but "impersonally" in empowering the creativity of the creaturely responses to the divine "letting be"; or, if we are unhappy about depersonalizing the Spirit's creative work in chemical and cosmic evolution, we push the analogy between theological and empirical approaches and say that the Priestly "faith perspective" allows us to see divine intentionality unfolding in the creaturely domain on the one hand even as the scientific and "naturalistic perspective" allows us only to identify the efficient and material causal trajectories of emergent processes on the other. The former would in effect be a metaphysical claim about the modality of the Spirit's "working" in natural history, while the latter only allows for an analogy between the two "languages" of science and faith so long as the "faith perspective" is not taken literally. Either response addresses Clayton's concern so long as we assume not a literal (read: historical-scientific) correlation between the seven days of creation and the evolution of the world, but a literary-theological

61. This point is made by Westermann, *Genesis 1–11*, p. 123, following Franz Delitzsch. See also Alexei V. Nesteruk, "Design in the Universe and the Logos of Creation: Patristic Synthesis and Modern Cosmology," in *Design and Disorder: Perspectives from Science and Theology,* ed. Niels Henrik Gregersen and Ulf Görman (London and New York: T. & T. Clark, 2002), pp. 171-202, especially 198: "all things are differentiated in creation and at the same time the principle of their unity is that they are differentiated. In particular, it provides a common principle for the unity of intelligible and sensible creation."

reading of the Priestly narrative somewhat like the one I am providing here.[62]

This leads, thirdly, to our observation regarding the interactivity and cocreativity between the divine and the creation.[63] There are not only the commandment breathed out by and from God and the responsive performance of the created order throughout the creation narrative, but at a few points God even seems to allow the creation to take the initiative. So, while in each case God "lets be" or allows the creation to organize and produce, not in all cases is the "let there be . . ." followed by the statement that God then acted. Thus God actively makes the firmament and separates the waters (1:6); God makes the great lights and sets them in the skies (1:16-17); God creates the great sea monsters and the birds of the sky (1:21); and God makes the animals on the ground (1:25). But in some cases God creates and makes by saying (emphases mine): "Let the earth *put forth* vegetation: plants *yielding* seed, and fruit trees . . . that *bear* fruit" (1:11); "Let the waters *bring forth* swarms of living creatures" (1:20); and "Let the earth *bring forth* living creatures of every kind" (1:24). In the first and third cases (but not the second), God's command is followed by an "And it was so," before indicating God's response and activity. Further, on the third day, the dry land is allowed to appear and God proceeds only then to call it Earth (1:9-10). Subsequently, the earth itself is said explicitly to bring forth vegetation (plants, fruits, and trees), and God responds evaluatively, seeing this to be good (1:11-12).

Hence the text emphasizes, on the one hand, God as reactive — seeing, naming, and responding to creation — and, on the other, creation's own

---

62. In doing so, however, we must not bifurcate theology and science as if they were completely disparate arenas. The languages are distinct, but their references *may* overlap and it requires patient translation to determine if indeed such overlap occurs. And the problem is not only on the theological side, but also on the scientific: while there is general agreement about the general shape of the theory of evolution, for example, evolutionary studies are filled with debates among scientists about many of the particulars. So, any theology in dialogue with science works best when neutral with regard to which particular theory is finally decided to provide a better scientific explanation of how things come to be. Here, I follow Michael Heller, *Creative Tension: Essays on Science and Religion* (Philadelphia and London: Templeton Foundation Press, 2003); in his very helpful chapter 2, "On Theological Interpretations of Physical Creation Theories" (especially pp. 13-15), he suggests that this route is better than to univocally equate a theological idea with a specific scientific theory.

63. Here, I have been greatly helped by Michael Welker, "What Is Creation? Rereading Genesis 1 and 2," *Theology Today* 48 (1991): 56-71; and Welker, *Creation and Reality*, trans. John F. Hoffmeyer (Minneapolis: Fortress, 1999).

environmental activity and agency in bringing forth and (re)producing various heterogeneous forms of life processes. The Creator-creature distinction certainly should not be blurred — that is the main point of the creation account. At the same time, it is also the case that God creates by calling forth the orders of creation as cocreators and enabling the various levels of creation, to use Clayton's language, to participate in the processes of production and reproduction. That the narrative indicates some domains to be more active and others more passive in the creative process may correlate with the observation in emergence theory that there is no monolithic law of causality operative throughout the various levels of creation. Some would suggest that in this reading the debate over evolution shifts to a different plane since the created order may be considered not only to be fully gifted with evolutionary capacities from the beginning,[64] but also to be equipped to make whatever adjustments are needed along the way. While this would reflect the unfathomable creativity and resourcefulness of the divine wisdom, it would also be open to the charge of deism — unless (as I suggest here) creation's work is set within a robust pneumatological framework that preserves the ongoing creative activity of God *(creatio continua)*. The pneumatological hypothesis I am proposing is that the processes of separation, differentiation, division, and distinction seen in the creation narrative reflect the character of *ruach Elohim* clearly articulated elsewhere in Scripture as the dynamic, particularizing, relational, and life-giving presence and activity of the Spirit of God.[65]

Even as Clayton acknowledges that the emergence of mind provides the kind of data for strong emergence lacking in physical, chemical, and biological processes, so also, I contend, the creation of living creatures and *ha'adam* on days five and six provides insights into a more robust pneumatological theology of creation consonant with emergence theory than that which is described about the previous days. For starters, the biblical narrative acknowledges the dependence and interconnectedness between the human spirit and its material substrate in a way that is consistent with the emergent monist thesis. In the Jahwist account (2:7), *ha'adam* is said explicitly to be formed out of and thereby emergent from the dust

64. E.g., Howard Van Til, "The Fully Gifted Creation ('Theistic Evolution')," in *Three Views on Creation and Evolution*, ed. J. P. Moreland and John Mark Reynolds (Grand Rapids: Zondervan, 1999), pp. 159-218.

65. These categories are not, of course, entirely absent from the creation narrative. I develop the biblical background in *Spirit-Word-Community: Theological Hermeneutics in Trinitarian Perspective* (Aldershot, UK, and Burlington, VT: Ashgate, 2002), chapter 1.

of the ground.[66] *Ha'adam*, however, becomes a living being only with the breath of the Lord. This is certainly consistent with the rest of the biblical witness (e.g., Job 34:14-15; Eccles. 12:7; Ps. 104:28-29; Ezek. 37:1-14; Luke 23:46; Rom. 8:11 and 18-23). A canonical hermeneutic enables a combined reading of the Priestly and Jahwist creation accounts that in turn sustains a robust pneumatological theology with regard to the creation of human beings, but one that does not minimize the physical and embodied aspect of what it means to be human. That other creatures are also said to have the breath of life (1:30), but yet not of the same order as *ha'adam*, is also suggestive of the fact that there are increasingly complex levels of the emergence of spirit within the biological domain, each interacting with its environments in various ways.

Further, "enspirited" creatures are empowered with lesser or greater capacity to act as causal agents. This is most clear in the case of *ha'adam*, who is commanded to take responsibility for the creation and is hence considered to be under personal and purposive obligation. Further, that the fish of the sea and the birds of the air are also blessed and commanded to be fruitful and multiply (1:22) points to a certain impersonal yet real capacity they possess to respond to the divine mandate.[67] In this sense, living creatures in general and human beings in particular represent the unfinished dimension of the creation, with the potential to fulfill creation's reason for being, but also with the potential, given the greater dimension of freedom humans are endowed with, to perhaps sabotage the divine intentions. It is noteworthy that the phrase "And it was so" does not follow the

66. So Claus Westermann's conclusion — "The person as a living being is to be understood as a whole and any idea that one is made up of body and soul is ruled out" (*Genesis 1–11*, p. 207) — effectively undercuts the dominant dualistic reading of the tradition that defines human nature in terms of material bodies plus eternal souls. I further develop the details of this philosophical anthropology elsewhere; see Yong, "*Pneuma* and *Pratityasamutpada*: Neuropsychology, the Christian-Buddhist Dialogue and the Human Person," *Zygon* 40, no. 1 (2005): 143-65.

67. I suggest, building on the observation of Lawson Stone — e.g., see Lawson G. Stone, "The Soul: Possession, Part, or Person? The Genesis of Human Nature in Genesis 2:7," in *What about the Soul? Neuroscience and Christian Anthropology*, ed. Joel B. Green (Nashville: Abingdon, 2004), pp. 47-61, especially 51-52 — that the fish and the birds are also addressable by God because they also have the breath of life in them (1:30). This does not, however, turn animals into moral creatures, which is what distinguishes *Homo sapiens* from their closest cousins, which has an impact on how we are to understand the nature of evil; I say more about this, especially the issue of what some call "natural evil," in the last section of the next chapter.

creation of *ha'adam* as it does other acts of creation (vv. 7, 9, 11, 15, 24, and 30). While this may dovetail with Clayton's rejection of the causal closure of the world, at least for the prehominid levels of emergent realities, it certainly implies the open-endedness rather than definiteness of the human path or way of being.[68] This ambiguous nature of what it means to be human may be the reason why God does not specifically see and immediately pronounce *ha'adam* as good, as God had done with the work of days three through six.[69] The later narrative of the "fall" (Gen. 3) reflects human freedom exercised *against*, rather than in harmony with, the nature of things, thereby breaking the relationships among human beings with God, creation, and each other.

Finally, *ha'adam* is created as a relational creature, representing the divine image and likeness. Of course, the divine relationality in the creation narratives derives not from the allegedly proto-Trinitarian "Let *us* make . . ." (1:26) but from the God-world and God-humankind relationships. More specifically, the divine image is revealed in the creation of *ha'adam* as male and female. Here, the testimony of the later biblical traditions that the Spirit makes present the divine love within human hearts (Rom. 5:5) and replicates the fellowship of the triune God amidst the people of God (2 Cor. 13:13) fills out the pneumatological content of *ha'adam* given the breath of life to embrace each other as well as the Creator. And of course, human relationality does not stop with God and human beings. Rather, as a close reading of 1:26b-30 reveals, the sexual differentiation of *ha'adam* points both to interpersonal sociality and to intercreaturely relationality. *Ha'adam* as male and female are told not only to multiply and fill the earth, but also to subdue and care for the created order.[70] This clear relationship among human beings, the animals, and the earth itself, not to mention the formation of *ha'adam* from the dust of the ground, reflects the symbiotic and ecological character of what it means to be hu-

---

68. See Robert Sacks, "The Lion and the Ass: A Commentary on the Book of Genesis (Chapters 1–10)," *Interpretation: A Journal of Political Philosophy* 8, nos. 2-3 (1980): 29-101, especially 38-39.

69. See Leo Strauss, "On the Interpretation of Genesis," *L'Homme* 21, no. 1 (1981): 5-20, especially 18-19.

70. This point is clearly argued by Welker, *Creation and Reality,* pp. 64-69. See also John McIntyre, *The Shape of Pneumatology: Studies in the Doctrine of the Holy Spirit* (Edinburgh: T. & T. Clark, 1997), pp. 190-93, for the thesis that "The Holy Spirit is God the Creator himself setting us in a right and responsible relation to the animal and natural order" (quote from p. 93).

man. In this reportrayal of the doctrine of creation, the interdependence of the physical, environmental, biological, mental, and (even) spiritual realms of creation can be seen as suggestive of the hierarchically and pluralistically ordered yet complexly interconnected vision of the world enunciated in emergence theory that is open, in Clayton's terms, to transcendence. A pneumatological reading of the creation narratives is thus consistent with contemporary perspectives, discussed in chapter 3, that go beyond traditional (Platonist and, especially, Cartesian) dualist definitions of humans as "embodied souls" toward ontological, holistic understandings of human beings as emergent, interpersonal, interrelational, and cosmologically and environmentally situated creatures.[71]

The Spirit of Evolutionary Emergence and the Eschaton: A Teleological Account

This final section of this chapter is devoted to accomplishing two objectives related to the methodological and theological theses of this volume: to specify how a pneumatological theology of creation further justifies a pluralistic and interdisciplinary scientific research program, precisely what is called for in Clayton's emergence hypothesis, and to more explicitly identify how the preceding pneumatological reading of the creation narratives contributes toward the formulation of a more robust theology of evolutionary emergence. Moving in reverse order, I deal with the latter theological issue first.

I have already noted Clayton's reticence to say too much about theology given his desire to make as strong a philosophical argument as possible to the scientific community. As a theologian speaking first and foremost to other theologians interested in engaging the sciences, however, I am also concerned that Clayton's theory pass muster from a biblical and theological point of view. Hence I propose that the pneumatological theology of creation presented here contributes to emergence theory at three levels.

---

71. E.g., Joel B. Green, "'Bodies — That Is, Human Lives': A Re-examination of Human Nature in the Bible," in *Whatever Happened to the Soul? Scientific and Theological Portraits of Human Nature,* ed. Warren S. Brown, Nancey Murphy, and H. Newton Malony (Minneapolis: Fortress, 1998), pp. 149-73, and Green, "What Does It Mean to Be Human? Another Chapter in the Ongoing Interaction of Science and Scripture," in *From Cells to Souls — and Beyond: Changing Portraits of Human Nature,* ed. Malcolm Jeeves (Grand Rapids and Cambridge: Eerdmans, 2004), pp. 179-98.

First, it brings philosophical theory and biblical text together in mutually beneficial ways: on the one hand, the Scriptures are illuminated against the backdrop of the emergentist hypothesis; on the other hand, a specific instantiation of an abstract theory is provided by way of an analogical reading of the ancient creation narratives. Second, the much richer detail of a pneumatological theology of creation can supplement and in that sense fill out the theological content of Clayton's emergence metaphysics. While this may be risky within the broader theology and science dialogue (see below), it is nevertheless true that the theologians in the conversation need to find ways of saying more theologically without undermining the discussion with the scientists. I trust that the merits of a pneumatological perspective for this interchange are clear.

Most importantly, and thirdly, I believe that a pneumatological approach provides some relief to the strain imposed by the acknowledged theological dualism in Clayton's theory of emergence. Recall that Clayton was led to this position in order to avoid an immanentist construal of God as finally dependent on the world similar to how human consciousness is dependent on its material substrate. From the angle of the *ruach Elohim* hovering *over* or moving *upon* the primordial chaos, this transcendental aspect of divine presence and activity is certainly justified. On the other hand, from the angle of the breath of life given to and operative *in* creatures and *ha'adam*, the *ruach Elohim* is also present and at work from within the creaturely domain. A pneumatologically informed metaphysic, in other words, requires us to hold the immanent and transcendent aspects of divine presence and activity together, regardless of how tempted we are to privilege one over the other. This way forward, I suggest, enables the theistic dimension of Clayton's metaphysic to fit more coherently within his hypothesis since the final conceptualization requires not a one-sided theological dualism, but rather opens up to a theological *nondualism* whereby God is neither merely immanent nor merely transcendent on the one hand, and neither merely emergent nor merely purposive and personal on the other.[72]

72. At one point, I found curious Clayton's suggestion that he has explored a "view of the God-world relation that radicalizes the immanence of God" (*Mind and Emergence,* p. 187). I wondered if he did not mean "transcendence" of God since I did not see where he had proposed a radical account of divine immanence in his book. Elsewhere, Clayton has developed a panentheistic theology the details of which have been left out of *Mind and Emergence,* no doubt given his focused attempt to convince scientists of the emergence hypothesis. Whether or not one agrees with a panentheistic construal of the God-world rela-

I have argued so far, especially in chapters 3–4 above, that divine action may be fruitfully reconceived in pneumato-eschatological terms, and that the pentecostal experience of the Spirit provides confirmation that this is vouchsafed to us from God's future and draws us into the coming kingdom. In light of the gains made in this chapter, then, I wish to programmatically sketch a pneumatological theology of divine action as occurring proleptically across the scope of the natural history of the world. I propose that there are four stages of what might be called special divine action — stretching across what the theological tradition has called the work of creation and redemption — all of which await the hoped-for consummation God intends to bring about, albeit in different respects.

1. Primordial creation. The first stage might be understood in terms of the *ruach Elohim* hovering over the face of creation and bringing order out of chaos. Told from the standpoint of the cosmological and natural sciences, as summarized in the standard account at the beginning of this chapter, it is arguable that the gaps of the narrative will be increasingly filled. Seen from the eyes of faith, however — from the perspective of the eschatological purposes of God — each disciplinary perspective represents a different set of tongues that opens up and clarifies the creative works of God in the history of the cosmos. Eschatologically put, it is the work of the Spirit to remain "hidden" amidst the natural processes of the world, all the while immanently shaping the evolutionary unfolding of the material world according to the final intentions of God. The primordial creation thus proleptically anticipates the new creation of the heavens and the earth.

2. Emergence of life. The second stage could be seen in the *ruach Elohim*'s bringing forth increasing complexity in sentient organisms, the giving of the breath of life, and the emergence of living creatures, culminating (so far) with humankind. As a theologian, I suggest the following three summary provisional claims in response to the standard account detailed above: (1) Whatever science finally uncovers about the origins of life and the evolutionary history leading up to *Homo sa-*

---

tionship, this enables recognition of God's responsiveness and relatedness to the world. On Clayton's panentheism, see Clayton, *The Problem of God in Modern Thought* (Grand Rapids: Eerdmans, 2002), and Philip Clayton and Arthur Peacocke, eds., *In Whom We Live and Move and Have Our Being: Panentheistic Reflections on God's Presence in a Scientific World* (Grand Rapids: Eerdmans, 2004).

piens should not be incompatible with the pneumatological theology of divine action proposed here since the latter relies on a teleological rather than efficient mode of causality. (2) Precisely because this is a pneumatological explication of divine action, it is a theological rather than scientific perspective; hence it presumes eyes of faith shaped by the broader narrative of God as creator, redeemer, and perfecter of the world. (3) From an eschatological perspective, a finely tuned universe that anticipated human life, also known as the Anthropic Principle, can be understood as a cosmic type of the proleptic action of God so that the transition from complexity to life and the various processes of evolutionary convergence are signs foreshadowing in general the redemptive transformation of living creatures in the age to come.[73] The emergence of life thus proleptically portends the resurrection of living, conscious, and embodied beings in the eschaton.[74]

73. Some might wonder: What about the fall of humanity and original human sin vis-à-vis an evolving creation? I have given a preliminary response to this issue elsewhere — e.g., *Theology and Down Syndrome: Reimagining Disability in Late Modernity* (Waco, TX: Baylor University Press, 2007), pp. 162-65 — but will add here that the fall of the "first Adam" can be understood only eschatologically in light of the "second Adam." In that case, the historicity of the first Adam is less the issue than is the teleological vision of the kingdom that structures the pneumatological imagination. Hence, final salvation is not a restoration to a primordial garden, but the garden and the emergence of *ha'adam* are but a proleptic anticipation of what God's creative and redemptive purposes are designed to accomplish. I sketch this minimalist account not over and against, but alongside of and intended as complementary to, other proposals responding to this issue of original sin and the Fall in an evolutionary world. See, e.g., Jerry D. Korsmeyer, *Evolution and Eden: Balancing Original Sin and Contemporary Science* (New York and Mahwah, NJ: Paulist, 1998); Patricia A. Williams, *Doing without Adam and Eve: Sociobiology and Original Sin* (Minneapolis: Augsburg, 2001); and Daryl P. Domning, *Original Selfishness: Original Sin and Evil in the Light of Evolution* (Burlington, VT, and Aldershot, UK: Ashgate, 2006), all of whom advocate reconceiving the doctrine of original sin in a way that locates the "fall" in the evolutionary consequences of the instincts of sentient creatures toward self-preservation and reproduction.

74. Thus does the renowned Christian evolutionary paleontologist Simon Conway Morris suggest a positive answer to the provocative question in the title of his essay "Does Biology Have an Eschatology, and If So Does It Have Cosmological Implications?" in *The Far-Future Universe: Eschatology from a Cosmic Perspective,* ed. George F. R. Ellis (Philadelphia and London: Templeton Foundation Press, 2002), pp. 158-74. One of my students, Bradford McCall, is working on a dissertation precisely on this topic, with the tentative title "God in an Evolutionary World: Toward a Teleological Model of Divine Action in the Science and Theology Dialogue," in which he attempts to show how teleological notions in the evolutionary history of biology can be understood in terms of the pneumatological eschatology that has been argued here.

3. Election of and covenant with Israel. The history of Israel in all its complexity can be told from two perspectives. One, utilizing the various historiographical methods, involves both insider (emic) and outsider (etic) perspectives on the story of this people. This set of narratives has been and can be tremendously illuminating about ancient Israel, and we should not underestimate its methodological power. The other, however, understands the narrative of ancient Israel teleologically, in faith, as proleptically signifying and even initiating the next steps of God's covenantal redemption of humanity and the world that had been created. God's special election of one was for the explicit purpose that "all the families of the earth shall be blessed" (Gen. 12:3). The miracles of the Red Sea, of the manna from heaven, of the prophetic works and announcements regarding the apocalyptic Day of Yahweh, etc., therefore cannot be understood apart from the larger story of God's pneumatologically immanent actions within the world to redeem the whole of creation (including the lion and the lamb, etc.).[75] The election of and covenant with Israel thus proleptically initiate the social, communal, and covenantal character of the new creation.

4. The incarnational and pentecostal events. I treat these two events together because they belong together inasmuch as it is the risen Christ who pours out the Spirit to the world (Acts 2:33). This fourth stage thus intensifies the era of redemption, including both the Holy Spirit's activity in the incarnation, death, and resurrection of the Son of God and then the Son's outpouring of the Spirit on all flesh (Acts 2:17-21). If the election of Israel resulted in the emergence of a social and communal God-consciousness in the human race, then the election of Jesus as the Christ and the gift of the Holy Spirit enabled the emergence of God-consciousness in individual human hearts and minds. These are thus the days between the times, rife with the signs of the kingdom amidst the people of God, yet still anticipating the fullness of the kingdom to be ushered in. They are the days after the resurrection of Jesus but before the final resurrection. In the eschatological scheme of things, the God who comes to us from the future will judge, redeem,

---

75. I speak here of divine immanence following John R. Levison, *Filled with the Spirit* (Grand Rapids: Eerdmans, 2009), who discusses the "holy spirit" (uncapitalized) in ancient Israel as indistinguishable, by and large, from the human spirit. I am not presuming, however, that Levison would agree with the rest of my pneumatological considerations.

and transform the past, and this happens in part now in and through the ministry of the Spirit-empowered church. In this sense, the future of creation will yet be *ex vetere* (from the old).[76] The incarnation and Pentecost thus proleptically not only anticipate the redemption of creation, living creatures, and covenantal communities, but also point toward the communion that all things will share with the Father, through the Son, and in the Holy Spirit, even as the world itself will become an inhabitation of the triune God.[77]

To be sure, the pneumatological theology of divine action outlined in the preceding is no more than suggestive; but perhaps this also can serve as a promissory note or down payment anticipating further elaboration on a teleological reading of natural and human history. If the second law of thermodynamics insists that only open or dissipative systems can generate order, then the resurrection suggests that the world is open to God's future, even as the church may be the clearest proleptic medium announcing and enacting at least the general details of the coming kingdom. In the meanwhile, let us recall that the Divine Action Project sought a noninterventionist yet objective account of special divine action. My claim is that within a regularist account of natural laws, and abstaining from insisting that these special divine activities involve any insertion of energy into the world, no scientific identification of divine intervention in the world is required. Yet each of these stages or events is objectively accountable for, to some degree or other, utilizing various scientific and historiographical tools.

But in the end, the specialness of these divine activities can be affirmed only eschatologically and in faith: apart from a broader teleological framework within which we can understand how these events are significant, we would not even bother to claim that God or the Spirit had acted or is acting in them. When framed eschatologically and teleologically, however, these can be understood as four special activities of God's Spirit — in the creation of the world, in the emergence of life and complexity, in

76. Some of the ideas in this paragraph derive from George L. Murphy, "Hints from Science for Eschatology — and Vice Versa," in *The Last Things: Biblical and Theological Perspectives on Eschatology,* ed. Carl E. Braaten and Robert W. Jenson (Grand Rapids: Eerdmans, 2002), pp. 146-68.

77. As beautifully argued by Frank D. Macchia, *Justified in the Spirit: Creation, Redemption, and the Triune God,* Pentecostal Manifestos 2 (Grand Rapids and Cambridge: Eerdmans, 2010).

the history of Israel, and in the Christ event (that includes the returning of the Spirit to the world at Pentecost) — that proleptically and generally herald the salvific plans of God that will be finally accomplished in the age to come. Each subsequent stage provides new perspective on the prior stages, even as, for Christians, the apostolic witness sheds new light on the Hebrew Bible (called the Old Testament). Put in terms of emergence theory, each divine act unpredictably ushers in something novel in the world, supervenes upon the former act/s, and fulfills and completes them in light of the eschatological intentions of God. If Morowitz is right to say that "Evolution is the overall process, while emergence characterizes the punctuations,"[78] then on my eschatological account, the kingdom is the goal and these four stages of special divine action are the major anticipatory events. Put in pentecostal terms, salvation is the intended goal for humankind, while conversion, regeneration, sanctification, Spirit-baptism, etc., are the intensifying experiences toward that end.[79]

Speaking in more formal theological terms, given the patristic principle of *opera Trinitatis ad extra sunt indivisa* (the economic works of the Trinity are undivided), both the creative and redemptive actions of God participate in the perfecting (eschatological) work of the triune God. This is because all the works of God are directed toward an eschatological realization. Hence the works of the Spirit in creation (the first two stages of the ordering of cosmic history, and of the emergence of complexity and life) and in redemption (in the next two stages of Israel's calling, and the incarnation and Pentecost events) are weaker and stronger instantiations, respectively, of the proleptic principle. Each of these special divine activities anticipates the eschatological intentions of God from various periods of (cosmic, natural, and human) history and hence gradually unveils the final purposes of God. With the life, death, and resurrection of Christ and with the outpouring of the Holy Spirit on the world, however, the final age has begun to arrive. Hence the anointed Messiah and the ecclesial fellowship of the Spirit both provide illuminating lenses through which to understand more explicitly how the creative works of God can now be understood in light of the coming kingdom.[80]

78. Morowitz, *The Emergence of Everything*, p. 37.

79. I argue this in my work *The Spirit Poured Out on All Flesh: Pentecostalism and the Possibility of Global Theology* (Grand Rapids: Baker Academic, 2005), chapter 2.

80. This would be, as Keith Ward suggests, to measure divine action as generating value rather than according to the terms of efficient or material causation; see Keith Ward, "Divine Action in an Emergent Cosmos," in *Scientific Perspectives on Divine Action: Twenty Years*

Before we conclude this chapter, however, we must return to the methodological issue, which has to do with Clayton's concern that too much theological discourse will wreck the theory of emergence in terms of its dependence upon scientific data and its intention to more coherently explain and in that sense empower scientific inquiry. This is an important matter that needs to be attended to. At one level, if we assume the category of "spirit" to be metaphysically opposed to "matter" (as do most natural scientists, but not so many social scientists), then it may be difficult to advance the theology and science conversation by injecting a dose of pneumatological theology. On the other hand, if we agree that ontologically distinct and ontologically plural realities do not necessarily require a dualistic metaphysic — witness Clayton's emergent monism thesis — then there is no a priori reason why the inclusion of a nuanced pneumatological theology of creation need sabotage the theology and science dialogue. On the contrary, in conclusion here, I suggest three ways in which a pneumatological perspective actually further legitimates what Clayton wishes to do, namely, to undergird a sufficiently robust research program that would enhance scientific inquiry.

First, recall that the creation narrative read in pneumatological perspective sees the *ruach Elohim* as both presiding over and empowering from within the processes of differentiation, separation, and particularization that constitute the days of creation. I have already suggested (chapter 2) that this denotes the differentiation-in-unity of Spirit. In the biblical narrative, we find this feature of the Spirit even more emphatically pronounced, as in the multiplicity of tongues somehow harmoniously giving glory to God and as in the plurality of members each playing a distinctive and indispensable role in the edifying of the one body.[81] I suggest that, transposed into a metaphysical key, a pneumatological theology of creation further secures the ontological pluralism articulated in Clayton's theory of emergence. This provides theological legitimacy for the plurality

---

of *Challenge and Progress,* ed. Robert J. Russell, Nancey C. Murphy, and William R. Stoeger (Vatican City State: Vatican Observatory Publications; Berkeley, CA: Center for Theology and the Natural Sciences; and Notre Dame, IN: University of Notre Dame Press, 2008), pp. 285-98.

81. See Michael Welker's discussion of the Spirit as a multicontextual and polyphonic presence in his essay "The Spirit in Philosophical, Theological, and Interdisciplinary Perspectives," in Michael Welker, *The Work of the Spirit: Pneumatology and Pentecostalism* (Grand Rapids and Cambridge: Eerdmans, 2006), pp. 221-32, especially 228; cf. also Welker, *God the Spirit,* trans. John F. Hoffmeyer (Minneapolis: Fortress, 1994).

of disciplines in the sciences, even while it holds forth the complementarity principle (introduced in chapter 1) that anticipates the various disciplines that provide distinctive but essential perspectives on reality. From an epistemological vantage point, such multidisciplinarity would neither break down reductionistically (so that any one discipline could claim a final, total word) nor result in disciplinary isolation (because each discipline supposedly deals with methods and realities incommensurable with the others); rather the *ruach Elohim* that hovers over the waters and is also the breath of life brings about an inter- and transdisciplinary perspective directed toward the scientific quest for truth in the long run.[82]

Within this framework, then, science explores the creative activity of God utilizing various disciplinary tools and perspectives, guided by its methodological naturalism. Thus science is purposefully limited to descriptive claims about replicable inquiries presuming a causal sequence that can be observed in some sense. Science can therefore only propose testable hypotheses about

- the emergence of the cosmological constants from out of the big bang singularity;
- the emergence of biological life out of the chemical substratum; and
- the emergence of mental life (consciousness, morality, and spirituality) from out of the biological, etc.

Theology can go further, in faith, to assert divine activity at each of these emergent levels (and more) and in providentially sustaining the world and its creatures even within these levels. While the designs of the world can be understood in terms of their various functions at the scientific level, the final cause or ultimate telos of things, even the universe as a whole, can only be a theological matter.[83]

---

82. My reference to the "long run" is inspired by Charles Sanders Peirce's theory of truth; see Yong, "The Demise of Foundationalism and the Retention of Truth: What Evangelicals Can Learn from C. S. Peirce," *Christian Scholar's Review* 29, no. 3 (Spring 2000): 563-88.

83. Thus does Old Testament scholar John H. Walton, *The Lost World of Genesis One: Ancient Cosmology and the Origins Debate* (Downers Grove, IL: IVP Academic, 2009), argue that the Genesis narrative should be interpreted teleologically in terms of God's functional creation of a world that can serve as his temple or inhabitation, a reading that complements rather than rejects scientific explanations and resonates with my emergentist interpretation provided here. From a theological perspective, as John F. Haught, *Christianity and Science:*

Second, a pneumatological theology of creation would reaccentuate the biological and especially psychological and humanistic sciences that risk being neglected in the theology and science conversation, the agenda of which is often dictated by those engaged in the physical and natural sciences. Clayton does acknowledge that "theists have traditionally claimed that there are analogies between human persons, and in particular human minds, on the one hand, and God, understood as divine mind of Spirit, on the other."[84] Of course, this is in part the reason why the status of the psychosocial sciences has been perennially devalued by those who equate true science with the natural sciences. But only a dogmatic scientism would arbitrarily terminate this conversation and reject the possibility of the human sciences contributing to what truly counts as knowledge. Further, the fascinating strides made in the biological sciences in the last generation and the recognition and articulation of the "hard problem" of consciousness both also provide clues, I suggest, to the mystery of psyche and spirit in creation. Not surprisingly, the category of spirit cannot be exorcised from this conversation since it will often reappear under another name. As slippery as it is, of course, spirit needs to be "disciplined" from other perspectives. But this, as I see it, is precisely the task, at least in part, of the various social and humanistic sciences.

Last, I propose that spirit serves as a limit category that continually calls the scientific enterprise forward beyond itself. For science to fulfill its promise, it has to go where the trail of discovery leads. The fertility of spirit as a philosophical and even empirical category points to both the problem and the promise of a pneumatological contribution to the theology and science conversation. On the one side, the challenge is how to engage spirit conceptually and empirically since when something can mean so many things, it may end up meaning nothing. On the other side, the human spirit of curiosity and inquiry continues to respond to the wondrous spirit of creation. Philip Clayton's theory of emergence is one attempt to depict the openness of the world to its future. It will surely be revised going forward, even as it is always possible that as a paradigmatic theory, it will be undermined as a whole as a scientifically viable model in the future. That

---

Toward a Theology of Nature (Maryknoll, NY: Orbis, 2007), advocates, we should develop a "layered explanation" that preserves room for natural, personal, and teleological explanations; in the end, "As far as Christian theology is concerned, however, it is in no way contrary to scientific accounts of life's emergence to attribute the existence of life ultimately to the vitalizing power of the Holy Spirit" (pp. 142 and 151).

84. Clayton, *Mind and Emergence,* p. 183.

is, of course, always the risk in the theological adaptation of philosophical ideas or scientific theories. Still, I have always claimed that a pneumato-logical theology — in this book, of creation — is venturous, flexible, always "on quest,"[85] and thus would affirm this openness even while it enlists, continuously, the aid of the sciences and empowers scientists to explore the shifting edges of this ever-evolving world whatever they be and the frontiers of knowledge wherever they are. In this process, who knows if we might catch a whiff of the wind of God that blows where she wills?

85. My research has long been motivated by a "pneumatology of quest"; for my initial articulation of this idea, see *Spirit-Word-Community,* pp. 21-23 and passim.

6 A Spirit-Filled Creation?

Toward a Pneumatological Cosmology

But just how open is either Clayton's research paradigm or the pneumatologically inspired one being formulated in this book? Open enough for proposing in the theology and science conversation a consideration of a spirit-filled cosmos? Notice, I did not capitalize "spirit" in the last sentence, which suggests that I'm thinking more about other spirits, whatever these may be, than about the Holy Spirit. This is not an idle or merely abstract question since, for pentecostals, if not also for many, even most, Christians, the world is a complex "place," inhabited by innumerable spiritual powers and forces. Yet such a densely populated universe is incomprehensible to the naturalistic and materialistic mentality of modern science, which in most circles believes that the premodern beliefs in angels and demons — not to mention the Holy Spirit herself! — were exorcised by the Enlightenment.[1] Is the emergentist and evolutionary cosmology articulated in the preceding chapter capable of helping us to bridge this divide?

This chapter is dedicated to exploring the viability of an emergentist cosmology for rethinking the nature of spiritual realities. To date, most emergentist philosophies and theologies have been content to argue for the emergence of human minds (spirits) while recognizing in faith the ontological and primordial reality of divine mind (even the Holy Spirit). I am going out on a limb to propose a pneumatological or spirit-filled cosmology in dialogue with the philosophy and science of emergence. Our in-

---

1. See Robert Muchembled, *A History of the Devil: From the Middle Ages to the Present,* trans. Jean Birrell (Cambridge and Oxford: Polity Press, 2003), chapter 5.

quiry will proceed in four steps — the four sections of this chapter. We begin with an overview of pentecostal and charismatic views of the spiritual realm, in particular focusing on beliefs in angels and demons (fallen angels), and ancestor spirits. The next two sections will attempt to engage these matters scientifically in terms of extant empirical research in dialogue with the parapsychological sciences, and theoretically in terms of philosophical interpretation of and (some) biblical reflection on the data. Along the way we will need to confront criticisms by those in the theology and science dialogue about the wisdom of linking the pneumatological theology of science and creation proposed in this book with that of work in the anomalistic sciences, and then tentatively suggest next steps in this discussion in a way that respects the means and accomplishments of science on the one hand but does not bar the way of scientific inquiry on the other.[2] The concluding section will present a set of speculative hypotheses that can be understood to summarize an emergentist pentecostal cosmology, one that reconsiders the pluralistic nature of the spiritual dimensions of the world in the light of modern science rather than reiterating a premodern and prescientific worldview.

I cannot overemphasize, however, that our path of inquiry is fraught with both scientific and theological problems. I have decided to press through such a set of potential landmines, while being sure to register here the apprehensiveness with which we are proceeding. My major reason for persisting is that we have been swimming against the current all along in this first monograph devoted to the interface of pentecostalism and science, and thus should not but address this contentious issue since the belief in a spirit-filled cosmos is endemic to both pentecostal spirituality, at least as popularly conceived, and Christian life in general. Hence any claim that pentecostal perspectives might actually have something to contribute to the theology and science dialogue would be empty if we skirted this problematic set of topics altogether. To my knowledge, what I will be proposing in this chapter — an emergentist theology of spirit beings informed by scientific perspectives — is the first of its kind. My hope, however, is that in the process of this discussion, scientific perspectives can

2. Charles Peirce insisted that our prejudices often barred the way to ongoing inquiry; see my discussion of Peirce's fallibilism in my essay "The Demise of Foundationalism and the Retention of Truth: What Evangelicals Can Learn from C. S. Peirce," *Christian Scholar's Review* 29, no. 3 (Spring 2000): 563-88, and my book *Spirit-Word-Community: Theological Hermeneutics in Trinitarian Perspective* (Aldershot, UK, and Burlington, VT: Ashgate, 2002), especially chapter 6.

help exorcise the fluff of spirits that plague at least the naive pentecostal-charismatic imagination; but simultaneously, perhaps even here a pneumatological "assist" might help us get beyond a reductionistic, positivistic, and scientistic paradigm toward one in which the strong emergence of the spiritual dimensions of human experience is taken seriously enough to hold forth the promise of rigorous scientific investigation.

A Spirit-Filled World: Angels, Demons, and Spirits in the Pentecostal Imagination

In my first book, I presented in broad strokes the "spirit-filled" pentecostal imagination, one that includes not just the Holy Spirit but also angels, demons, and other spiritual beings and powers.[3] Therefore the following will do no more than survey pentecostal beliefs and practices vis-à-vis these presumed realities.

We begin with angels. Pentecostals around the world believe in angels not only because the Bible talks about them, but also because they claim to have been vigilant about showing hospitality to strangers, and "by doing that [they] have entertained angels" (Heb. 13:2) themselves. Some pentecostals also claim to have received help from angels, as promised in Scripture: "Are not all angels spirits in the divine service, sent to serve for the sake of those who are to inherit salvation?" (Heb. 1:14).[4] The various accounts of angels throughout the pentecostal canon within the canon, the book of Acts, lead pentecostals to expect angelic deliverances, guidance, comfort, and even justice (i.e., Acts 12:23, which says, "an angel of the Lord struck him [Herod] down, and he was eaten by worms and died"), as was recorded of the experiences of the earliest Christians. In short, pentecos-

---

3. See Yong, *Discerning the Spirit(s): A Pentecostal-Charismatic Contribution to Christian Theology of Religions* (Sheffield: Sheffield Academic Press, 2000), pp. 127-32, 234-55, 294-308, and passim.

4. From the inspirational genre, see James O. Russell and Georgia Smelser, *The Coal Miner Preacher: A Testimony of Healings, Miracles, Angels, and Prophecies* (Hazelwood, MO: Word Aflame Press, 1993), and Steven W. Brooks, *Working with Angels: Flowing with God in the Supernatural* (Shippensburg, PA: Destiny Image Publishers, 2007). Of course, pentecostals are not the only Christians, much less the only kinds of religious or nonreligious people, who believe in angels in general, and in guardian angels more specifically; enter "guardian angels" on the search line at Amazon.com and it will be apparent that this is a widespread belief.

tals expect angelic interventions today, as extensions of the grace of God in their lives.[5]

But alongside benevolent angels are malevolent spirits or demons. The satan or the devil is a real personal and spiritual being, and his demons unceasingly do his work of stealing, killing, and destroying (cf. John 10:10a and Heb. 2:14b).[6] Hence the world of demonic creatures is ultimately responsible for sickness, disease, misfortune, temptation, trials, suffering, failure, tragedy, sinful behaviors and consequences, and all that is opposed to the holiness, righteousness, and peace of God.[7] Demonic entities thus torment human beings, either by oppressing or by possessing them, although there is some debate among pentecostals about this matter, as there is about the extent of demonic powers over Christian believers.[8] Certainly across the global South, spirit possession is phenomenologically prevalent, either by the Holy Spirit or by other — lesser and demonic — spirits.[9]

Besides angels and demons, however, pentecostals of various stripes also believe in all kinds of intermediary, disincarnate spirit beings. Often these are spirits of recently dead or long-dead ancestors, separated from their bodies but still capable of interacting with, and often tormenting, their living descendants; this is particularly prevalent in regions of the global South among pentecostal groups whose indigenous worldviews include the spirits of deceased ancestors possibly interacting with the day-to-day lives of their descendants.[10] In traditional religions, such spirits need

5. A formal doctrinal overview can be found in Carolyn Denise Baker, "Created Spirit Beings: Angels," in *Systematic Theology*, ed. Stanley Horton, rev. ed. (Springfield, MO: Gospel Publishing House, 1995), pp. 179-94.

6. Pentecostals would be inclined to agree with much of the contemporary restatement of the traditional demonology by Stephen F. Noll, *Angels of Light, Powers of Darkness: Thinking Biblically about Angels, Satan, and Principalities* (Downers Grove, IL: InterVarsity, 1998). See also Peter Kreeft, *Angels and Demons: What Do We Really Know about Them?* (San Francisco: Ignatius, 1995).

7. Pentecostals would be very sympathetic with Gregory A. Boyd's *God at War: The Bible and Spiritual Conflict* and *Satan and the Problem of Evil: Constructing a Trinitarian Warfare Theodicy* (Downers Grove, IL: InterVarsity, 1997 and 2001, respectively), even if some might take issue with Boyd's advocacy of open theism.

8. See Opal L. Reddin, ed., *Power Encounter: A Pentecostal Perspective*, rev. ed. (Springfield, MO: Central Bible College Press, 1999).

9. Felicitas D. Goodman, *How about Demons? Possession and Exorcism in the Modern World* (Bloomington and Indianapolis: Indiana University Press, 1988), especially chapter 4, and passim.

10. As detailed, e.g., in Julie C. Ma, *When the Spirit Meets the Spirits: Pentecostal Ministry among the Kankana-ey Tribe in the Philippines*, Studies in the Intercultural History of

to be placated or appeased, so that their ongoing journey in the spirit world of the afterlife can proceed, and so that their living descendants will no longer be troubled. Pentecostals, however, recommend exorcism at least on two grounds: that demonic spirits have appeared in the form of deceased ancestors, even as angels of light (2 Cor. 11:14), and thus need to be expelled; and that the Bible prohibits mediumistic interactions with the dead (e.g., Lev. 19:31; 20:6; 20:27; Deut. 18:10-11; 1 Chron. 10:13), and therefore these alien intrusions should not be needlessly entertained.[11]

Exorcisms therefore are practiced across the pentecostal world. In most cases the ritual formula is simple: "in the name of Jesus," following the apostolic guidelines (Acts 16:18). However, local or regional variations color what ends up being a broad spectrum of pentecostal rituals of deliverance.[12] In some cases, sacramental objects may be utilized (as in Saint Paul's handkerchiefs; Acts 19:12), while in other cases, certain forms of prayer and fasting (following Mark 9:29 in the Textus Receptus) will be more normative. In all cases, however, pentecostals believe that the exor-

---

Christianity 118 (Frankfurt am Main: Peter Lang, 2000), chapter 4; Allan Anderson, *Zion and Pentecost: The Spirituality and Experience of Pentecostal and Zionist/Apostolic Churches in South Africa* (Pretoria: University of South Africa Press, 2000), chapter 6; and J. M. Heredero, S.J., *The Dead Rescue the Living: Spirit Possession in a Gujarati Christian Community* (Anand, India: Gujarat Sahitya Prakash, 2001).

11. Pentecostals are deeply informed by popular evangelical and fundamentalist literature on these matters, from the older works of Kurt Koch to the newer writings of apologists like Dave Hunt. A fairly evenhanded evangelical treatment with which many pentecostals would be sympathetic is David Burnett, *World of the Spirits: A Christian Perspective on Traditional and Folk Religions* (2000; reprint, Oxford: Monarch Books, 2005). A more sophisticated treatment linking the spirit-filled world with the paranormal and pentecostal-charismatic spirituality (at least as understood by most laypeople in the movement), although somewhat at odds with the overall trajectory of my argument here, is Marguerite Shuster, *Power, Pathology, Paradox: The Dynamics of Evil and Good* (Grand Rapids: Academie Books, 1987).

12. See, e.g., David Maxwell, *African Gifts of the Spirit: Pentecostalism and the Rise of a Zimbabwean Transnational Religious Movement* (Oxford: James Currey; Harare, Zimbabwe: Weaver Press; and Athens: Ohio University Press, 2006), chapter 4; Mechteld Jansen, "Deliver Us from Evil: Deliverance Prayers in Three African Christian Communities in Amsterdam," in *A Moving God: Immigrant Churches in the Netherlands,* ed. Mechteld Jansen and Hijme Stoffels, International Practical Theology 8 (Münster: LIT, 2006), pp. 197-218; and Opoku Onyinah, "Deliverance as a Way of Confronting Witchcraft in Contemporary Africa: Ghana as a Case Study," in *The Spirit in the World: Emerging Pentecostal Theologies in Global Context,* ed. Veli-Matti Kärkkäinen (Grand Rapids: Eerdmans, 2009), pp. 181-202. A sociologist's account of exorcism in the North American context is Michael W. Cuneo, *American Exorcism: Expelling Demons in the Land of Plenty* (New York: Doubleday, 2001), part III.

cism of evil spirits will result in health, well-being, and even prosperity and success. If the devil and his demons intend to afflict, oppress, and destroy, God has come to give life, and do so more abundantly (John 10:10b).

Last but certainly not least, brief mention must be made of the pentecostal understanding of spiritual warfare. At least two forms of this set of discursive practices can be identified. In the North American context, the notion of spiritual warfare includes, at least on occasion, elaborate understandings of how specific societal ills are demonically perpetrated. Thus, for example, there is the spirit of alcoholism, or the spirit of greed, or the spirit of sexual immorality (Hos. 4:12 and 5:4), etc.,[13] often linked to geographical locations — following the biblical references to the prince of Persia or the prince of Greece (Dan. 10:20) — under the control of such malevolent demonic entities. Spiritual warfare waged against such social ills must therefore engage the principalities and powers behind such phenomena, whatever else we might wish to do to transform society. On the other hand, across the global South, spiritual warfare practitioners often understand the demonic principalities and powers in terms of the forces that resist the evangelization of any region.[14] In these cases, spiritual warfare prayer undermines the grip that these demonic powers are thought to have over the lives of the unevangelized so that the message of the gospel can be effectively communicated and embraced.

At one level, the preceding pluralistic cosmology of the pentecostal imagination sits well with classical Christian beliefs about a spirit-filled world. In large part this is because the traditional Christian angelology (the doctrine of angels) and demonology (the doctrine of demons) were firmly wedded to the substance ontologies of nonmaterial entities developed by the ancient Greeks.[15] Hence the idea of disembodied spirits —

13. As depicted in Thomas D. Pratt, "The Need to Dialogue: A Review of the Debate on Signs, Wonders, Miracles and Spiritual Warfare in the Literature of the Third Wave Movement," *Pneuma* 13, no. 1 (1991): 7-32, especially 28-29 n. 152.

14. C. Peter Wagner and his many authored and edited books on the topic have led the way. See also Paul Alexander, *Signs and Wonders: Why Pentecostalism Is the World's Fastest Growing Faith* (San Francisco: Jossey-Bass, 2009), chapter 6. An ethnographic study is Virginia Garrard-Burnett, "Casting Out Demons in Almolonga: Spiritual Warfare and Economic Development in a Maya Town," in *Global Pentecostalism: Encounters with Other Religious Traditions,* ed. David Westerlund (London and New York: I. B. Taurus, 2009), pp. 209-25. Pentecostal influence on global evangelicalism can be seen in Chuck Lowe, *Territorial Spirits and World Evangelization* (1998; reprint, Ross-shire and Kent, UK: Mentor/OMF International, 2001).

15. An earlier survey cutting across various world religious traditions, even if in outdated

good and bad, angelic and demonic — has not been particularly problematic until modern times. While some have noted that the rejection of angels and demons because they are noncorporeal rather than material entities also requires the rejection of classical theism because of its emphasis on the transcendence of God, few classical theists today have spent much time thinking about either angelology or demonology. The primary options today seem to be: (1) accept naturalism and reject angels and demons; (2) accept theism but explain angels and demons using psychosocial (or other modern scientific) categories;[16] (3) accept theism but (in this case) ignore the whole question of angels and demons;[17] and (4) accept God, angels, and demons as supernatural entities, basically unrevised from the classical ontology. (1) leads to materialism; (2) is potentially reductionistic at the metaphysical level; (3) is theologically irresponsible; and (4) is premodern and uncritical.

How then do we rethink cosmology, if at all, not only in light of pentecostal spirituality and piety, but also because the explosive growth of Christianity across the global South is taking place largely among those with similar sensibilities?[18] While the rest of this chapter can be considered a preliminary response to this question, in the next few paragraphs I want to begin our reply in dialogue with a philosopher who seems to be one of the few pentecostal scholars or academics to have taken this question seriously.

Trained in the tradition of analytic philosophy, Phillip Wiebe is a phi-

---

demonological categories, is Paul Carus, *The History of the Devil and the Idea of Evil from the Earliest Times to the Present Day* (1900; reprint, New York: Bell Publishing Co., 1969). For the most comprehensive history see the multiple volumes by Jeffrey Burton Russell.

16. For example, Pascal Boyer, *Religion Explained: The Human Instincts That Fashion Gods, Spirits, and Ancestors* (London: William Heinemann, 2001), especially chapter 4, "explains" gods and spirits within an evolutionary social-psychological-cognitive framework, noting how such beliefs emerge out of inferential reasoning processes to serve human adaptive purposes. See also Boyer, *The Naturalness of Religious Ideas: A Cognitive Theory of Religion* (Berkeley: University of California Press, 1994); Michael A. Persinger, *The Neuropsychological Bases of God Beliefs* (New York: Praeger, 1987); and Ilkka Pyysiäinen, *How Religion Works: Towards a New Cognitive Science of Religion* (Leiden and Boston: Brill, 2003).

17. This is the standard strategy for contemporary theology — e.g., Daniel Migliore, *Faith Seeking Understanding: An Introduction to Christian Theology,* 2nd ed. (Grand Rapids: Eerdmans, 2004), broaches neither the doctrine of angels nor of demons.

18. As documented by Philip Jenkins, *The Next Christendom: The Coming of Global Christianity* (Oxford: Oxford University Press, 2002), and Jenkins, *The New Faces of Christianity: Believing the Bible in the Global South* (Oxford: Oxford University Press, 2006).

losopher of religion at Trinity Western University who spent many of his adult years worshiping in churches in the Pentecostal Assemblies of Canada. In terms of empirical methodology, Wiebe's work, laid out in his first book on Christian faith in the age of science, is suggestive of one way forward.[19] In this volume Wiebe explores the rationality or reasonableness (not truth) of theism as a postulated theory to explain extraordinary events of an "intersubjectively observable kind."[20] Within this matrix, Wiebe discusses paranormal events that are suggestive of the existence of what he calls "suprahuman intelligences."[21] Wiebe's goal here is not to defend the veracity of such paranormal events — the examples include biblical phenomena and other events attested to independently by multiple witnesses — but to suggest that if such events occurred, they would provide "the necessary (and sufficient) grounds for advancing theism."[22] The empirical methodology, however, is what is most important for us: paranormal phenomena testified to by more than one witness (thus intersubjectively observed) are less liable to be frauds or hoaxes, and thus more deserving of consideration and requiring nonmaterialistic forms of explanation.

Following this, Wiebe applied his empirical method to an investigation of the visions of Jesus in the New Testament and in Christian history and contemporary times.[23] In reflecting philosophically on his survey of christic visions, Wiebe critically interrogates various theories proposed in response — for example, supernaturalism (including classical orthodoxy, angel mediation theories, and Swedenborgianism), mentalism (disembodied soul, psychic, Jungian archetypal, stress, mental event, and psychoanalytic theories), and neurophysiological hypotheses (of apparitions as hallucinations, and pharmacological, perceptual release, information processing, and overactive reticular system theories) — finding each of them wanting in various respects. He thus proposed tentatively in conclusion a theory of transcendence not as a replacement of but as a supplement to existing scientific accounts for the variegated apparitions of Jesus, and outlined avenues for further research.[24] Such an account would include, at

19. Phillip H. Wiebe, *Theism in an Age of Science* (Lanham, MD: University of America Press, 1988).

20. Chapter 7 of *Theism in an Age of Science* is titled "Intersubjectively Observables."

21. Wiebe, *Theism*, p. 113.

22. Wiebe, *Theism*, p. 115.

23. Phillip H. Wiebe, *Visions of Jesus: Direct Encounters from the New Testament to Today* (New York and Oxford: Oxford University Press, 1997).

24. Wiebe, *Visions of Jesus*, pp. 216-19.

least for Christians (and certainly for pentecostals), the role of the Holy Spirit in bringing about such visions of Jesus.[25]

Wiebe's most recent book, *God and Other Spirits,* extends the line of thinking opened up in both earlier volumes by elaborating upon and defending a fairly traditional theology and ontology of created (evil) spirits.[26] This volume presents the argument that an empirical approach to human experiences of transcendence — which includes not only God, but also angels and other (evil) spirits — provides the best way forward for contemporary philosophy of religion. In an overview of what he calls "intimations of evil" preserved in the Bible, prevalent throughout Christian history, and reported by contemporaries, Wiebe suggests that the paradigmatic cases that invite some theory of transcendence involving a more pluralistic cosmology (to use my term) are those that connect two or more distinctive persons or groups of entities that are otherwise disconnected and that are corroborated by multiple witnesses (i.e., "intersubjectively observed").

There are both biblical examples — for example, Legion's request to enter a herd of pigs, and the herd's subsequent stampede into the sea, as reported by the swineherds (Mark 5)[27] — and other accounts that fit these criteria. In a well-known contemporary report involving Leo the exorcist, the spirits being exorcised from an older man told Leo that if cast out, they would enter a young man known to Leo. Leo proceeded to cast out the spirits along with ordering them to stay away from the young man. However, he was called within thirty minutes by the young man's mother, and upon visiting the young man, was told in a threatening voice "that he had heard from the older man a short while ago . . . , 'We told you we would get him, didn't we?'"[28] While these "intimations of transcendence" do not

25. Wiebe, *Visions of Jesus,* pp. 160-64.

26. Phillip H. Wiebe, *God and Other Spirits: Intimations of Transcendence in Christian Experience* (Oxford: Oxford University Press, 2004).

27. Of course, there are various other possible readings of the destruction of pigs: as an antitype of the destruction of Pharaoh's army; as a foreshadowing of Jesus' atoning sacrifice; as confirming the success of Jesus' exorcism; or as evidence of Jesus' eschatological victory. See the various essays, especially those by Ken Frieden, "The Language of Demonic Possession: A Key-Word Analysis," and Carol Schersten LaHurd, "Biblical Exorcism and Reader Responses to Ritual in Narrative," in *The Daemonic Imagination: Biblical Text and Secular Story,* ed. Robert Detweiler and William G. Doty, AAR Studies in Religion 60 (Atlanta: Scholars, 1990); cf. Michael Willett Newheart, *My Name Is Legion: The Story and Soul of the Gerasene Demoniac* (Collegeville, MN: Liturgical Press, 2004). In any case, Wiebe's observations would persist if we take the narrative at face value.

28. Wiebe, *God and Other Spirits,* p. 12.

provide conclusive "proof" in the mathematical sense for the existence of spiritual beings, Wiebe suggests that they resist purely materialistic or reductionistic explanations.

Following out his empirical approach to religious experiences of transcendence, Wiebe proposes a sophisticated theory of spirits that he claims is best able to do justice to the described data. While there is a clear admission that we know far too little about spirits and the spiritual realm to conclude definitively that they are either "natural" or "supernatural" entities, the plausibility and coherence of his theory of transcendence suggest that the conceptual resources of orthodox Christian faith provide even better overall elucidation of human intimations of transcendence than naturalistic counterparts.

Wiebe's thoughtful yet empirical approach to the demonic deserves consideration by pentecostals, especially given the emphasis in the tradition on the discernment of spirits. How else can "intimations of transcendence" be engaged except by careful discernment, and is this not what Wiebe proposes as empirical engagement? Of course, from within the realm of pentecostal experiences various questions persist as we wade through the massive numbers of reports regarding experiences of the holy, of the demonic, and of the transcendent, so prevalent in these circles. On the one hand, does not the fantastic nature of many of these accounts strain the principle of credulity — the idea that things are probably the way they are reported to be unless we have good reason to doubt this — even one so finely nuanced as Wiebe's? On the other hand, does not his proposal beg the coherentist question regarding how "intimations of transcendence" are often embedded within narrative/theoretical frameworks, which he also acknowledges? More important may be the practical and even ethical question regarding the instinctive pentecostal response to exorcise the demonic rather than merely hypothesize about, study, or understand that reality. At the same time, how pentecostals go about "casting out the evil one" and releasing those oppressed by the devil is dependent at least in part both on their ontology of the demonic and on what kind of intimations of transcendence are discerned to be operative.

I propose that critical pentecostal perspectives should be brought to bear on the following discussions: on the phenomenology, ontology, and the cosmology of spirits; on manifestations of the demonic, both at the personal and at the social level; and on the rituals of exorcism.[29] But more

---

29. My own preliminary attempts to rethink some of these matters can be found in

importantly for our purposes, Wiebe's emphasis on an empirical approach to the realm of spiritual or transcendent beings should be pressed into service to temper the tendency in pentecostal circles to talk about the proverbial "demon behind every tree." This means, minimally, that psychopathological and sociological interpretations of the demonic will invite dialogue with the psychosocial sciences in order to develop more sophisticated understandings of the human encounter with the spiritual dimension of reality. But going even further, it also suggests that there will be theological implications for how we understand the nature of the spirit world once we open up to a serious engagement with the sciences on these matters.

But what is one to say about the preceding overview of the spirit-filled pentecostal cosmos from the perspective of the dialogue between theology and science? Understandably, little work has been done at the interface of these topics, for a number of reasons. First, as already noted, the notion of disincarnate spirits is thought to be a remnant of the superstitious premodern mind that scientific advances have exorcised from modern life. In effect, however, such may be no more than a modern prejudice, although the way forward does not necessarily mean a naive return to and retrieval of the ancient worldview. Even the growing reflection on the nature of evil in scientific and evolutionary perspective has rarely, if ever, tackled the obvious theologically connected questions about the relationship of evil to the biblical symbols of the satan and the devil, not to mention "his" demons.[30]

"Going Where the Spirit Goes . . . : Engaging the Spirit(s) in J. C. Ma's Pneumatological Missiology," *Journal of Pentecostal Theology* 10, no. 2 (April 2002): 110-28; "The Demonic in Pentecostal-Charismatic Christianity and in the Religious Consciousness of Asia," in *Asian and Pentecostal: The Charismatic Face of Christianity in Asia,* ed. Allan Anderson and Edmond Tang (Oxford and Kuala Lumpur: Regnum International, 2005), pp. 93-127; and "Spirit Possession, the Living, and the Dead: A Review Essay and Response from a Pentecostal Perspective," *Dharma Deepika: A South Asian Journal of Missiological Research* 8, no. 2 (2004): 77-88. The following pages attempt to further these reflections in dialogue with the sciences.

30. The only three exceptions about which I am aware: (1) an early book whose science is seriously dated: George Francis Millin, *Evil and Evolution: An Attempt to Turn the Light of Modern Science on the Ancient Mystery of Evil,* 3rd ed. (New York and London: Macmillan, 1899; reprint, Charleston, SC: BiblioLife, 2010); (2) an unorthodox (for Christian theological purposes) Manichean explication of the satan as the dark side of God: David Ash, *The Role of Evil in Human Evolution: Exposing the Dark to Light* (Rondebosch, South Africa: Kima Global Publishers, 2007); and (3) a recent book by Stephen Webb, to which I will return later in this chapter. Otherwise, the literature is multiplying, but none discuss the demonic (or the angelic) with any seriousness — e.g., Richard W. Kropf, *Evil and Evolution* (Cranbury, NJ, and London: Associated University Presses and Fairleigh Dickinson University Press,

Second, and perhaps more justifiably, the principle of methodological naturalism (see above, chapter 1) has successfully limited what science has to say about nonmaterial realities. On the other hand, scientific research has also become more and more adept both at investigating "matters" at the edge of the natural world (witness, for example, developments in quantum mechanics), and at exploring and understanding the complexity of the world in both its material and nonmaterial dimensions. In particular, parapsychologists have been at the forefront of such scientific research over the last century. Is it possible that pentecostals and others in the theology and science discussion who are interested in rethinking the notion of a pluralistic cosmology might be aided by advances in this field of inquiry?

In Search of Spirits: What Might Research in Parapsychology Tell Us?

Before proceeding, we need to confront the elephant in the room, as the figure of speech goes: Why should we, in this initial monograph on pentecostal theology and science, risk tarnishing the project as a whole by associating ourselves with the field of parapsychology whose scientific credentials are disputed, at best, in the broader science community? In its worst forms, parapsychological investigations devolve into no more than paranormal inquiries into what skeptics have rightly called not science but nonsense.[31] Part of the problem is that too many books by advocates discuss topics like UFOs and cryptozoology and include encountering aliens and tracking beasts and wild monsters.[32] But even if we could eliminate delusion and control for fraud, doesn't too much still go on in what is also

---

1984); Timothy Anders, *The Evolution of Evil: An Inquiry into the Ultimate Origins of Human Suffering* (Chicago and La Salle, IL: Open Court, 1994); Michael A. Corey, *Evolution and the Problem of Natural Evil* (Lanham, MD: University Press of America, 2000); Cornelius G. Hunter, *Darwin's God: Evolution and the Problem of Evil* (Grand Rapids: Brazos, 2001); Christopher Southgate, *The Groaning of Creation: God, Evolution, and the Problem of Evil* (Louisville and London: Westminster John Knox, 2008); and Gaymon Bennett et al., eds., *The Evolution of Evil*, Religion Theologie und Naturwissenschaft/Religion Theology and Natural Science 8 (Göttingen: Vandenhoeck & Ruprecht, 2008), among others.

31. As labeled by editor in chief of *Skeptic* magazine, Michael Shermer, *The Borderlands of Science: Where Sense Meets Nonsense* (Oxford and New York: Oxford University Press, 2001), p. 23.

32. E.g., Kenneth Partridge, ed., *The Paranormal*, Reference Shelf 81:5 (New York and Dublin: H. W. Wilson Co., 2009), part V.

called the anomalistic sciences for the mainstream scientific community to take seriously, and do not parapsychological inquiries repeatedly step over the line demarcating scientific orthodoxy from pseudoscience?[33] In that case, is not the mere fact that I am entertaining data from the field of parapsychology already an indictment on my attempt to engage in a serious dialogue with the sciences?[34]

Let me first present four reasons for proceeding down this risky path. First, while respecting the domains of the sciences as well as their methodological naturalism, I think the scientific bias against parapsychology is derived from an underlying commitment toward a nonscientifically determinable materialistic philosophy or metaphysics rather than the result of an honest examination of carefully conducted case studies and the experimental evidence.[35] Things are changing, however, as can be seen in the

33. See Patrick Grim, ed., *Philosophy of Science and the Occult* (Albany: State University of New York Press, 1982); Terry O'Neill and Stacey L. Tipp, eds., *Paranormal Phenomena: Opposing Viewpoints* (San Diego: Greenhaven Press, 1990); and Henry H. Bauer, *Science or Pseudoscience: Magnetic Healing, Psychic Phenomena, and Other Heterodoxies* (Urbana and Chicago: University of Illinois Press, 2001), among a long list of older analyses of these matters. But note James McClenon's *Deviant Science: The Case of Parapsychology* (Philadelphia: University of Pennsylvania Press, 1984), which provides an insightful sociological assessment of how parapsychologists have gone about their work and of the mounds of experimental data that have been produced, both of which combine to suggest why parapsychological inquiry has not been so easily dismissed by the broader scientific community even after over a century of investigations (at the time of McClenon's writing), when most such processes of delegitimation usually occur within the span of fifteen to twenty years.

34. I consider myself admonished by University of Maryland (Baltimore County) philosophy professor Stephen E. Braude, whose parapsychological inquiries after receiving tenure (as of the mid-1970s) resulted in his being marginalized by those he had otherwise thought were colleagues, most of whom reacted in this way only because of prejudice and not because they were more knowledgeable than he about the issues at hand; see Braude's latest book, *The Gold Leaf Lady and Other Parapsychological Investigations* (Chicago and London: University of Chicago Press, 2007), pp. xiv-xxi.

35. As the prominent psychologist Donald Hebb confessed as far back as 1951: "why do we not accept ESP [extrasensory perception] as a psychological fact? Rhine has offered us enough evidence to have convinced us on almost any other issue. . . . I cannot see what other basis my colleagues have for rejecting it. . . . My own rejection of [Rhine's] views is — in the literal sense — prejudice"; see Donald O. Hebb, "The Role of Neurological Ideas in Psychology," *Journal of Personality* 20 (1951): 35-55, at 45, cited in Harvey J. Irwin and Caroline A. Watt, *An Introduction to Parapsychology,* 5th ed. (Jefferson, NC, and London: McFarland and Co., 2007), p. 251. The reference to Rhine is to J. B. Rhine (1895-1980), who founded and operated the parapsychology laboratory at Duke University, and was also the founder and first editor of the *Journal of Parapsychology.*

Parapsychological Association having been an affiliate member of the prestigious American Association for the Advancement of Science since 1969. Second, since pentecostals are new to the theology and science discussion, if in fact the turn to parapsychological research is a wrong one, then we can make our way best by observing what has gone awry in this field that has long aspired to attain scientific credibility. But this leads, third, to my wager: that if we examine the scientifically reputable parapsychological literature impartially, we will realize that there is not only much to learn from developments in this arena, but also, for those who are apologetically motivated, that our historical polemics against psi (short for psychic) phenomena have been woefully misinformed — for example, popular pentecostal apologetics, following traditional conservative evangelical or fundamentalist leads, have typically dismissed paranormal phenomena as fraudulent at best or as "tricks of the devil" designed to deceive the unsuspecting at worst — and need to be disciplined by the accumulated research. But most importantly, for purposes of this book, I believe that all those engaged in the theology and science dialogue have a stake in this discussion if for no other reason than to develop new modes of scientific inquiry that can engage with what pentecostals call, following the Bible, the reality of principalities, powers, evil spirits, and the demonic — what I've called a spirit-filled world.[36] The other alternatives, noted in the preceding section, are not viable options going forward. But the rationale in this paragraph is just an initial apologia; I hope it will be sustained as we make our way through the remainder of this chapter.

Let us now survey developments in the field of parapsychology. Here, I rely on the summaries of Charles Tart, a doyen in the field after having labored in it for over forty years, and Harvey Irwin, author of the major textbook in the discipline, which is in its fifth edition, coauthored with Caroline Watt.[37] We cannot survey everything in the field, so I focus on some of

---

36. Roman Catholic theologian John J. Heaney, *The Sacred and the Psychic: Parapsychology and Christian Theology* (New York and Ramsey, NJ: Paulist, 1984), was one of the first to wade into the intersection noted in his book's subtitle. The few reviews were positive and receptive, but the conversation has not continued. In the next section, I will review the work of David Ray Griffin.

37. See Irwin and Watt, *An Introduction to Parapsychology*. Tart has authored many scholarly books (by recognized academic publishers and university presses), including two classic texts in the field: *Altered States of Consciousness: A Book of Readings* (New York: Wiley, 1969), and *Transpersonal Psychologies* (New York: Harper and Row, 1975), both with many reprinted editions. I rely here on his most recent volume, *The End of Materialism: How Evi-*

the major psi phenomena that are arguably relevant to pentecostal spirituality, beginning with what Tart calls "the big five": telepathy (the extrasensory communication of thoughts or feelings), clairvoyance (the remote nonsensory awareness, viewing, or perceiving of physical events), precognition (the antecedent knowing of things), psychokinesis (the ability to affect or move objects by mental effort), and psychic healing (the ability to heal through mental effort).[38] There is neither space nor need to detail the many experiments that have been performed. Interested readers can consult the sources cited.[39] I only summarize here what I am inclined to note as a pentecostal scholar interested in the dialogue between theology and science.

Telepathy. Sustained research over the last century and a half has weeded out fraudulent scenarios and conducted rigorous experiments in which alleged telepathically gifted percipients were able to correctly identify information in the minds of senders even though the former were shielded from the latter so that there was no known way of communication between the persons. The success rates were too high to be relegated to pure chance, and some of these studies have been replicated. All indications are that extrasensory perception (ESP) exists.

Clairvoyance. Similarly, putatively clairvoyant individuals have performed much higher than statistically expected by chance in identifying the ordering of shuffled decks of cards when shielded from the shuffler; in this case, of course, the card shuffler kept the deck facedown throughout, so that the viewer would not be able to access the order of the cards by ordinary means. Other experiments involving randomly chosen target locations visited by the experimenter have also been correctly identified by clairvoyant viewers too exactly to be deemed coincidental.

Precognition. Tart cites a study of 309 separate investigations of precognition by 62 investigators and involving 50,000 subjects from 1935 to

---

dence of the Paranormal Is Bringing Science and Spirit Together (Oakland: New Harbinger Publications, 2009). A well-respected earlier introduction with fairly strong scientific credentials is Carroll B. Nash, *Parapsychology: The Science of Psiology* (Springfield, IL: Charles C. Thomas, 1986), while a more recent, evenhanded, and valuable textbook is Jane Henry, ed., *Parapsychology: Research on Exceptional Experiences* (London and New York: Routledge, 2005).

38. See Tart, *The End of Materialism,* chapter 5.

39. Unless otherwise noted, I rely primarily in the following on Tart, *The End of Materialism,* chapters 6–10, and various sections of Irwin and Watt, *An Introduction to Parapsychology,* chapters 4–7.

1987, reported in 113 articles, and constituting a composite database of almost 2 million trials.[40] The conclusion was that "The combined results of the studies produced odds against chance of 10 septillion to 1. . . . [It's] preposterous to believe that these cumulated precognition results were due to chance."[41] Various follow-up analyses that have isolated other variables that could have impacted the result of this study have been conducted, and the overall conclusions have been repeatedly validated.

Psychokinesis. Here again, whether it is moving objects or influencing the roll of dice or the toss of coins to a greater degree than probable just merely based on chance, repeated experiments have demonstrated the reality of psychic powers. Thus, not only is the proverbial "mind over matter" suggested, but also that minds can affect material realities from a distance. Most researchers are convinced that such capacities cannot be explained in terms of electromagnetic influences, although there is no agreement on how to otherwise positively account for such phenomena.[42]

Psychic healing. Here I limit myself to comments on recent parapsychological research, fully aware of the long history of discussion of such phenomena in theosophical, spiritualist, and Christian Science circles against which pentecostals have long reacted. Still, the scientific data is suggestive. Tart and Irwin and Watt cite the work of McGill University experimental morphologist Bernard Grad on plant and animal restoration in response to the laying on of hands of a reputed psychic healer.[43] Irwin and Watt conclude that many such studies may combine to "provide some evi-

40. C. Honorton and D. C. Ferrari, "Future Telling: A Meta-Analysis of Forced-Choice Precognition Experiments, 1935-1987," *Journal of Parapsychology* 53 (1989): 281-308. To be sure, it is highly improbable that all the studies in this meta-analysis meet acceptable research standards, but it is also too easy, not to mention unscientific, for the skeptic to reject the implications of such a study simply because some of these investigations may be unreliable.

41. Tart, *The End of Materialism,* p. 133.

42. In his *Limits of Influence: Psychokinesis and the Philosophy of Science* (New York and London: Routledge and Kegan Paul, 1986), Stephen E. Braude proposes, in his quest for a theory of psychokinesis (PK), that the attempt to identify PK processes at the microphysical or psychological level is misguided since PK does "not *reduce* to some set of underlying phenomena" (p. 246, italics in original). I return later to suggest an emergentist theory of psi phenomena in general.

43. See Bernard Grad, "Some Biological Effects of the 'Laying On of Hands': A Review of Experiments with Animals and Plants," *Journal of the American Society for Psychical Research* 59 (1965): 95-127, and "The Biological Effects of the 'Laying On of Hands' on Animals and Plants: Implications for Biology," in *Parapsychology: Its Relation to Physics, Biology, Psychology, and Psychiatry,* ed. G. R. Schmeidler (Metuchen, NJ: Scarecrow Press, 1976), pp. 76-89.

dence on the question of the effect of human intentionality upon another's health."[44]

Thus Tart summarizes about "the big five": "The findings of scientific parapsychology force us to pragmatically accept that minds can do things . . . that cannot be reduced to physical explanations, given current scientific knowledge or reasonable extensions of it."[45]

But what are the reigning parapsychological interpretations of the psi phenomena?[46] A number of theories have arisen regarding the mediation of ESP, some of which no longer command much attention. The theory of electromagnetic radiation once generated scientific attention, but repeated investigations have failed to identify brain wave radiation correlatable with psychic phenomena or sufficiently powerful to produce documented psi results. In its place, energy field theories have hypothesized that quantum effects can pass through solid objects, but research has not been able to identify such energy fields to date. More recently, observational theories, built on quantum mechanical notions relating the collapse of the probability wave function to outside observations of the system, suggest that psychic experiences are similar "effects" of the percipient's consciousness; but the application of otherwise experimentally suggestive data to psi phenomena is contested, even as such accounts inevitably take on the metaphysical baggage and debates that continue to rage in the field of quantum mechanics.[47] In terms of the experiential phase of psi (assuming that mediation of ESP were somehow possible), proposals have included a sixth-sense theory (which lacks experimental rigor), memory models (which have much going for them, but remain insufficiently comprehensive in explanatory scope), and a psi-mediated instrumental response theory, related to individual adaptations to external situations/stimuli (with research ongoing in this area). In addition, there are also noncybernetic theories such as Jung's synchronicity hypothesis about acausally connected yet meaningful or significant events,[48] although some think this notion of

44. Irwin and Watt, *An Introduction to Parapsychology,* p. 115.

45. Tart, *The End of Materialism,* p. 241.

46. See Irwin and Watt, *An Introduction to Parapsychology,* chapter 15, for an overview.

47. Some of the issues are summarized by Douglas M. Stokes, *The Conscious Mind and the Material World: On Psi, the Soul, and the Self* (Jefferson, NC, and London: McFarland and Co., 2007), chapter 2, "Mind and the Quantum."

48. Most recently argued for at length by Victor Mansfield, *Synchronicity, Science, and Soulmaking: Understanding Jungian Synchronicity through Physics, Buddhism, and Philosophy* (La Salle, IL: Open Court, 1998), and Joseph Cambray, *Synchronicity: Nature and Psyche*

meaningful coincidences is tautological, not explanatory. Finally, of course, there are skeptics who think all such phenomena are frauds or can be explained away (reduced to underlying mechanistic or materialistic processes); others think sound scientific explanations will eventually be found.

In sum, the data begs for nonmaterialistic interpretations, but most of the theories on hand remain partial at best. But now I wish to complicate matters further by turning to even more controversial aspects of the parapsychological sciences precisely to get at the larger questions motivating our discussion in this chapter regarding the nature of a spirit-filled and pluralistic cosmology. I am referring to parapsychological studies of disembodied psychic phenomena, mediumships, and poltergeist experiences, many of which are based on eyewitness and case study accounts rather than on laboratory or experimental evidence.[49] Let me, again, briefly summarize notable developments (from my pentecostal vantage point) in the field, before highlighting what their import may be for thinking about the cosmological matters at hand.[50]

Disembodied psychic phenomena. The data here is indicative of the possibility of spiritual or psychic existence apart from human embodiment. Out-of-body experiences (OBEs) suggest that human minds both can be located apart from their bodies and can even perceive this extrabodily environment, and near-death experiences (NDEs) are accounts — many clinically recorded — of people who have been near to death or declared physi-

---

in an Interconnected Universe (College Station: Texas A&M University Press, 2009). See also Ira Progoff, *Jung, Synchronicity, and Human Destiny: Noncausal Dimensions of Human Experience* (New York: Delta Books, 1973).

49. Yet as Braude, *The Gold Leaf Lady and Other Parapsychological Investigations*, urges, we should not be too quick to dismiss the empirical evidence afforded by eyewitness accounts, which remain the standard in the fields of ethnography and anthropology. This approach is significant from a pentecostal perspective that appreciates the evidential role of testimony.

50. Although we will return to the topic momentarily when discussing the work of David Ray Griffin, here I leave out parapsychological studies of reincarnation that are treated in most texts in the field primarily because I think they raise more complicated issues of a related yet distinct order than what I am attempting to address. Further, even if reincarnation were demonstrable, the fact that people can be "born again" in later lives would speak to the possibility of future incarnational existence but still not address what I am discussing in this chapter regarding a nonmaterialistic and pneumatological cosmology. For a book-length discussion, see Sylvia Cranston and Carey Williams, *Reincarnation: A New Horizon in Science, Religion, and Society* (New York: Julian Press, 1984).

cally dead, and survived or (were) resuscitated to tell of their experiences "on the other side."[51] Of course, naturalistic explanations have been proffered, including how OBEs can be triggered by drug use, or how NDEs are related to the brain being deprived of basic life functions. Yet even after factoring in for such possibilities, and also in light of my own stance that scientific explanations at any level do not necessarily eliminate higher-level analyses, I am open to the hypothesis, suggested by some parapsychologists, that both of these combine to suggest the ontological existence of disincarnate spiritual entities. From this has emerged what those working in the parapsychological sciences have called the survival hypothesis, the idea that disembodied consciousnesses may survive bodily death, at least for some time. There are also, in addition to the above, after-death communications and apparitions, wherein messages from deceased people are received by those who remain alive, and sightings of the same are received. This phenomenon touches on the question of mediumships.

Mediumships and related phenomena. This phenomenon is not limited to Western societies, but is prominent also in indigenous cultures and throughout the global South. But even if fraud were controlled for — and many solid investigations appear successful in ruling this out — the question of what precisely is occurring in mediumistic situations is debated. The obvious response, if we take the claims of mediums at face value, is that they are in contact with spirit beings, usually those of deceased individuals. But parapsychological evidence is incapable of distinguishing conclusively that claim from the "super-ESP" theory in which mediums may simply be telepathically or psychokinetically engaged with other living mentalities (although in this case we are resorting to explaining one set of anomalistic phenomena with another, even if these are Tart's "big five"). Still, the latter super-ESP hypothesis is generally thought insufficient for explaining both the accuracy and amount of information related to other lives and the more detailed mannerisms and finely honed skills reflective of those lives exhibited by mediums.[52] A tentative conclusion as suggested

51. For reasons related to the biblical intimation that the dead do not return to report back to the living (e.g., Luke 16:30-31), an evangelical medical doctor also thinks that apart from the few biblical exceptions, near-death experiences are not strictly accounts of life after death; see Michael Sabom, *Light and Death: One Doctor's Fascinating Account of Near-Death Experience* (Grand Rapids: Zondervan, 1998), pp. 196-98.

52. These skills include xenoglossy, the speaking in a language unlearned by the speaker while being possessed or inhabited by the spirits of deceased persons. The most well-documented and investigated cases remain those of Ian Stevenson, *Xenoglossy: A Review and*

by historian and psychologist Alan Gauld is that "in the present state of our knowledge some sort of survival theory gives the readiest account of the observed phenomena, [although] many issues remain undecided."[53] And if we were to proceed tentatively with Gauld and expand the sphere of mediumship to include the phenomenon of trance possession in shamanistic cultures of indigenous Euro-America and the global South, then alongside the channeling of spirits of deceased individuals in the Western world we would have to consider the manifest apparitions of a wider range of spiritual entities, including not only celestial beings but also animal spirits.[54] Anthropological research, of course, while neglecting in large part the mediumship phenomenon in industrial societies, has long been at the forefront of studying spirit possession in shamanist ecstasy and flight.[55] Of course, reference to such anthropological literature raises immediately all the questions regarding participant ethnography that have perennially persisted regarding the objectivity of ethnographic fieldwork.

Poltergeist phenomena. Originally a German word, *poltergeist* translates roughly into English as referring to noisy spirit manifestations. While Tart does not discuss this issue specifically, Irwin and Watt do have a chapter on it and it is mentioned in most other serious scientific discussions of parapsychology.[56] Its phenomenology involves movement of objects, hearing of noises, incendiary eruptions, water seepage or inundations (less frequent), bites/scratches/pinches, demonic persecution, electronic phenomena (increasing in prevalence as we have moved further into the infor-

---

Report of a Case (Charlottesville: University Press of Virginia, 1974), and *Unlearned Language: New Studies in Xenoglossy* (Charlottesville: University Press of Virginia, 1984), who believes these to be skills not telepathically communicable or extrasensorily perceptible, and thus serve as "important evidence for the survival of human personality after physical death" (*Unlearned Language*, p. 158). More on the survivalist hypothesis in the next section.

53. Alan Gauld, *Mediumship and Survival: A Century of Investigations* (London: William Heinemann, 1982), p. 262.

54. This would include the phenomenon of spirit surgeries and spirit healing conducted by doctors in trances putatively guided by the spirits of deceased individuals; see the discussion in Sidney M. Greenfield, *Spirits with Scalpels: The Culturalbiology of Religious Healing in Brazil* (Walnut Creek, CA: Left Coast Press, 2008), part I.

55. Most recently and comprehensively discussed in the third edition of I. M. Lewis's classic text, *Ecstatic Religion: A Study of Shamanism and Spirit Possession* (New York and London: Routledge, 2003).

56. Hundreds of cases are also well documented in William G. Roll, *The Poltergeist* (Metuchen, NJ: Scarecrow Press, 1976), and Alan Gauld and A. D. Cornell, *Poltergeists* (London and Boston: Routledge and Kegan Paul, 1979).

mation age), etc., following places or people. Some of the theories suggested have been: fraudulent activity, misinterpretations (for physiological or psychological reasons), subconscious psychokinetic manifestations (also known as the *recurrent spontaneous psychokinesis* theory), or neurological explanations. Or, perhaps, as common folklore has perennially taken it, poltergeists are the manifestation of deceased persons who have not rested in peace.[57] Once fraud is controlled for and misinterpretations corrected, the class of inexplicable phenomena is suggestive yet remains inconclusive regarding the survival or life-after-death hypothesis in particular and for thinking about the spiritual domains of the world more generally.

In Tart's perspective, then, the combination of survivalist and mediumship phenomena, when added to the "big five," provides prima facie evidence for overturning the Western scientific and materialistic worldview. But skeptics of course have perennially argued that work done in the parapsychological arena is spurious or pseudoscientific.[58] Yet demographic analyses substantiate neither the social marginality hypothesis (that only socially nonadapted people claim to have or have psychic experiences) nor the cognitive deficits theory (that psi phenomena follow only people with lower intellectual or reasoning skills).[59] Yes, worldview and personality factors do show some correlational signs (i.e., beliefs in psi tend to have preceded experiences of such), and there is "general support

57. David J. Hufford, "An Experience-Centered Approach to Hauntings," in *Hauntings and Poltergeists: Multidisciplinary Perspectives,* ed. James Houran and Rense Lange (Jefferson, NC, and London: McFarland and Co., 2001), pp. 18-40.

58. There are many works, especially published by members of the Skeptics Society and the Committee for Skeptical Inquiry, as well as by Prometheus Books. While I would not dismiss these "skeptical" arguments aprioristically, they should be taken with a grain of salt. Some of the most radical have even been identified as skeptical "fundamentalists" given their questionable motivations and methods — as detailed by Richard S. Broughton, *Parapsychology: The Controversial Science* (New York: Ballantine Books, 1991), pp. 81-86. Further, though parapsychological endeavors should certainly not be exempt from critical assessment, yet in some cases, as David J. Hess, *Science in the New Age: The Paranormal, Its Defenders and Debunkers, and American Culture* (Madison: University of Wisconsin Press, 1993), suggests, debunkers are much closer to the parapsychologists, not to mention the practitioners of psi phenomena, than they realize. Yet for an interesting probabilistic and statistical analysis of some aspects of the anomalistic sciences written without the polemic but clearly undertaken to defend the integrity of the scientific endeavor, see Georges Charpak and Henri Broch, *Debunked! ESP, Telekinesis, and Other Pseudoscience,* trans. Bart K. Holland (Baltimore and London: Johns Hopkins University Press, 2004).

59. Irwin and Watt, *An Introduction to Parapsychology,* pp. 225-27 and 229-31.

for the psychodynamic functions hypothesis" that suggests that experiences of the paranormal often work to enable psychological adaption and to compensate for the personal sense of a loss in control.[60] But worldview and personality factors are not isolatable in terms of one-to-one causal relations vis-à-vis psi phenomena, even as it has also been shown that there is low correlation between paranormal beliefs or experiences and the chronically anxious or otherwise psychologically disturbed.[61]

Before moving on, I want to briefly discuss the work of Dean Radin, who received his Ph.D. in psychology from the University of Illinois, Champaign-Urbana, and then had appointments at Princeton University, the University of Edinburgh, and the University of Nevada before taking the position as senior scientist at the Institute of Noetic Sciences (IONS) in 2001 (also serving since as an adjunct faculty in the Department of Psychology at Sonoma State University). His work is intriguing because of his research at the interface of consciousness and quantum physics.[62] In his first book, Radin suggested at the end of a long investigation that quantum physics might be helpful for providing an overarching theoretical framework for untangling the scientific mysteries of psi phenomena.[63] Just as a photon is describable as a wave and as a particle, both true at the same time, although not measurable as such, so also consciousness might have complementary states, correlating, let's say, between a receiver and a percipient (in telepathy, clairvoyance, or precognition). Further, quantum nonlocality — the paradoxical yet demonstrated idea that quantum objects spatially separated from each other may be able to influence each other simultaneously, contrary to the physical laws pertaining to classical mechanical objects — is suggestive of the primordial entanglement of the universe, an entanglement and instantaneous relationality called attention to by psychokinetic and psychic healing phenomena.[64] Thus conscious biological systems that are "exquisitely sensitive to certain kinds of information" may be interacting with their not-so-immediate environments, re-

---

60. Irwin and Watt, *An Introduction to Parapsychology,* p. 234.

61. Irwin and Watt, *An Introduction to Parapsychology,* pp. 227-29 and 233.

62. A previous, less rigorously formulated, attempt to link the paranormal and the new physics is Lawrence LeShan, *The Medium, the Mystic, and the Physicist: Toward a General Theory of the Paranormal* (New York: Viking Press, 1974). A number of LeShan's suggested analogies are philosophically and theologically problematic.

63. Dean J. Radin, *The Conscious Universe: The Scientific Truth of Psychic Phenomena* (New York: HarperEdge, 1997).

64. See Radin, *The Conscious Universe,* pp. 281-84.

ceiving and "teleporting" information without any passage of time or expenditure of energy.[65]

Radin's next book further explores such a quantum interpretation of psi.[66] In addition to Tart's summary of meta-analytical studies of precognition experiments (mentioned above), Radin provides an overview of the field based on a meta-meta-analysis of 1,019 controlled laboratory experimental case studies involving almost 40,000 sessions, 2.6 million dice tosses, and over 1.1 billion randomly generated number analyses, with odds against chance so large (13×10^{104} to 1) that the results are "unlikely to be due to coincidence or dumb luck."[67] Radin first summarizes the various quantum theories of psi, which include the observational theory, which we briefly noted.[68] Also discussed are the pragmatic information model, wherein psi effects are complementary nonlocal correlations between states of reality and perceiving minds, and the weak-quantum theory, which builds off the analogy between psychotherapeutic transference (projected from client to therapist) and countertransference (from therapist to client) phenomena to suggest a model for psi interactions. Especially intriguing is the holographic universe paradigm of quantum physicist David Bohm (1917-1992). In Bohm's theory, all things are implicated in an undivided holistic realm from out of which is explicated our ordered world of commonsense observations and perceptions. The human brain thus can be mapped so that its information reception, storage, and trans-

---

65. See Radin, *The Conscious Universe,* pp. 285-86, citing C. H. Bennett et al., "Teleporting an Unknown Quantum State via Dual Classical and EPR Channels," *Physics Review Letters* 70 (1993): 1895-99.

66. Dean I. Radin, *Entangled Minds: Extrasensory Experiences in a Quantum Reality* (New York: Paraview Pocket Books, 2006).

67. Radin, *Entangled Minds,* p. 276. Table 14-1 on p. 276 summarizes the experimentally documented odds against chance: 2.2×10^{10} to 1 for dream psi; 3.0×10^{10} to 1 for Ganzfeld psi; 8.5×10^{46} to 1 for conscious detection of being stared at; 2.6×10^{76} to 1 on dice psychokinesis; and 3,052 to 1 for randomly generated numbers psi.

68. Radin also suggests how the Stapp–von Newmann interpretation of quantum mechanics, featuring the conscious observer's knowing as the center of the theory, is amenable to an account of psi phenomena both in terms of the brain's high sensitivity to atomic-level events given its own neural and synaptic constitutedness and in terms of the possibility now that "one person's mind/brain can cause the probabilistic brain states of another person or another object (or other human organs, like the gut), to preferentially collapse into selected states" (*Entangled Minds,* p. 260). To the degree that I understand what Radin is here suggesting — and that I am including this in a footnote rather than discussing this in the main text should be indicative of my sense of ignorance — I think this can be understood as a variant of the observational model.

mission processes are implicated within the world's events. A parapsychological interpretation is that psi phenomena are conscious explications of such interactions. Yet as a psychologist, Radin realizes that we need a multidimensional or multidisciplinary model, one that combines physics with neuroscience and psychology.

The kind of research that Radin is engaged in is still fairly novel in the field, and developments in this area are worth watching carefully. So while we should be cautious about basing too much on this data, at the present it is nevertheless appropriate to tentatively suggest that Radin's proposal is consonant with an emergentist view of psi phenomena. Physics provides an ontological context for psi events; neuroscience describes how the "hardware" of such events functions; and psychology reveals how conscious minds enable the interface of brains and the worlds they inhabit. Each provides complementary, although nonreductive, analyses of the phenomenon. Radin's point is that minds are entangled, both with other minds and with other realities in the world. It's just that we have been wired to be most conscious about the things that matter most to us (those things and realities that we are closest to), so that inevitably what is more distant only occasionally, and very ambiguously, bubbles to the surface of our consciousness. In the end, though, Radin stays more at the level of the physics and psychology of consciousness. This is helpful for our realization about the pervasive role of human consciousness in the world,[69] but does it shed any light at all on the possibility of there being other conscious or spiritual beings besides ourselves? Might a more explicitly emergentist account do better?

Psi, Principalities, and Powers:
The Emergence of a Spirit-Filled World

In the preceding section we attempted to cover a good deal of highly controversial scientific and theological ground in a very short space. My goal, however, is to ask what, if anything, science might contribute to our understanding of what I have called a spirit-filled cosmology. And since scientific research on this matter has not been accomplished in relationship to pentecostalism, the closest related field of research is parapsychology.

---

69. As also suggested by Minas C. Kafatos and Robert Nadeau, *The Conscious Universe: Parts and Wholes in Physical Theory* (New York: Springer, 2000).

What then are the implications of such parapsychological data for pentecostal theology in particular and perhaps for the Christian theological enterprise as a whole? Let me suggest that such psi and ESP phenomena, if scientifically confirmable, have implications for our understanding of charismatic manifestations in at least the following ways. If ESP is scientifically measurable, there are at least parallels here to, if not also implications for how to comprehend, such charismatic or spiritual gifts as the word of wisdom. Further, the science of precognition may also be suggestive for considering the charisms of words of knowledge or prophecies of future events. Last but certainly not least, establishing the scientific bases for psychokinesis and psychic healing may also illuminate pentecostal-type manifestations like miraculous healings. My claim is *neither* that these psi incidents are exact parallels to charismatic manifestations *nor* that the possibility of scientific investigation of the former might produce irrefutable evidence of the Holy Spirit's working through the latter. As I hope I have already made clear in the preceding chapters, since science cannot identify a causal joint for divine action, the work of the Spirit can only be understood eschatologically and teleologically in faith. Rather my point here is that the parapsychological sciences may shed some light on the natural processes that mediate what pentecostal Christians call in faith the charisms of the Spirit.

Further, from a pentecostal perspective, survivalism, mediumship, and poltergeist phenomena are suggestive in other respects. Most obviously, these experiences and encounters indicate that there is much more to the cosmos than is initially perceived, and that there may be spiritual agencies at work in the world besides human and divine persons. Theologically, for pentecostals, such realities are usually understood in terms of their dominant angelologies or demonologies. Thus encounters with the disincarnate and disembodied spirits are dualistically construed as interactions with either benevolent spiritual beings (angels) or malevolent spiritual entities (demons). OBEs and NDEs are otherwise understood as admonishing experiences allowed by God to redirect the course of people's lives. But beyond these responses, the preceding discussion shows the potential relevance of parapsychological research for attempts to understand pentecostal spirituality scientifically.[70]

---

70. As Michael Grosso notes, "In the near-death experience, we have a modern empirical model for understanding early Christian conversion and Pentecostal experiences," and "Parapsychology gives an empirical basis for religious claims and constructs." See Grosso,

I cannot here resolve the question about parapsychology's scientific status (this must be left to scientists in general, and psychologists in particular, to adjudicate). But if pentecostals align themselves with the skeptic's perspective that parapsychology is a pseudoscience rather than legitimately scientific, pentecostals will also have to concede that from that same skeptical perspective, pentecostalism, pentecostal experience, and pentecostal spirituality are similarly suspect. The reductionist knife cuts both ways: it explicates parapsychological phenomena either as fraudulent or in terms of natural forces that are not yet known on the one hand, even while it similarly dismisses pentecostal claims on the other. From a rationalistic and scientistic perspective, if psi phenomena, ghost hunting, shamanism, and disembodied spirit beings are rejected as superstitions of unenlightened mythology, then, some might argue, so are the claims of pentecostalism.[71]

Whither then the dialogue between pentecostalism and science, given this parapsychological intervention (some might say detour!)? I propose in this section to build toward an emergentist interpretation of psychic phenomena within a broader pluralistic cosmological framework in conversation with the philosopher of religion and theologian David Ray Griffin,

---

"Miracles: Illusions, Natural Events, or Divine Interventions," *Journal of Religion and Psychical Research* 20, no. 4 (1997): 182-97, quotes from 191 and 189, respectively.

71. Pentecostals may cringe at this claim, but this charge is potentially unnerving also for theists in general. E.g., David Christopher Lane, *Exposing Cults: When the Skeptical Mind Confronts the Mystical* (New York and London: Garland, 1994), includes pentecostal glossolalia alongside Da Free John, UFO religion, and Asian Indian gurus among the many other movements to be exposed. Other book-length "exposés" that are less polemical but nevertheless skeptical include Ian Cotton, *The Hallelujah Revolution: The Rise of the New Christians* (Amherst, NY: Prometheus Books, 1996), and Roland Howard, *Charismania: When Christian Fundamentalism Goes Wrong* (London: Mowbray, 1997); see also Joe Nickell, *Looking for a Miracle: Weeping Icons, Relics, Stigmata, Visions, and Healing Cures* (Amherst, NY: Prometheus Books, 1993), chapter 5. My citing these authors is not so much an indication that I agree with their criticisms — although I do think there is much pentecostals can learn from these critics — as to make the point that from the skeptical perspective, pentecostalism and psi phenomena are at similar, if not equivalent, levels. There are, of course, other issues to consider, such as the types of evidence, besides scientific ones, that might separate pentecostal spirituality from these other phenomena. The eschatological framework I am suggesting for the arguments of this book as a whole, for example, might be suggestive of how there are broader assumptions in place that are relevant for how not only pentecostals but also Christians and other monotheists might engage with this issue. The rest of this book provides, at least indirectly and in an ad hoc manner, a pentecostal apologetic on this matter.

and the biblical scholar Walter Wink. My goal is to lay the theological ground for the speculative pneumatological cosmology to be sketched in the final section of this chapter.

David Ray Griffin is a longtime faculty member at Claremont Graduate School who has worked from the beginning within a Whiteheadian philosophical and cosmological framework.[72] At about the peak of his scholarly career in the mid-1990s — from which he does not seem to have descended, given his output over the last decade[73] — he published a formidable philosophical and theological analysis of parapsychology.[74] I will review Griffin's accomplishments in this volume, showing how he takes us beyond the work of Radin and the parapsychological community in thinking theologically about a pluralistic cosmology.

Griffin locates his proposals both against traditional theism's dualistic construal of human spirits and divine transcendence on the one hand, and against contemporary science's reductionistic materialism and positivism on the other hand. His goal is to find a middle way between an intuitionist supernaturalism and an atheistic, materialistic, and sensationist naturalism — the doctrine that all knowledge results from mere physical sensation. However, this dichotomy is not the only one bequeathed by modernity; a modernist mentality has also arbitrarily separated the natural (inanimate) and human (animate) worlds, the world of facts and that of values, the domain of experience and that of matter, mind, and spirit.[75]

72. His earliest and most influential books were a new and corrected edition (with Donald W. Sherburne) of Whitehead's classic *Process and Reality: An Essay in Cosmology* (New York: Free Press, 1978); *A Process Christology* (Philadelphia: Westminster, 1973); *God, Power, and Evil: A Process Theodicy* (Philadelphia: Westminster, 1976); the coauthored (with John Cobb) *Process Theology: An Introductory Exposition* (Philadelphia: Westminster, 1976); and two edited books: again, with Cobb, *Mind in Nature: Essays on the Interface of Science and Philosophy* (Washington, DC: University Press of America, 1977), and *Physics and the Ultimate Significance of Time: Bohm, Prigogine, and Process Philosophy* (Albany: State University of New York Press, 1985).

73. Much of Griffin's work in the last ten years has focused on exposing what he believes to have been a government cover-up related to the September 11 tragedy. The position that Griffin has taken may mar his legacy in the long run, but it does not touch on the major aspects of his work that I am drawing on and engaging, which was published long before. Still, Griffin has not left his philosophical and theological work behind — e.g., Griffin, *Whitehead's Radically Different Postmodern Philosophy: An Argument for Its Contemporary Relevance* (Albany: State University of New York Press, 2007).

74. David Ray Griffin, *Parapsychology, Philosophy, and Spirituality: A Postmodern Exploration* (Albany: State University of New York Press, 1997).

75. For the record, Griffin defends a version of the supervenience model of the mind-

Against these dualistic assumptions, Griffin proposes an emergentist panexperientialism that redefines all created realities in terms of *how* (not whether or not) they experience the world.[76]

Human beings have a complexity to their experiences that rocks do not have, but to conclude that rocks have no experiences at all means both that they do not exert causal influence in the world (which they do) and that they are incapable of being experienced (which is counterintuitive to our own encounters with rocks). Now of course, rocks do not experience the world as humans do. Rather, following Whiteheadian interpreter Charles Hartshorne, Griffin urges that only "compound individuals" with an emergent "dominant member" have higher-level experiences of individuality, spontaneity, and self-determination, and this would include humans plus other sentient beings (like animals).[77] Otherwise, aggregate societies of multiplicities (e.g., rocks, tables, stars) do not experience the world in like manner, although they are experienceable by other things.

What does all this have to do with psi phenomena? Besides presenting the standard evidence for parapsychological phenomena, Griffin provides an extended argument for life after death drawing from five kinds of phenomena: mediumistic messages, possession-type cases, reincarnation, apparitions, and out-of-body (and near-death) experiences.[78] With regard to mediums, Griffin agrees with most investigators of the phenomenon that regular telepathic or ESP communications are incapable of account-

---

brain relationship; see his *Religion and Scientific Naturalism: Overcoming the Conflicts* (Albany: State University of New York Press, 2000), chapters 6–7; *Reenchantment without Supernaturalism: A Process Philosophy of Religion* (Ithaca, NY, and London: Cornell University Press, 2001), chapter 3; and the book-length argument of *Unsnarling the World-Knot: Consciousness, Freedom, and the Mind-Body Problem* (Berkeley: University of California Press, 1998), chapter 10.

76. Griffin's discussion of emergence is specifically elaborated upon in *Parapsychology, Philosophy, and Spirituality*, pp. 124-28. At one level, Griffin's panexperientialism, informed by Whitehead's philosophy of organism, is attractive in terms of its promise to bridge the metaphysical gap between mind and matter. I am more comfortable embracing an emergentist cosmology that can include the panexperientialist thesis — if borne out by inquiry in the long run — rather than one that relies on a metaphysical intuition that is still contested at present.

77. Griffin cites Hartshorne's "The Compound Individual," in *Philosophical Essays for Alfred North Whitehead*, ed. Otis H. Lee (New York: Longmans, Green, 1936), pp. 193-220. For further discussion, see also Griffin, *Unsnarling the World-Knot*, chapter 9.

78. The overall evidence for telepathy, clairvoyance, and other psi capacities is presented in Griffin's *Parapsychology, Philosophy, and Spirituality*, chapter 2; the argument for life after death proceeds over chapters 4–8.

ing for what manifests in at least some of the most well-documented cases: the depths of memories, similarity of mannerisms, extensiveness of intellectual knowledge and other types of skills, overall purposes, cross-correspondences of messages through multiple mediums at the same or during a similar period of time, and drop-in communicators, where the spirits of deceased people emerge in séances intended to contact other personalities. Parallels include similarly inexplicable cases in which deceased (or displaced) spirits take either temporary possession of or are more permanently reincarnated in other subjects (the latter case often involving younger children who would be, arguably, less capable of perpetrating hoaxes). Griffin then examines putatively veridical apparitions wherein living subjects claim to come into knowledge about their deceased relatives (usually) or friends directly from them, and such information is verified and of the type unattainable by other means, and allegedly collective apparitions involving manifestations of a single spirit to more than one person. Finally, veridical cases are also identified in OBEs and NDEs, which leave those with such experiences convinced about the possibility of postmortem survival, feeling, perception, and even limited forms of agency apart from their bodies.

Materialistic theories, Griffin avers, are not capable of producing satisfactory explanations of these phenomena. Of course, Griffin also realizes that none of these phenomena, even if real, demonstrate conclusively that there is life after death. However, if there are no other viable explanations (and there are not),[79] then when combined they show, he argues, at least the possibility that "the person (the mind or the soul, with or without some kind of nonphysical body) can exist apart from the physical body."[80]

Recall, however, that Griffin was led to examine parapsychological material in his quest for a *via media* between dualistic and supernatural-

79. Alan Gauld, "Survival," in *Parapsychology: Research on Exceptional Experiences,* ed. Jane Henry (London and New York: Routledge, 2005), pp. 217-23, especially 220.

80. Griffin, *Parapsychology, Philosophy, and Spirituality,* p. 263. Note the important role that Whitehead's philosophical framework provides for Griffin's analyses. Apart from such supporting metaphysical assumptions, other scholars are less likely to conclude that scientific evidence for life after death is convincing — e.g., David Lester, *Is There Life after Death? An Examination of the Empirical Evidence* (Jefferson, NC, and London: McFarland and Co., 2005). A debate format, covering much of the parapsychological evidence, is Rebecca K. O'Connor, ed., *Is There Life after Death?* (Farmington Hills, MI: Greenhaven Press, 2005). After twenty-five years of studying and thinking about parapsychological evidence, Stephen E. Braude, *Immortal Remains: The Evidence for Life after Death* (Lanham, MD: Rowman and Littlefield, 2003), comes to similar, albeit perhaps more tentative, conclusions than Griffin.

istic theism on the one hand and a positivistic and materialistic scientism on the other. Whitehead's philosophy of organism that understood reality to be constituted by dynamic yet momentary occasions of experience (technically called *actual occasions*) provides, for Griffin, a philosophically plausible framework to make sense of such phenomena at least along the following lines. In particular, Whitehead's theory of prehension suggested that (human) sense experience is derived (emergent, even) from a more fundamental nonsensory perception of the world. For human beings, such occurs mostly subconsciously or unconsciously, the clearest instance of which is our encounter with our own past through our "memory."[81] In fact, all things are constituted prehensively, that is, in some ways (passively) being produced by and in other ways (actively) incorporating other contiguous and noncontiguous events. Contiguous prehensions include the mind-body relation while noncontiguous relations include not only our memories but also our prehending other minds. The result is what Griffin calls a form of mind-brain interactionism, but one that avoids both dualism on the one hand and reductionist materialism on the other.[82]

What Griffin does is apply Whitehead's theory of prehension to parapsychological phenomena by developing a novel hypothesis regarding how human beings can interface with disembodied spirits. What Griffin calls "retroprehensive inclusion" involves the prehension of prior memories and experiences that are not our own, including intellectual information (knowledge *that*), interactive skills (knowledge *how*), mannerisms, personalities, and even intentional purposes.[83] This framework would not only account for psi phenomena inexplicable through telepathy and ESP, but also explain in the survivalist thesis how other disincarnate entities can persist and reemerge through mediums, possession phenomena, apparitions, or reincarnation.[84] (Might it even shed some light on the biblical indication that the "spirit and power of Elijah . . . will go before" Jesus [Luke 1:17], empowering his ministry and work?) Griffin concludes, given the

---

81. Griffin, *Parapsychology, Philosophy, and Spirituality,* pp. 38-40.

82. See also Griffin, *Whitehead's Radically Different Postmodern Philosophy,* chapter 3.

83. Griffin, *Parapsychology, Philosophy, and Spirituality,* pp. 155-56, and passim.

84. Griffin does note that disincarnate personalities that "survive" typically involve those who have experienced violent deaths or had manifested an intense holding on to life resulting in "unfinished business" at the time of death that in turn perpetuates their paranormal manifestations (*Parapsychology, Philosophy, and Spirituality,* pp. 193, 204-5). This is consistent with folklore and other anthropological research among indigenous traditions about the encounter with spirits of deceased human beings.

principle of parsimony or simplicity, that the survivalist hypothesis has a strong case, a case buttressed by the fact that "when the five kinds of phenomena are taken collectively . . . , some of them provide support for elements of the others."[85]

In the end, the cash value of these deliberations for Griffin is a robust, naturalistic, but not materialistic spirituality. Within the process cosmological framework, human selves are emergent self-determining souls that prehend themselves (their memories), others, the world, God, and even other spiritual realities, and through such prehensive occasions they encounter and create value in the world. Such evaluative enhancements are not limited to our embodied life spans, but may persist after we die as our disincarnate spirits continue to interact with and influence others and the world.[86]

Griffin's proposals are intriguing because of the possibilities they elicit for a pneumatologically informed cosmology that can account for, rather than exclude, psi phenomena. The doctrine of emergent panexperientialism begs for further exploration concerning the convergence of the traditionally disparate natural, human, and spiritual domains. While Griffin's primary focus is on how a panexperientialist perspective illuminates the processes of what modernity had defined as the merely natural world, I suggest that panexperientialism also helps us to rethink what premodernity had defined as the transcendent or spiritual world. If in Griffin's emergentist cosmology there are no purely inanimate natural entities, in a pneumatological cosmology there are no purely transcendental spiritual beings (except God, of course). More precisely, inasmuch as Griffin's panexperientialism does away with the ontological dualism between the natural and human worlds, I propose that when extended toward cosmological matters within an emergentist frame of reference, it also does away with the ontological dualism between the earthly and spiritual realms.

What I mean is that Griffin's process cosmology is capable of providing a metaphysical account not just for the existence of the disincarnate spirits of the dead but also for a spirit-filled world.[87] There are two aspects

85. Griffin, *Parapsychology, Philosophy, and Spirituality,* pp. 266-67.

86. Griffin, *Parapsychology, Philosophy, and Spirituality,* chapter 9, "Parapsychology and Postmodern Spirituality"; see also Griffin's introductory chapter, "Postmodern Spirituality and Society," in *Spirituality and Society: Postmodern Visions,* ed. Griffin (Albany: State University of New York Press, 1988), pp. 1-31.

87. I have always insisted that process philosophy and cosmology are consistent with Christian faith; where I part ways with the process tradition is in terms of its dipolar theism,

to this proposal. On the one hand, if human minds are considered as emergent properties or capacities constituted by but irreducible to the brain and the body, then psychic interactions can be similarly considered as emergent realities constituted by but irreducible to the complex interrelations of two or more mental sequences, whether conceived individually (as referring to specific persons) or corporately (in this case involving group activities and histories). On the other hand, if human spirits are emergent realities that are capable of surviving and indeed survive after bodily death, then I suggest that, as pentecostal and charismatic spirituality assumes, angels (as servants of God to human beings) and demons (as agents of destruction in human lives and societies) are similarly emergent spirits that can and indeed do "survive" the disintegration of their originary material or sentient "parts." Is it plausible to suggest that angels and demons — among the many other ancestral, animal, and nature spirits in the pentecostal imagination — are not necessarily transcendental entities (as Wiebe suggests) but emergent spiritual realities that constitute the complex fabric and web of human experience?

For help in this cosmological reimagination, I suggest consulting the work of biblical scholar and longtime Auburn Seminary professor Walter Wink on the biblical data on the principalities and powers.[88] For Wink, the biblical references to such powers — including angels and demons, authorities, heavenly rulers, etc.[89] — should be understood less as personal disincarnate spirits and more as fallen cosmic structures and forces. More importantly, they represent the various social, economic, and political aspects of what Wink calls the "world domination system." As such, they are violent and destructive realities that require not only socio-ethical critique but also a nonviolent praxis and spirituality of resistance.[90]

---

defending instead a more robustly Trinitarian understanding of God as much more coherent — see Yong, *Spirit-Word-Community,* chapter 3.

88. See especially Wink's trilogy *Naming the Powers: The Language of Powers in the New Testament* (Philadelphia: Fortress, 1984); *Unmasking the Powers: The Invisible Forces That Determine Human Existence* (Philadelphia: Fortress, 1986); and *Engaging the Powers: Discernment and Resistance in a World of Domination* (Minneapolis: Fortress, 1992). A summary statement is Wink, *The Powers That Be: Theology for a New Millennium* (New York: Doubleday, 1998).

89. In *Naming the Powers,* pp. 13-38, Wink devotes detailed attention to the language of power in the Christian Testament: *archē* and *archōn, exousia, dynamis, thronos, kyriotēs,* and *onoma.*

90. I have previously engaged with Wink's theology of the powers in my *Discerning the Spirit(s): A Pentecostal-Charismatic Contribution to Christian Theology of Religions* (Shef-

Wink's basic thesis is that the biblical language for the powers names and identifies our experience of and engagement with realities that have both inner and outer aspects. "As the inner aspect they [the powers] are the spiritualities of institutions, the 'within' of corporate structures and systems, the inner essence of outer organizations of power. As the outer aspect they are political systems, appointed officials, the 'chair' of an organization, laws — in short, all the tangible manifestations which power takes."[91] Both aspects go together and neither can be in isolation from the other. The powers are thus heavenly and earthly, spiritual and material, divine and human, invisible and structural. But they are also good as well as potentially evil. Wink notes that the biblical *mythos* clearly identifies the powers — including the satan himself, at least in his origins if not also at the end — as servants of God.[92] The emergence of evil is best related in the myth of the primeval fall. Historically, however, human choices play a decisive role in the origin and perpetuation of demonic powers.[93] For Wink, then, there are powers at work in the world, some of which are demonic in character; yet none of these operate apart from the oversight and ultimate control of God. But once unleashed — or, to use my conceptualization: once emergent — these powers potentially attain a life of their own, capable of influencing and interacting with concrete historical structures, institutions, organizations, nations, and even persons and church movements.

In his assessment, then, the biblical principalities and powers refer to a wide range of realities, in some cases to human institutions, in others to cosmic elements, and in a third instance to personified structures like the law or even death. So if "demons" are the inner personal or collective dimensions of outwardly destructive behaviors and manifestations, the biblical "angels" of churches can be identified with and understood as the edifying personality, vocation, or ministry of their congregations (e.g., Rev. 2–3).

---

field: Sheffield Academic Press, 2000), pp. 128-29 and passim, and *In the Days of Caesar: Pentecostalism and Political Theology — the Cadbury Lectures, 2009* (Grand Rapids: Eerdmans, 2010), chapter 4.2.3. Nigel Wright, *The Satan Syndrome: Putting the Power of Darkness in Its Place* (Grand Rapids: Zondervan Academie, 1990), is another evangelical scholar who has found Wink helpful, although appropriating his work in different ways.

91. Wink, *Naming the Powers,* p. 5. See also Wolfhart Pannenberg, *Toward a Theology of Nature: Essays on Science and Faith,* ed. Ted Peters (Louisville: Westminster John Knox, 1993), chapter 6, for a more philosophical and theological discussion of the inner, psychic, and spiritual dimension of things, in dialogue with Teilhard de Chardin.

92. Wink, *Unmasking the Powers,* pp. 9-22.

93. Wink, *Unmasking the Powers,* pp. 30-39.

Yet — and this is important — this is not merely a demythologizing hermeneutic that reduces the principalities and powers to social or ecclesial con-
ventions. Rather, the principalities and powers are

> the invisible, intangible interiority of collective enterprises, the invari-
> ant, determining forces of nature and society, or the archetypal images
> of the unconscious, all of which shape, nurture, and all too often cripple
> human existence. These mighty Powers are still with us. They are not
> "mere" symbols — that too is the language of the old worldview that is
> passing, for we now know that nothing is more powerful than a living
> symbol. As symbols they point to something real, something the
> worldview of materialism never learned to name and therefore never
> could confront.[94]

From a critical pentecostal perspective, Wink is to be applauded in
what he affirms — especially his retrieval and socioeconomic-political reinterpretation of the biblical powers and his development of a theology of
praxis to inform our contemporary response — even if he may need to be
challenged in what he denies regarding the personal character of these
powers. Any pentecostal theology of discernment of spirits can certainly
gain from a close reading of Wink's reconstruction of the biblical powers,
especially in terms of balancing out the sometimes excessive individualism
that permeates popular pentecostal demonology. Further, pentecostal rites
of exorcism could also be enriched and transformed with the help of
Wink's understanding of the powers as constituting the structures of our
world domination system. In both cases — of discernment and exorcism
— pentecostal praxis would be empowered to engage with far more than
the forces of evil that operate at the level of the individual (as important as
that may be). Rather, insofar as the biblical powers are further understood
within an emergence and supervenience model of the God-world relationship, to that degree pentecostal discernment and exorcism could engage
with the entire range of evil powers, from those functioning at the individual level to those structuring institutional, social, international, and other
corporate relationships.[95] On the other hand, of course, the personal char-

94. Wink, *Unmasking the Powers*, p. 173.
95. This balance between an individualistic and corporate demonology is best seen in
the work of Thomas J. Csordas, *The Sacred Self: A Cultural Phenomenology of Charismatic
Healing* (Berkeley: University of California Press, 1994), especially chapter 7. In Csordas's
analysis of Catholic charismatic ritual exorcism, the demonic is often comprehensible as a

acter of especially angels need not be denied, especially since a supervenience model of the spirit/mind-brain relationship could also support a more classical understanding of spirit beings. This view would require a kind of hermeneutical sophistication, but nevertheless recognizes how the cosmic forces of destruction do manifest themselves through and engage with personal beings like ourselves.

But what I want to take from Wink, in combination with Griffin's contributions, are the basic building blocks for an emergentist cosmology, one that features emergent spiritual dimensions rather than a merely materialistic world. On the one hand, Griffin's nondualistic and nonsupernaturalistic defense of the survival hypothesis is suggestive for an ontology of disembodied spiritual realities. On the other hand, Wink's reinterpretation of the biblical materials regarding principalities, powers, and the demonic is also suggestive of the reality of emergent spiritual forces. Put together, the spirit-filled cosmos of the pentecostal-charismatic imagination can be understood within an emergentist framework to account for at least the following two levels of spiritual realities:

- personal spirit-beings constituted initially by physical bodies, but irreducible to them and capable of surviving the death of such bodies, at least for a period of time; and
- corporate spirit-beings constituted initially by corporate realities, but irreducible to them and capable of surviving the dissolution of such realities, at least for a period of time.

How theologically plausible is such a cosmological hypothesis in light of emergence theory and the insights of the parapsychological sciences?

Speculative Theses for a Pluralistic Cosmos

Adam Frank has noted that "Modern cosmology is our culture's origin story. It is the science of the universe entire, and its purview embraces the

---

collective representation of the conflicted/alienated self-in-society. Hence, the phenomenology of charismatic demonology calls attention to the physical, psychiatric, and social conflicts/disabilities that are being negotiated by individuals in charismatic communities, and exorcisms are a socio-emotional process of self-(re)formation and communal (re)formation. While Csordas's analysis does not account entirely for charismatic phenomena, it illuminates the dialectic between an individualistic and a social interpretation of the demonic.

origin of all space, time, matter, and energy."[96] What then would a late-modern or postmodern cosmology look like from a pentecostal perspective? In this section, I want to provisionally draw to a close our discussions in this chapter at the intersection of pentecostal-charismatic beliefs in a pluralistic or spirit-filled world and the paranormal phenomena studied by the parapsychological sciences by presenting a pneumatological cosmology, informed in part by our late-modern or postmodern situation and intuitions.

Let me clearly say that this is a piece of speculative theology, albeit one that I believe is warranted (or warrantable) by Scripture, philosophical and theological considerations, and scientific perspectives, all understood within the emergentist, pneumatological, and eschatological frame of reference proposed in this book. Hermeneutically, let me also clarify that I provide scriptural citations not necessarily because I think they have to be interpreted as I am suggesting, but because I think the following speculative hypotheses are sufficiently vague to be able to account for the scriptural data, at least as presented at this level of generality. Philosophically, I am also aware that various metaphysical issues will need to be adjudicated, but I present these recommendations as heuristic proposals within the emergentist framework that has been developed. There are ten theses for consideration toward what I call a pluralistic cosmology.

Thesis 1: The triune God is the only necessary, transcendent, and purely spiritual reality. This is, of course, an article of faith that answers to one biblical description, one theological achievement, and one philosophical or metaphysical hypothesis. Biblically, the author of the Fourth Gospel records Jesus' claim that "God is spirit [*pneuma*], and those who worship him must worship in spirit and truth" (John 4:24). Theologically, the affirmation here is that God is triune, understood as Father, Son, and Holy Spirit, although the three persons of the classical confession should be understood theologically and relationally in a way that preserves the unity or oneness of God, rather than ontologically in a way that divides the threeness of the divine persons.[97] Philosophically, the claim that the triune God is a necessary being responds to the metaphysical question, Why is

96. Adam Frank, *The Constant Fire: Beyond the Science vs. Religion Debate* (Berkeley: University of California Press, 2009), p. 144.

97. Here, of course, I am sensitive to the position of Oneness Pentecostals, who constitute almost one-fourth of the global renewal movement; see my *The Spirit Poured Out on All Flesh: Pentecostalism and the Possibility of Global Theology* (Grand Rapids: Baker Academic, 2005), chapter 5.

there something rather than nothing? The answer, in faith, is that God is the necessary ontological reality from out of which all things derive. As a theological hypothesis, nothing in thesis 1 contradicts science. Science simply does not present reasons for or against this proposition. Put positively, such an understanding of God can even be seen to be consistent with modern science.

Thesis 2: The creation narrative reveals that the triune God creates all things as good and brings about order and complexity by Spirit *(ruach* or *pneuma)* and Word (through divine speech).[98] Here I am building on my reading of the Genesis narrative in chapter 5, but formalizing this as a theological and metaphysical claim with regard to three specific aspects of the created order in dialogue with the proposals in the preceding section. First, the form of the Word is revealed in the incarnation, the enfleshment, of God in Christ — which theologically means that the template for the creation, its means, and its goal, is Christ (Col. 1:15-20 and Heb. 1:2). Thus, creation by the Word of God involves not just God speaking but God forming and making distinct, particular, and concrete material and fleshly things.

Second, given divine creation by Spirit and Word, all things are constituted, as Wink suggests, not only by their outward concrete and material aspect but also by an inner dynamic, spiritual, and interrelational dimension.[99] In what Griffin calls compound individuals — for example, animals that have an emergent dominant member capable of higher-level experiences of individuality, spontaneity, and self-determination — the inner relational dynamic emerges as a sentient form of life, constituted by but irreducible to the sum of the bodily parts. In *Homo sapiens,* this inner dynamic emerges as the self-conscious spirit, also constituted by but irreducible to the sum of the brain and bodily parts in their interaction with their environment.

Finally, all things in their embodied and concrete particularity and in

---

98. Divine creation through Word and Spirit is an Irenaean doctrine, which I have elaborated pneumatologically in my *Spirit-Word-Community,* chapter 2.

99. These are my theological renditions of what my *Doktorvater* Robert Cummings Neville, *Recovery of the Measure: Interpretation and Nature* (Albany: State University of New York Press, 1989), chapter 5, calls the conditional and essential features of all things. Elsewhere — e.g., in my *Spirit-Word-Community,* part I — I have developed a Trinitarian ontology from Charles S. Peirce's triadic metaphysics, but that added argument will only complicate our discussion here. For our present purposes, it is enough for me to highlight at least this dyadic aspect of all created realities.

their dynamic and relational-spiritual aspects were originally created good (Gen. 1:4, 10, 12, 18, 21, 25, and 31). This means that the processes of divine creation, which include the evolutionary history of this world (according to the standard account presented in chapter 5), produced only good things. In this frame of reference, then, evil is an inaccurate theological descriptor for the developments — that is, predation, animal suffering, death, and even species extinction — that occurred prior to and contributed to the arrival of *Homo sapiens.*[100]

100. This is not to minimize the plague, predation, pain, parasitism, and death that occurred in the world before the coming of *ha'adam.* On this issue, Stephen Webb, *The Dome of Eden* (Eugene, OR: Cascade Books, 2010), has recently retrieved, updated, and expanded upon the ancient gap or chaos-restitution theory regarding the fall of the satan between Gen. 1:1 and Gen. 1:2 to resolve the problem of natural evil, especially these violent and cruel aspects of animal life before the fall of humankind, by developing a novel proposal of how the perennially mysterious dome or firmament of Gen. 1:6-8 served to demarcate and shield the paradisiacal evolution in the Garden of Eden from the satanically infected process "red in tooth and claw" outside. Webb is one of the very few theologians to take the doctrine of the satan seriously in order to account for the long history of evolutionary violence and death prior to the arrival of humanity, and those involved in the theology and science dialogue should read this book. The prose is engaging, and even detractors will be forced to think through many issues in light of Webb's trenchant analyses, especially of Darwinian evolution as a metaphysically naturalistic hypothesis. Because his very creative and ingenious argument came to my attention as I was completing my manuscript, I cannot engage it at length here. Suffice it to make the following observations. With regard to the dome theory, there persist for me exegetical questions about how his reading makes sense of the wider creation narratives, theological questions left over from the long history of the fall of angels paradigm, and wider scientific questions — behind and beyond the evolution of animals, i.e., regarding cosmological interstellar, planetary, geospheric, and geological formation — that now arise. With regard to the fall of angels thesis, Webb presents as valuable a protological (origins-related) account as anyone, but I think my eschatological framework makes better sense of the cryptic biblical references to the angelic fall motif — which is contrasted to the authority and salvation of believers by Jesus (Luke 10:18-20) and related to the struggle of human and salvation history (Rev. 12:13-17), precisely my point in thesis 6 — while avoiding unwarranted speculation about pre-Adamic-lapsarian evolution (since even the enigmatic Jude 6 indicates that the lapsed angels have been "kept in eternal chains in deepest darkness for the judgment of the great day," rather than that they remained free to roam around and infect the process of animal evolution with suffering). Last but not least, with regard to the nature of what Webb calls natural evil, my initial response is to read Rom. 5:12 — "just as through one man sin entered the world, and death through sin, and thus *death spread to all men,* because all sinned" (NKJV, italics added) — as referring to human rather than animal death, and secondarily, to think about animal predation, etc., in nonmoral terms, thus obviating the need for a theodicy before the fall. On this final issue, I remain unconvinced not only by Webb but also by R. Paul Thompson, "An Evolutionary Ac-

Thesis 3: God is the primordial source of the transcendentals, for example, the good, the beautiful, and the true, but the dialectically oppositional aspects of the axiological, alethic, aesthetic, moral, and spiritual dimensions of the world only fully emerge in the cosmos with the appearance of *Homo sapiens*, supervening upon their relationships. The temptation to sin is certainly personified in the Bible — for example, through the craftiness of the tempting serpent in Genesis 3:1 — but such is really birthed out of freedom "by one's own desire" and according to the "cravings that are at war within" us (James 1:14; 4:1). Sin is thus a theological reality that identifies humanity's conscious rebellion against and falling out of relationship with God, resulting in the emergence of evil:

- what is good and valuable can be misused and devalued with the manifestation of sin;
- what is beautiful can be perverted and become ugly through sin;
- what is true and right can be rendered false and enacted incorrectly by sin; and
- what is spiritually in harmony with God can be alienated by sin.

In short, sin enters the world through the destructive choices and behaviors of self-conscious human beings who refuse to worship God, who live in enmity with others, and who become estranged from the created environment. Philosophically speaking, just as consciousness supervenes upon the states of the brain (see chapter 2), so also sin is a supervenient reality, constituted by but irreducible to the human experience of broken and distorted relationships. There is no separate "fall of angels" in the creation narrative, at least not one that occurred prior to the emergence of *ha'adam* (although see thesis 6 below).

Thesis 4: The emergence of spirit in humanity intensified further the spiritual dimension already latent in the very fabric of our interrelational cosmos. Insofar as human beings have developed as personal and spiritual creatures, to that extent the world and all its parts now also come alive spiri-

---

count of Evil," in *Philosophy after Darwin: Classic and Contemporary Readings*, ed. Michael Ruse (Princeton and Oxford: Princeton University Press, 2009), pp. 533-49, who suggests a population concept of evil such that whatever enhances population perpetuation is good and whatever does not do so is evil. In a future book with the working title of *God Is Spirit, God Is Love: Love in the Power of the Spirit* (Waco, TX: Baylor University Press, forthcoming), I intend to address these matters at greater detail in developing a theology of love informed in part by altruism studies in evolutionary biology.

tually in relationship to human sensibilities, intentions, and activities. If the primordial entanglement of the universe illuminates, at least in part, human psychic accomplishments, then the spiritual nature of the cosmos emerges out of discursive human interactions with the world. So, for example,

- we feel awe and an emergent spiritual sense of wonder when staring out over the Grand Canyon, sitting beneath the Redwoods, or peering through a telescope into the Andromeda Galaxy, or we sense the spiritual sublimity of sacred places as Jacob did at Bethel, locations wherein portals into the transcendent or numinous presences emerge that overwhelm our normal sensory perceptions;
- we interact spiritually with the dynamics of nature, as did the ancients (and some moderns) in their following of stars,[101] as did ancient seafarers in their understanding of the calm of the storm as spiritually potent and significant, or as did Native Americans with their rain dances, etc.; and
- we develop deep relationships with animals, whether domesticated in farms or kept as pets in our homes, often making connections with these forms of sentient life that are suggestive of an emergent sense of spiritual engagement (e.g., as in the four animal spirits in Ezek. 1).

101. The Matthean reference to the wise men from the East, also known as magi or astrologers, following the star of Bethlehem is the clearest case (Matt. 1:18–2:12). A natural astronomical explanation for the star, one that leaves aside rather than reduces the biblical view, is Mark Kidger, *The Star of Bethlehem: An Astronomer's View* (Princeton: Princeton University Press, 1999). From the standpoint of faith, one largely consistent with (even supervening upon, in my terms) Kidger's research but concluding that the biblical account is fully consonant with the contemporary astronomical sciences, is the study by the Vatican Observatory astronomer Gustav Teres, S.J., *The Bible and Astronomy: The Magi and the Star in the Gospel* (Budapest: Springer, 2000). A classic theological interpretation of the stars is E. W. Bullinger, *The Witness of the Stars* (1893; reprint, London: Lamp Press, 1954). Intriguingly, then, the blurred lines between ancient astronomy and historic and contemporary astrology would again raise theological questions. In view of our discussion in the preceding chapter regarding the Genesis narrative, however, Nahum M. Sarna, *Genesis: The Traditional Hebrew Text with the New JPS Translation* (Philadelphia, New York, and Jerusalem: Jewish Publication Society, 1989), p. 10, notes that the plain, matter-of-fact mention of the creation of the luminaries of the sky, without any further discussion, "constitutes a tacit repudiation of astrology" (citing Jer. 10:2 as well). From a cautious philosophical perspective, see Stephen Braude's discussion of astrology in *The Gold Leaf Lady,* chapter 8. A sympathetic and brief review of the scientific aspects, albeit arriving at negative conclusions, is David Groome, "Astrology," in *Parapsychology: The Science of Unusual Experience,* ed. Ron Roberts and David Groome (London: Arnold; New York: Oxford University Press, 2001), pp. 60-73.

As discussed at the end of chapter 3, this is not just a subjectivistic way of engaging the world so that its "spiritual dimension" becomes only a projection or extension of our own consciousness. Rather, the emergence of human spirituality is constituted at least in part by these dynamic interactions with the natural world so that the latter is not merely inert matter but is itself attunable to or prehensible by our knowing, feeling, and doing. And to the degree that human beings have emerged with the capacity to choose for either good or evil, to that same extent the spiritual dimensions of the world also are potentially benevolent or malevolent.[102]

Thesis 5: Angelic spirits, then, are emergent benevolent realities that minister the salvific grace of God to human lives.[103] Although proposed tentatively, nothing in the Genesis 1–2 narrative suggests that purely spiritual (disembodied) beings were included in the work of divine creation.[104] Just as the human spirit emerges from and supervenes upon the embodied relations that constitute our existence, so also, I suggest, do benevolent spiritual realities emerge from the complex material and personal relationships through which God's redemption is at work.[105] If

102. This is suggested, for example, by the biblical references to evil spirits said to be from or under the command of God (e.g., Judg. 9:23; 1 Sam. 16:14-23; 18:10; 19:9) — unexpectedly since God is usually understood as good — or to "angels of the Lord" that engage in behaviors like lying usually associated with the devil who is the father of lies (John 8:44; cp. 1 Kings 22:21-23 and Ps. 78:49). There are also destroying angels from God, although mostly these represent either God's deliverance of his people or divine judgments on unrighteousness (e.g., 2 Sam. 24:15-17; 2 Kings 19:35; 1 Chron. 21:12; 2 Chron. 32:21; Acts 12:23).

103. For a traditional explication of this biblical definition, minus the "emergent" aspect, see Peter S. Williams, *The Case for Angels* (Carlisle, UK, and Waynesboro, GA: Paternoster, 2002).

104. The indication in the letter to the Hebrews that human beings have been made "for a little while lower than the angels" (Heb. 2:7 — although the Masoretic Hebrew text of Ps. 8:5, the LXX version of which is quoted here, says: "a little lower than God/gods") does not require that angels were created prior to or emerged before humanity; that same logic would say, incoherently, that since animals are a little lower than humans, the latter were created prior to or emerged before the former.

105. Part II of Geddes MacGregor, *Angels: Ministers of Grace* (New York: Paragon House, 1988), also discusses a similar idea of "angels as an evolutionary possibility." But rather than viewing angels as posthuman emergent realities, MacGregor suggests instead that their evolutionary history (perhaps off wholly different lineages) has resulted in their advanced powers, far superior to human beings, just as human evolution has distanced us from our closest cousins. I am intrigued by MacGregor's suggestions, although he provides little empirical perspective to make the notion plausible. I note, however, that MacGregor also believes, as do I, that psychical research has a bearing on our thinking about angels and other spiritual or immaterial creatures (see *Angels,* chapter 16).

such is indeed the case, then angels may be understood as manifestations that are

- personal, as recorded across the biblical traditions when they appear in the form of human beings (e.g., Dan. 8:15 and Luke 1:19 regarding Gabriel),[106] as "guardian angels" (Matt. 18:10), and as strangers whom we entertain unawares (except retrospectively in faith), with their personal features here defined not in terms of the Cartesian cogito but in terms of the emergent interpersonal character of human relationships;[107]
- ecclesial, as angels of the churches, as identified by the Apocalypse (Rev. 2–3), thus identifying the emergent spiritual character of congregations, communities, and corporate groups of people;
- institutional, social, or national, as perhaps (1) what Saint Paul called principalities, powers, thrones, authorities, and rulers (1 Cor. 2:6-8; Eph. 3:10; 6:12; Col. 1:16); (2) what the biblical authors identified as the princes of Persia and of Greece (Dan. 10:20) or as Michael, the prince of the people of God (Dan. 12:1; cf. Rev. 12:7);[108] or (3) what the an-

106. Gabriel's character in Daniel as a messenger and harbinger of information, in contrast to the archangel Michael's "divine warrior" role, is consistent with his bringing good tidings in Luke; for discussion of Gabriel's role in Daniel, see Benedikt Otzen, "Michael and Gabriel: Angelological Problems in the Book of Daniel," in *The Scriptures and the Scrolls: Studies in Honour of A. S. Van Der Woude on the Occasion of His 65th Birthday,* ed. F. García Martínez, A. Hilhorst, and C. J. Labuschagne, Supplements to Vetus Testamentum 49 (Leiden: Brill, 1992), pp. 114-24, especially 121-22.

107. This may explain the practices of ancestor veneration and worship, especially if ancestors are confused with angelic spirits who have also been — incorrectly — worshiped (Col. 2:18). But see also the fascinating study of Stephen L. Young, "They Will Shine Like the Stars of Heaven: Early Jewish Angelic Resurrection and Exaltation-of-the-Righteous Traditions in Their Hellenistic Matrix" (master of theology thesis, Westminster Theological Seminary, 2008), who shows that prevalent across the later Second Temple Jewish literature was an apocalyptic and eschatological expectation that God "will exalt the righteous to be like the angels, share in angelic identity, transform them to be like the angels, have communion with the angels, and/or become angelic priests" (p. 3). In this case, then, the lines between the spirits of the deceased righteous and angelic spirits are blurred indeed, precisely what one would expect if my hypothesis regarding the emergence of spirit beings is anywhere close to the mark.

108. In an intriguing article, Colin Nicholl argues that "the restrainer" of the second Thessalonian letter can be understood as referring to the archangel Michael. If this is the case, then, similar to how disincarnate human spirits can retain a more or less effective presence and activity either before or after death, so also might the effectiveness of spirit beings

cient Near Eastern world understood as the divine council or assembly of the gods, members of whom may have been "assigned to" (or supervened upon) the nations of the world (Deut. 32:8; 1 Kings 22:19-20; Job 1:6; 2:1; Ps. 82:1, 6)[109] — each of which thus represents the emergent tribal, corporate, and national consciousness of people groups, the inner dynamics of networks (i.e., the spirit of educational institutions), the various manifestations of civil society (i.e., spirits of communities and voluntary associations), and the comprehensive structures of economic relations (i.e., the spirits of capitalism, socialism, or the global economy);[110]

- terrestrial, as spirits shaped by geographical or topographical regions — for example, the angels "at the four corners of the earth" and the "angel ascending from the rising of the sun" in the Apocalypse (Rev. 7:1-2), or "the angel of the waters" (Rev. 16:5) — or by natural terrestrial phenomena like winds, flame, and fire (Judg. 13:20; Heb. 1:7),[111]

---

of corporate entities like nations, in this case, Israel itself, be minimized or even negated. See Nicholl, "Michael, the Restrainer Removed (2 Thess. 2:6-7)," *Journal of Theological Studies*, n.s., 51, no. 1 (2000): 27-53.

109. These go also by many other labels in the Hebrew Bible, including "sons of the gods" (Ps. 29:1; Gen. 6:2, 4), "holy ones" (Job 5:1; Ps. 89:6-7; Zech. 14:5), and even just plainly "gods" (*elohim* or *ha-elohim* — Exod. 15:11; Pss. 95:3; 96:4; 135:5; 136:2; and many other texts). See, e.g., E. Theodore Mullen Jr., *The Divine Council in Canaanite and Early Hebrew Literature,* Harvard Semitic Monographs 24 (Chico, CA: Scholars, 1980), and Michael S. Heiser, "Deuteronomy 32:8 and the Sons of God," *Bibliotheca Sacra* 158, no. 629 (2001): 52-74; cp. also Mark S. Smith, *The Early History of God: Yahweh and the Other Deities in Ancient Israel,* 2nd ed. (Grand Rapids and Cambridge: Eerdmans; Dearborn, MI: Dove Booksellers, 2002).

110. In my *In the Days of Caesar,* chapter 4, I argue at length in dialogue with the relevant biblical and theological studies literature that the biblical powers refer at least in part to the social, economic, and political structures that shape human existence, and that while fallen in some respects, they can be redeemed in order to accomplish again what they were intended to do.

111. Two additional comments are noteworthy regarding Heb. 1:7. First, Koester's commentary connects this text with Ps. 148:8, "fire and hail, snow and frost, / stormy wind fulfilling his command," leading him to suggest that "God made natural elements like wind and fire into his servants"; see Craig R. Koester, *Hebrews: A New Translation with Introduction and Commentary,* Anchor Bible 36 (New York: Doubleday, 2001), p. 194. The point is to highlight the emergence of angelic spirits from or in association with natural phenomena. Second, does the windlike character of angels suggest that they were originally created as disembodied spirits? But to make angels as spirits does not necessarily deny their emergence, just as the making of human spirits supervenes upon rather than rejects their prior bodies and brains. As important, the point of Hebrews is not to provide a scientific or ontological description of the origins of angels, but to emphasize that unlike God's unique Son, angels "are

thus being constituted by but ultimately irreducible to environmental phenomena and processes;

- celestial, as spirits of the heavenlies — what the Bible often calls the hosts of heaven (e.g., Isa. 40:26; Luke 2:13)[112] — perhaps emergent from the intergalactic constellation and alignment of the stars (Job 38:7), especially vis-à-vis the salvation history events on earth, and once emergent, representing the celestial and cosmic worship that surrounds the eschatological throne of God (Heb. 12:22; Rev. 5:11).[113]

In sum, then, angelic spirits are emergent from their material substrates, constituted by but also thereafter irreducible to their outward physical forms. On the one hand, as agents of God who assist in the salvation of personal beings, they also are personal realities; on the other hand, as emergent from the complex matrices that constitute human relationships and their multiple environments, what we call angels are higher-level transpersonal or suprapersonal realities, constituted by and supervening upon the human relations from which they derive. Yet once emergent, they are irreducible to their underlying parts, even to the point of being capable of exercising "top-down" influence and agency in relationship to their lower-level realities.

---

like wind or fire, not eternal"; see Ben Witherington III, *Letters and Homilies for Jewish Christians: A Socio-Rhetorical Commentary on Hebrews, James, and Jude* (Downers Grove, IL: IVP Academic; Nottingham, UK: Apollos, 2007), p. 129.

112. There is an ancient tradition that links the origins of angels to the Genesis narrative in terms of God's creating the stars. On the one hand, this would locate the origins of such spiritual beings in the primordial divine creation, but on the other hand, this would go even further to sustain my emergence hypothesis since it would link angelic realities to the trillions of stars in the cosmos. In any case, there is little distinction in the ancient mind between the physical objects of the heavens (the stars) and spiritual beings: "these two were closely related"; see Verlyn D. Verbrugge, "The Heavenly Army on the Fields of Bethlehem (Luke 2:13-14)," *Calvin Theological Journal* 43, no. 2 (2008): 301-11, at 304.

113. Although it is also certainly possible that humankind's degeneration leads them to worship these hosts of heaven rather than their Creator (see Deut. 4:19-20; 2 Chron. 33:3-5; Jer. 7:18; 8:2; 19:13; Zeph. 1:5; Acts 7:42), this would be ironic, as these hosts of heaven were created to worship the Creator (Neh. 9:6; Ps. 97:7). In any case, the New Testament recognizes this plurality of cosmic beings while insisting on their subordination under what might be called the monotheistic principle of the sovereignty of the God of Christ: "Indeed, even though there may be so-called gods in heaven or on earth — as in fact there are many gods and many lords — yet for us there is one God, the Father, from whom are all things and for whom we exist, and one Lord, Jesus Christ, through whom are all things and through whom we exist" (1 Cor. 8:5-6).

Before moving on, I need to be clear about what it means to speak of angels as emergent beings. The closest analogy we are working with is the emergence of the mind or the spirit from the brain/body and its environment. We can say that without the brain, there is no mind or spirit, yet we cannot thereby reduce consciousness (or the spiritual person) to the brain's synaptic interactions. Therefore, I am also saying that without the various underlying material — that is, human and relational — substrates, there are no angels; yet I am also strongly insistent against reducing angelic spirits to their constituent members, particularly in light of the causal capacities they wield over the underlying material parts. And most importantly, rather than concentrating protologically on the *how* of angelic origins and emergence, my focus in understanding the nature and function of benevolent spirit entities is eschatologically informed, with the discernment of angels enabled based on the role they play in the human experience of the redemptive purposes of God.

Thesis 6: Demonic spirits, then, are divergent (as opposed to *emergent*) malevolent realities that oppose the salvific grace of God in human lives.[114] Again, I make this proposal tentatively since the biblical basis for this theological notion is skimpy indeed, at least from a surface reading.[115] But just as the human spirit emerges from the socially and environmentally embedded brain and body, and just as angelic spirits emerge as supervenient upon the concreteness and complexity of our interpersonal, social, and cosmic relations, so also, I suggest, do demonic spirits emerge

114. What follows is very consistent with Thomas A. Noble, "The Spirit World: A Theological Approach," in *The Unseen World: Christian Reflections on Angels, Demons, and the Heavenly Realm,* ed. Anthony N. S. Lane (Carlisle, UK: Paternoster; Grand Rapids: Baker, 1996), pp. 185-223, which understands the fall of angels realistically as a powerful consequence of human projection.

115. What is clear is that the fundamental notion of the demonic in the New Testament derives in large part from apocalyptic literature that proliferated during the Second Temple period (536 B.C.E. to 70 C.E.) and represented, at least in part, the protests of a marginalized people against their oppressors; see Archie T. Wright, *The Origins of Evil Spirits: The Reception of Genesis 6.1-4 in Early Jewish Literature,* Wissenschaftliche Untersuchungen zum Neuen Testament 2.198 (Tübingen: Mohr Siebeck, 2005); Annette Yoshiko Reed, *Fallen Angels and the History of Judaism and Christianity: The Reception of Enochic Literature* (Cambridge and New York: Cambridge University Press, 2005); and T. J. Wray and Gregory Mobley, *The Birth of Satan: Tracing the Devil's Biblical Roots* (New York and Basingstoke, UK: Palgrave Macmillan, 2005), chapters 4–5. See also Paul D. Hanson, *The Dawn of Apocalyptic: The Historical and Sociological Roots of Jewish Apocalyptic Eschatology,* rev. ed. (Philadelphia: Fortress, 1979).

from and supervene upon the human experience of alienation that disintegrates personal lives and destroys human relationships in general and human well-being as a whole.[116] If such is indeed the case, then the demonic may be manifest

- archetypally as the primeval chaos (Gen. 1:2) and its concomitant destructive primordial sea dragons (e.g., Job 41; Ps. 89:10; Isa. 51:9),[117] or as the satan or the devil, the adversary or the accuser of humanity that contradicts all aspects of human flourishing;[118]
- antipersonally as various destructive powers — referring by the time of the early Christian era to gods or lesser (even animal) spirits, a wide range of malevolent beings, deceased souls, or irrational realities threatening human existence[119] — that tempt, test, and try humans in opposing their peace and prosperity; the result is the disintegration of human lives, the overwhelming of the subconscious and unconscious aspects of the ego by irrational forces, as depicted in the various biblical narratives (i.e., the Gerasene demoniac and the seven sons of Sceva),[120]

116. Pannenberg, *Toward a Theology,* p. 159, notes in passing that whereas spirit is concerned with unifying and forming wholes (thus the human mind, if intact, also perceives synthetic forms), evil spirits, by contrast, are disintegrative instead of integrative, disruptive rather than synthetic, divisive rather than holistic, etc.

117. Thus should the Old Testament Leviathan or Rahab be understood, in conjunction with the primeval waters and seas, as opposing the order of Yahweh; see Neil Forsyth, *The Old Enemy: Satan and the Combat Myth* (Princeton: Princeton University Press, 1987), especially parts I and II; cp. Jon D. Levenson, *Creation and the Persistence of Evil: The Jewish Drama of Divine Omnipotence* (New York: Harper and Row, 1987).

118. Thus "there is no single celestial *śāṭān*" in the Old Testament, as noted by Peggy L. Day, *An Adversary in Heaven: Śāṭān in the Hebrew Bible,* Harvard Semitic Monographs 43 (Atlanta: Scholars, 1988), p. 147, after a thorough examination of the relevant Hebrew Bible texts (Num. 22:22-35; Job; Zech. 3; and 1 Chron. 21:1–22:1).

119. See Anders Klostergaard Petersen, "The Notion of Demon: Open Questions to a Diffuse Concept," in *Demons: The Demonology of Israelite-Jewish and Early Christian Literature in Context of Their Environment,* ed. Armin Lange, Hermann Lichtenberger, and K. F. Diethard Römheld (Tübingen: Mohr Siebeck, 2003), pp. 23-41. That the demonic is sometimes conceived as supervening upon animals is clear from the biblical references to the serpent in the garden (Gen. 3), the devilish manifestation in the form of a lion (1 Pet. 5:8), and the "three foul spirits like frogs coming from the mouth of the dragon, from the mouth of the beast, and from the mouth of the false prophet" (Rev. 16:13).

120. In the case of the Gerasene, there is also some suggestion in the text that the Legion of demons were regionally assigned, as they begged Jesus "not to send them *out of the country*" (Mark 5:10, italics mine).

and in historical and contemporary accounts of demonic possession and oppression;

• socially, historically, politically, and economically in terms of the domination systems (this is from Wink, of course) — even "the spirit of the world" as a whole (1 Cor. 2:12) — that impoverish and undercut human lives (i.e., the haunted city of Babylon in Rev. 18:2), and in terms of the corrupt, violent, and genocidal governments that have undermined the fabric of human social life;

• regionally, geographically, terrestrially, or cosmically as forces of chaotic destruction, perhaps describing the degenerative expressions of the divine council (see previous thesis), the violent upheavals that disrupt human relations (e.g., volcanic eruptions, tsunamis, and earthquakes), or locales of concentrated evil (e.g., as Pergamum was identified as the satan's throne and "where Satan lives"; Rev. 2:13);

• anticelestially as fallen angels, intimated in Jesus' reference to the satan's falling from heaven (Luke 10:18; cp. Jude 6; Rev. 12:13) and developed in the Christian tradition as the deceiver who was in the Garden of Eden responsible for the fall of *ha'adam*.[121]

Insofar as demonic realities are emergent from and supervenient upon originally good things, they lack their own being or onticity and thus emerge only parasitically in and through the moral behaviors, actions, and intentions of free creatures. Hence in the grand Augustinian tradition, I view evil as privation, and the symbols of the satan, the devil, and the demonic as pointing to the perversion and negation of goodness,

---

121. While Justin Martyr was one of the first Christian apologists to equate the fallen angels of the Book of the Watchers tradition (*1 Enoch* 1–36) with demons and pagan deities — on this see Reed, *Fallen Angels and the History of Judaism and Christianity*, chapter 5 — Augustine was most responsible for developing this into the doctrine of the pre-Adamic fall of the satan himself and his angels, and he had to resort to all sorts of theological and philosophical gymnastics to pull it off — e.g., William S. Babcock, "The Human and the Angelic Fall: Will and Moral Agency in Augustine's *City of God*," in *Augustine: From Rhetor to Theologian*, ed. Joanne McWilliam (Waterloo, Ontario: Wilfrid Laurier University Press, 1992), pp. 133-49, especially 143-47. See also the broad scope of these developments in Henry Ansgar Kelly, *Satan: A Biography* (Cambridge: Cambridge University Press, 2006), while the reception and transformation of the archangel Michael during this same period is recounted in Thomas J. Kraus, "Angels in the Magical Papyri: The Classic Example of Michael, the Archangel," in *Angels: The Concept of Celestial Beings — Origins, Development, and Reception,* ed. Friedrich Vinzenz Reiterer, Tobias Nicklas, and Karin Schöpflin (Berlin and New York: Walter de Gruyter, 2007), pp. 611-27.

truth, beauty, and value created by God.[122] Unfortunately once emergent, they also are irreducible to their underlying parts. But to then say that demonic spirits are therefore capable, like benevolent spirit beings, of exercising "top-down" influence and agency in relationship to their lower-level realities would be to grant them more personal integrity than I believe they actually possess. I would prefer to say that at the more corporate, social, political, and economic levels, demonic realities wield massive destructive powers (as Tillich discerned during the interwar years),[123] as powers exponentially more devastating than when considered simply the sum of malevolence exercised at the personal or individual level.

Yet as parasitic and privative — ultimately nothingness in comparison to the goodness and reality of God — the reality of the demonic, like sin, escapes rational definition. Thus does the author of the second epistle to the Thessalonians refer to the "mystery of lawlessness" (2 Thess. 2:7), which is indicative of the inexplicability of demonic chaos and of the origins of evil.[124] Similarly, then, the demonic's irrationality means that it can never exist as authentically personal entities; rather, that which is demonic opposes, distorts, and destroys the integrity of personhood.[125] For all these reasons and more, we do not "believe in" the devil and his demons in the

122. While problematic at various levels, Sung Min Jeong's *Nothingness in the Theology of Paul Tillich and Karl Barth* (Lanham, MD: University Press of America, 2003) provides an overview of the basic thrust of this Augustinian theology of evil as privation as elaborated upon by two of the giants of twentieth-century theology.

123. See Paul Tillich, *The Interpretation of History,* trans. Elsa L. Talmey (New York and London: Charles Scribner's Sons, 1936), pp. 77-122.

124. Thus have some theologians suggested that we should move on from attempting to explain evil and engage instead with combating and resisting it; e.g., Terrence W. Tilley, *The Evils of Theodicy* (Washington, DC: Georgetown University Press, 1991).

125. Here is where I would otherwise differ from Richard H. Bell's otherwise fine study, *Deliver Us from Evil: Interpreting the Redemption from the Power of Satan in New Testament Theology* (Tübingen: Mohr Siebeck, 2007). Bell rightly resists that the satan is a mythical figure, although by this he is not merely following Bultmann's demythologization program but is rather recognizing the ontological status of evil as noumenal (rather than only phenomenal or supernatural — thereby also rejecting the natural-supernatural dualism). But Bell affirms a dualistic anthropology (rather than an emergentist one), which leads him also to affirm the personality and personal character of the demonic, whereas I suggest that the demonic is personal only to the extent that it is parasitic on human personality and that, in fact, the reality of the demonic is ultimately antipersonal, "seeking" as it were the disintegration and destruction of true personhood, especially as revealed in Christ (which Bell also asserts).

same way we might believe in (and trust) a personal — or better: suprapersonal — God.[126]

Thesis 7: But the good news is that the triune God continues to work to redeem the world incarnationally (Word) and pentecostally (Spirit), and in this dispensation, such is being accomplished through the church. Although God in himself is pure spirit (see thesis 1), God in relationship to the world in general and to humanity specifically exists incarnationally and personally in Jesus and dynamically in the Spirit. The redemptive work of the triune God inaugurated in the incarnational and pentecostal events of salvation history continues to the present through the church, the body of Christ and fellowship of the Spirit. In short, we can also speak in emergent terms of God's redemptive work, in the life of Christ — his ministry, death, resurrection, and ascension — in the complexity of the Pentecost event, and in the dynamic unfolding of the church as a transpersonal, social, economic, and political community.

The church as an emergent entity therefore is constituted by and supervenient upon yet irreducible to the sum of its (congregational, denominational, or ecclesial) parts, even as these lower-level parts are also emergent and complex realities constituted by but irreducible to the persons who are members.[127] If this is the case, however, then individual members and aggregate congregations all have their part to play in the redemptive work of God:

- human persons work while alive to embody and proclaim the gospel of the kingdom, and after their death, their spiritual legacy survives and continues to influence the work of others (quite apart from, al-

126. Thus Nigel Goring Wright, *A Theology of the Dark Side: Putting the Power of Evil in Its Place* (Downers Grove, IL: InterVarsity, 2003), rightly talks about "disbelieving in the devil" (chapter 2). Filling out what is here merely asserted, my student David Bradnick is currently writing a dissertation on an emergentist theology of the demonic tentatively titled "Loosing and Binding the Spirits: Towards an Emergentist Theology of the Demonic"; see also Bradnick's "A Pentecostal Perspective on Entropy, Emergent Systems, and Eschatology," *Zygon* 43, no. 4 (2008): 925-42.

127. My notion of the "emergent church" is an ontological description that is not equivalent to the "emerging church" phenomenon on the contemporary North American landscape. I am not necessarily opposed to the latter in general (even if I might disagree with some aspects of its manifestations), although I am certainly sympathetic to how some of its advocates — e.g., Bruce Sanguin, *The Emerging Church: A Model for Change and a Map for Renewal* (Kelowna, British Columbia: Copperhouse, 2008) — are open to thinking ecclesiologically in light of the theology and science conversation.

though not necessarily excluding their mediation through, psi activities and effects);

- institutions and associations, for example, churches, parachurch networks, nongovernmental organizations, are the dynamic and concrete realities whose mission is accomplished by the Spirit through various established offices — that is, within the church, via the official functions of apostle, prophet, evangelist, pastor, and teacher — even when their individual members might come and go;
- social, political, economic, and historical processes are also being redeemed by the triune God so that the purposes of the kingdom may be made more apparent.

My point here is that Christian redemption is not merely spiritual in terms of its constitutedness by our embodiment and our concrete relationships in the world; however, the supervening and emergent nature of the spiritual dimension means that it also cannot be cordoned off from these various historical and concrete manifestations.

Thesis 8: Negatively put, the redemptive work of the church involves participating in the life and ministry of Christ by the power of his Spirit and naming, resisting, and, where appropriate, exorcising the demonic and delivering the oppressed from its destructive powers. While such participation may occur perhaps through what Griffin calls a process of retroprehensive inclusion, what is important is that the followers of Christ are empowered, as was Christ himself, to accomplish the works of the kingdom, which involve redeeming the world and its creatures from the powers that oppose that kingdom. Most importantly, we insist in faith that the demonic has been exposed and defeated at least initially by the cross of Christ (Col. 2:13-15), and that its final elimination is anticipated in the eschatological renovation of the cosmos. In the work of Christ, the lying, murderous, and violent powers of the demonic have been unmasked.[128] In the gospel, then, the redemptive possibilities offered by God are manifest in anticipation of the coming kingdom. The satan and his demons should thus be given neither too much credit nor too much attention, although

---

128. Thus my speculative hypotheses so far are fully consistent with, for example, René Girard's anthropological theory of the satan as representing the cycle of mimetic violence that plagues human life, which is broken only by the gospel of Christ, who triumphed in the cross precisely because he refused to perpetuate the response of violence; see Girard, *I See Satan Fall Like Lightning,* trans. James G. Williams (Maryknoll, NY: Orbis; Ottawa: Novalis; Leominster, UK: Gracewing, 2001).

they also should not be completely ignored because of the very real havoc and destruction they wreak in the world.

Yet even with this final overcoming of the demonic in hand, there is nevertheless the work of resistance on this side of the eschaton, and this can occur variously through prayer, fasting, the charisms, spiritual warfare in its various guises, as well as through the methods of exorcism deployed by Jesus himself. If the traditional rite of exorcism was designed to expel evil and destructive spiritual realities from the lives of people, then contemporary rites expose and unmask the privative and perverted nothingness of demonic realities. Exorcisms thus can function at various levels:

- personally, resulting in the healing of fractured self-identities (e.g., in terms of Jungian theory);
- socially, resulting in reconciliation between people (i.e., in terms of the enactment of spiritual warfare against greed);
- politically, resulting in the shalom that includes justice (namely, in terms of undermining territorial spirits).[129]

To reiterate, exorcisms do not merely cast out an immaterial, personal being, but they also cleanse and restore originally good creations according to the purposes of God. In short, such an emergentist cosmology is not dualistic and does not depend on an ontology that distinguishes the spirit-filled world from its material domain, but is thoroughly realistic (rather than nominalistic) in terms of the spiritual powers and forces that supervene upon concrete historical realities, which divine redemption combats.

Thesis 9: The eschatological redemption of the triune God will involve concrete and material bodies and their emergent inner and spiritual aspects, both announced as good in the primordial creation. This involves

- the resurrection of human (and perhaps animal) bodies, healed souls, and reconciled spirits, so that what lives eternally are whole creatures rather than disembodied spirits (cf. Luke 24:39);
- the redemption of the communities that have constituted the people of God across space and time (including their various emergent principalities and powers, all of whom will have been restored to their divinely intended vocation);

---

129. For further discussion, I refer readers, again, to my *In the Days of Caesar,* chapter 4; see also Yong, *Discerning the Spirit(s),* chapter 8 and passim.

- the renewal, renovation, and re-creation of the material creation itself, so that the prayers of the cosmos for redemption will have been answered (Rom. 8:19-22) as the many levels of emergent realities are restored and redirected for the governance of the new heavens and the new earth.

Thesis 10: On the other "side," the recalcitrant, reprobate, and irredeemable powers will finally experience (self) destruction, also understood as the other side of the incomprehensible judgment of God. This represents the hell of the biblical traditions, which is merely the thermodynamically anticipated destiny of the unrighteous, unraveling as nondissipative chaotic systems that close in upon themselves, analogous perhaps to the "freeze" ending of the cosmological "freeze or fry" scenarios regarding the end of the world. The spiritual realities that freely choose to resist the love of God will ultimately find that they are "nothing" in comparison with what they could have been in the divine scheme of things. The "eternally lost" would include:

- those who somehow succeed in eternally rejecting the immeasurable love of God, thus suffering the disintegration of their personhood and their spiritual identities;[130]
- entire social groups that embody unrighteousness (e.g., Sodom and its fallen angel), who will not find a home in the new heavens and the new earth;
- all unrighteousness ultimately represented by the satan as that incomprehensible and irrational chaos that in their paradoxical freedom eternally resists God.

I present these speculative theses with the conviction both that they register pentecostal sensibilities in the theology and science dialogue, and that formulated in this way, they also show how contemporary theological and scientific perspectives can enable a better understanding of the spiritual dimensions of the world within which we live, move, and have our be-

---

130. I confess I do not know at present what to make of the cryptic reference in the Fourth Gospel that in that eschatological final hour, the graves will be emptied, "those who have done good, to the resurrection of life, and those who have done evil, to the resurrection of condemnation" (John 5:29). The doctrine of the resurrection of the body fits well within my emergentist eschatology, but not for those who will suffer what appears to be eternal condemnation.

ing.[131] But presenting such a spirit-filled cosmos begs further questions. In particular, the theses may confirm all the worst fears of those involved in the theology and science conversation that once the gates are opened to allow pentecostals around the dialogue table, the worst facets of the premodern worldview will be given a new lease on life and the many spirits of the pentecostal-charismatic imagination will be unleashed to wreak havoc on the scientific enterprise. There is some basis for this set of fears, especially when we explore the history of parapsychological science, or what the scientific establishment on its best days has labeled the "pseudosciences"!

I personally think that if our cosmos is truly spirit-filled (or infested!), then science should or will eventually find a way to research these realities. In doing so, research at the interface of science and spirit will need to in the long run triangulate around three data sets: (1) pentecostal-type spirituality and experience in all its messiness, including charismatic manifestations, deliverance, and exorcism, and a fully supernaturalistic world (here I resort to the pentecostal vernacular rather than the notions of spirit-filled world or pluralistic cosmos that I have been using throughout this chapter); (2) the consensus in modern science, including due consultation not only in the physical, natural, anthropological, and humanistic sciences, but also with awareness of the most recent developments in the parapsychological or anomalistic sciences; and (3) the biblical and theological considerations, including the historical and contemporary research and interpretation of the worldview of ancient Israel and the earliest Christian communities, and the ongoing discussions in pneumatology and its related topics. In the preceding pages, I have attempted such a triangulation involving the field of parapsychology that I hope will make possible further exploration on these matters. I am optimistic that this might be useful at some level for thinking about a spirit-filled world in a scientific context, especially when the latter is understood in the widest sense of inquiring about the world as a whole.

---

131. The issues raised in this chapter require more than one book-length discussion; I am currently working with two colleagues, Veli-Matti Kärkkäinen and Kirsteen Kim, on editing a volume devoted to these matters, tentatively titled *Loosing the Spirits: Interdisciplinary Perspectives on a Spirit-Filled World,* which will still be no more than an initial step toward filling this lacuna.

Epilogue

This book has argued two major and two subsidiary theses. The major theses are both methodological and theological. Methodologically, pentecostal spirituality provides a theological justification for the many sciences and disciplinary perspectives based on the metaphor of the many tongues of the Spirit manifest on the Day of Pentecost, and this in turn invites us to honor the integrity of the many sciences rather than to view them as competitors with or threats to theology;[1] theologically, pentecostal convictions regarding the Holy Spirit's presence and activity in the world prioritize a pneumatological approach to the theology and science dialogue, one that not only registers pneumatological categories in the discussion but also goes beyond that to suggest an entire pneumatological framework of inquiry.[2] The auxiliary theses expand on this pneumatological theology to propose an eschatological and teleological theory of divine action that locates and explains the Spirit's activity in the world in accordance with the work of Christ to establish the coming kingdom, and to suggest a pneumatological cosmology that recognizes the spirit-filled nature of the universe yet avoids any dualism between spirit and matter as well as providing means for us to engage such a pluralistic cosmos scientifically and navigate its forces ethically.

1. See also Yong, "Reading Scripture and Nature: Pentecostal Hermeneutics and Their Implications for the Contemporary Evangelical Theology and Science Conversation," *Perspectives on Science and Christian Faith* 63, no. 1 (2011): 1-13.

2. For aspects of such a pneumatologically conceived research program, see Yong, "Discerning the Spirit(s) in the Natural World: Toward a Typology of 'Spirit' in the Theology and Science Conversation," *Theology & Science* 3, no. 3 (2005): 315-29.

For my pentecostal readers, I hope the preceding pages have helped us to see scientific work as one of the charisms, broadly understood, that enable us to better understand our world and to live responsibly in it. Theology has nothing to fear from science, rightly understood, and much to glean from it. I also trust that what has been said in the foregoing will encourage pentecostals to take up the task of scientific inquiry, as well as engage theologically with the sciences. This is an important issue since, if the demographics are correct, pentecostalism is one of the fastest-growing religious movements in the world — and we need a theological understanding of the sciences that can help us navigate life in the twenty-first century.

For my nonpentecostal readers, I hope this book has shown how pentecostal perspectives bring certain issues to the forefront of the theology and science discussions, issues that are or should be of concern not just to pentecostals but to Christians in particular and even to theists, religionists, or the spiritually minded in general. These issues thus are suggestive of our common task. I have made various suggestions about how pentecostal insights can further the discussion, but if and how we proceed will depend on the community of scholars or inquirers engaged in these issues. And given the explosive growth of global pentecostalism, it does not appear that the world can avoid this phenomenon. Thus encounter and dialogue are unavoidable, but they need to be respectful of the worldview of the dialogue partners yet willing to honestly and critically discuss the differences involved.

What is at stake in the preceding discussion? I think at least three broad ethical implications flow out of the interface between theology and science in general and with regard to the account presented in this volume in particular. First, human beings are teleological creatures. The emergence of consciousness has brought with it intentionality, freedom, and responsibility. Hence, we are moral beings with moral obligations and liabilities, in relationship not only to one another but also to God as the creator and consummator of all things. There is therefore a general moral dimension to the human endeavor.

But second, we are biological, material, and embodied creatures on the one hand and imbued with creativity on the other hand. The next steps of human evolution are unpredictable given the technological advances we are poised to make. Yet these capacities raise critical questions not only about beginning-of-life and end-of-life care but also about the interface between humanity and technology and between human intelligence and artificial intelligence. There is therefore a very specific set of moral issues related to the nature of what it means to be human and its implications for how to value, nurture, and protect one another across the life span.

Last but not least, human beings are symbiotically related not only to the animal world but also to the environment in its many layers of complexity. While the science may be disputed by some (a minority), we ignore environmental and ecological issues at our own risk in the long run. Even if our dispensationalist eschatology led us to believe that the end is near, that does not justify environmentally harmful behaviors and ways of life. The eschatological renewal of the whole creation invites us instead to care for the world, to the best of our abilities — now greatly enhanced by science — even as our anticipation of the final resurrection motivates us to care for our bodies. There is therefore this wider domain of the web of life as a whole that beckons our moral response.

I have dared to suggest in the preceding how all this might unfold for pentecostals and their potential dialogue partners. Now my readers will need to discern what has been spoken, and respond as they see fit. May the winds of the Spirit continue to inspire this conversation.

Name Index

Subject Index

Adam. *See ha'adam*
altered states of consciousness, 41n.25, 42, 45-46
ancestor veneration, 214n.107
angelology, 178-93, 197, 204-5, 210n.100, 213-17; fall of angels, 155n.52, 219; Gabriel, 214n.106; Michael, 214n.108, 219n.121. *See also* demonology
anthropology, 124n.62, 140-41, 165; theological, 64
anti-intellectualism, 2-3
apocalyptic literature, 217n.115
apologetics, 14, 17, 77, 117, 186
apparitions, 180, 191-92, 200-201
applied sciences, 6-8
artificial intelligence, 227
Assemblies of God, 55
astronomy, 136, 212n.101

baptism of the Holy Spirit, 43, 74-75
big bang, 122, 128, 155
brain, 59-61, 64, 148, 202

causality, 88, 159; efficient, 165; downward, 81, 148-49; final, 88, 95, 120-21, 123-24, 143-44; mental, 60-62, 81, 95
cessationism, 37, 75
chance, 120-21, 127, 130, 137, 187-88

chaos, 79, 82, 109, 156, 210; classical, 81; creation out of, 156; primeval, 155-56, 163, 218
charismatic renewal, 37, 54, 57
charisms. *See* gifts
christology, 20-21, 84; Logos, 19. *See also* incarnation
church, 92, 167, 221-22
clairvoyance, 187
cloning, 84
Committee for Skeptical Inquiry, 193n.58
complementarity, 26-27, 143, 146, 170
complexity, 121, 135-36, 138n.9, 142n.18, 143, 146, 147, 164
concordism, theory of, 138n.9
consciousness, 60, 62-63, 148-49, 171, 194, 196, 227
Copenhagen interpretation, 79-80, 82-83
cosmogony, ancient Near Eastern, 152
cosmology, 85, 137-38; natural selection, 141; pneumatological, 31, 203, 226; process, 203; relational, 100
covenant, 128, 166-67
creatio ex nihilo, 155
creation, 16-18, 23-24, 26, 29, 169, 171; care of, 228; co-creation, 158-59; *con-*

tinua, 159; creativity, 147; Day-age
theory of, 3, 138n.9; days of, 157; out
of chaos, 156; progressive theory of,
138n.9. *See also* Gap theory
creationism, young earth, 4-5, 15

Darwinism, 3, 119, 146
deism, 81, 114, 159
demonology, 178, 178-79, 197, 204-6,
213n.102, 217-20
deprivation, social, 48-50, 69
determinism, 124n.62, 128; metaphysical, 119
dipolar theism, 203n.87
dispensationalism, 228
dissociation, psychological, 41-43
divine action, 31, 79-80, 97, 167; noninterventionist and objective 79-80,
97-99, 100, 112, 167; special, 164
divine council, 215, 219
divine healing, 5-6, 11, 55, 67
divine intervention, 74-75, 99, 100n.69,
114
dualism: anthropological, 60, 62; Cartesian, 145, 162; cosmological, 31; mental, 149-50; metaphysical, 13, 169; ontological, 149, 203; Platonic, 118-19,
160n.66, 162; substance, 145; theological, 151, 163. *See also* nondualism

eco-theology, 24
election, 166
emergence, 146; strong, 147, 149-50, 159,
175; weak, 147, 149-50
Enlightenment, 11, 52-53, 76, 173
environment, 228; theology of, 24
eschatology, 85-88, 228
ethics, 61, 227
Eucharist, 19, 22, 85
Evangelicalism, 4, 117, 113n.1, 138n.9,
177n.11, 186
evil, natural, 210n.100; privation theory
of, 219-20; problem of, 86, 94, 114
evil spirits. *See* demonology
evolution, 119; biological, 139; conver-

gent, 140; theistic, 5. *See also* Darwinism
exorcism, 177, 181-82, 206, 222-23
extrasensory perception, 187, 189, 191,
197, 200

fall, doctrine of, 165n.73, 210n.100
final cause. *See* causality, final; teleology
freedom, 19, 61, 63, 94-95, 107;
compatibilism, 78, 95-96; divine, 95;
double agency, 95-96, 99; libertarian,
61, 94-95
function, biological, 139, 141
fundamentalism, 2, 4, 11, 75

Gap theory, 3-4, 138n.9, 210n.100
Genesis, 16, 138n.9, 152-53, 170n.83, 209,
211, 213
gifts: charismatic, 74-75, 90, 92-93, 128;
spiritual, 74, 197, 223; Holy Spirit, 99
glossolalia, 11, 35, 38, 65-66, 93; psychology of, 66-67; sociology of, 67-68
God-of-the-gaps, 75, 79, 142n.18

ha'adam, 159-61, 163, 165n.73
healing, 100; psychic, 188, 194, 197. *See
also* divine healing
hell, 224
hermeneutics, 93
higher education, 2-6, 9
Holy Spirit, 23-26, 31, 67, 71, 125, 128-29.
See also baptism of Holy Spirit
human nature, 41, 60, 62, 160n.66
humanities, 4, 8-10

imagination, pneumatological, 26, 28
imago Dei, 94
incarnation, 20-21, 23, 84, 87, 166, 209
intelligent design, 138n.9, 142n.18
interactionism, mind-brain, 202
interdisciplinarity, 29, 58, 65, 71, 162
interventionism, 15, 74-76, 79, 90, 98,
116-17, 138n.9, 142n.18
Israel, 84, 166, 168, 215n.108, 225

Jesus Christ, ministry of, 89-90

Scripture Index